FROM THEN INTO NOW:
WILLIAM KENNEDY'S
ALBANY NOVELS

To Pat and Joan —
In thanks for all their
kindness, from picking me up at the
airport for my interview to the buying
of this very book

FROM THEN INTO NOW: WILLIAM KENNEDY'S ALBANY NOVELS

by

Christian Michener

Scranton: University of Scranton Press

Library of Congress Cataloging-In-Publication Data

Michener, Christian, 1963-
   From then into now : William Kennedy's Albany novels / by
Christian Michener.
      p.   cm.
   Includes bibliographical references (p.   ) and index.
   ISBN 0-940866-70-6 (hc). – ISBN 0-940866-71-4 (pbk.)
   1. Kennedy, William, (1928-   – Knowledge – New York (State)-
-Albany. 2. City and town life in literature. 3. Cities and towns
In literature. 4. Albany (N.Y.) –In literature. I. Title.
PS3561.E428Z79   1997
813'. 54–dc21   97-36308
                                                              CIP

Distribution
University of Toronto Press
250 Sonwil Drive
Buffalo, New York 14225

PRINTED IN THE UNITED STATES OF AMERICA

TABLE OF CONTENTS

ACKNOWLEDGMENTS

Portions of Chapter Three appear in altered form as "Martin Daugherty's Victories in *Billy Phelan's Greatest Game*" in *PLL: Papers on Language and Literature* 31.4 (1995): 406–29.

PERMISSIONS

I am also pleased to acknowledge the following for permission to reprint previously published material:

From *QUINN'S BOOK* by William Kennedy. Copyright © 1988 by WJK, Inc. Used by permission of Viking Penguin, a division of Penguin books USA Inc.

CHAPTER ONE

FROM THEN INTO NOW: THE ALBANY CYCLE

*I*t may be commonplace to describe the voice of a writer as "unique," but it would be difficult to find a more appropriate description for the work of William Kennedy, an author who could be situated with ease in numerous twentieth century literary traditions, either American or international, and who could just as easily be shown not to fit squarely in any tradition at all. Kennedy's work as a whole, with its collection of repeated characters and its use of a common setting, has most often been compared to that of William Faulkner; Kennedy himself is an admitted admirer of Gabriel García Márquez, an admiration evident in the magical nature of many of Kennedy's settings and characters; the nature of these very characters as working-class, less-than-honorable heroes evokes in turn comparisons to Theodore Dreiser or maybe Raymond Carver; in the stories themselves it would be difficult to find more direct allusions to any writer other than James Joyce, a consummate modernist novelist; and in an era celebrating the voices of numerous cultural traditions within the American literary experience, Kennedy contributes one of his own in the voice he gives to Irish (Catholic)-Americans. You could, in short, situate Kennedy as an important

1

member of any of these literary traditions, and yet in doing so you would simultaneously reveal that no one tradition adequately describes him. Kennedy's "unique" voice embraces and yet transcends literary categories and forebears to shape a room all his own in contemporary American letters.

The shape of such a room, it must be said, has often startled or confused Kennedy's readers. His immensely successful fourth novel, *Ironweed,* was rejected thirteen times before publication, and *Quinn's Book* and *The Flaming Corsage* in particular did not always receive favorable reviews. Attention from literary scholars too has been limited. The shape of Kennedy's work, the singularity of his endeavor, probably contributes to this reception. The work resembles American realism in its depiction of the struggles of working-class figures, but it's neither the cramped, minimalist work of much contemporary realism nor is it concerned with the societal or psychological pressures on characters such as those in the late twentieth century (middle-class) worlds of Updike or Cheever. Kennedy's style approaches magical realism in the way historical moments in his fiction transcend time and the dead appear without question among the living, but the work is also situated firmly in the real world of working-class New York. Kennedy's fiction is also "historical," but we are given no heavy dose of historical fact in order to reconstruct the past, no elaboration of data compiled simply to establish verisimilitude. And in a way his writing is modernist in its allusions to myths, its use of mythological narrative structures, and its appreciation of the role of the artist in making sense of the world, but it is equally postmodern in its toying with and distorting points of view and in using language to create improbable and uncertain ontological landscapes. Kennedy's work, in other words, extends several important literary traditions, both national and inter-national, and yet it reshapes them all into a vision unique to himself, a singularity which has not always been understood or appreciated.

This singularity is especially noteworthy when one considers that the setting of almost all of Kennedy's fiction is Albany, New York, a literary locale as improbable as Faulkner's Yoknapatawpha county. For Kennedy there are no grand European capitals, no mysterious African jungles, no limitless Western vistas: the landscape for him is the one carved out by and simultaneously carved into the working-class Irishmen of a small, proud American city. But Albany is not merely background; it is an integral part of Kennedy's novels and, in fact, one of the important reasons Kennedy's work is simultaneously both realistic and magical. In his collection of essays entitled *O Albany!*, Kennedy explains the relationship between his hometown of Albany and the books he writes, and in the process he also reveals how or why his work establishes itself at the crossroads of several literary traditions at once:

> [Albany] is centered squarely in the American and the human continuum, a magical place where the past becomes visible if one is willing to track the multiple incarnations of the city's soul. I confront even a single street corner and there emerges an archetypal as well as an historical context in which to view the mutations of its trees, its telephone poles.
>
> It is the task of this and other books I have written, and hope to write, to peer into the heart of this always-shifting past, to be there when it ceases to be what it was, when it becomes what it must become under scrutiny, when it turns so magically, so inevitably, from then into now. (7)

It is thus in peering into the past of Albany that Kennedy finds both the historical material of his working-class world and the inspiration for the magical places we read about in his novels.

This task that Kennedy has established for himself of peering into the past of Albany, and his resulting discovery of its historical and archetypal contexts, has resulted in his producing what has come to be known as his Albany cycle, the focus of this study. The cycle is a collection of novels about the city of Albany and about three Irish-Catholic families in particular: the Phelans, the Daugherty, and the Quinns. The novels do indeed peer into what is the American past—altogether they cover moments from the 1840s to 1958—but the stories within each of the novels also use the concept of history or of the past as one of the primary concerns of their narratives, revealing in the process the magical transformations of which Kennedy speaks, the way the past "turns so magically . . . from then into now," the way the past becomes the present or history becomes archetype, the eternal "now." Through the actions of characters delving into their pasts, through the conflating of the worlds of the living and the dead, and through the power of the world of eternal myth and art to transcend the categories of time, Kennedy's Albany novels dramatize and at times even enact the "task" he sees for himself in writing: to scrutinize the past, to confront history, at the moment it turns into the present and the archetypal.

The simplest and most obvious way in which the past is made present in Kennedy's narratives is through the lives of the characters in his novels. The pattern of most of the books of the cycle is structured upon a heroic quest by a character or characters into the past in order to resurrect, redeem, or purify that past. Perhaps only *Legs*, Kennedy's 1975 novel, does not follow this pattern, but this anomaly also occurs in a novel in which the real-life gangster Jack "Legs" Diamond, the main character in the book, is himself the very part of the past which is brought into the present: *Legs* is the dramatization of how Diamond, a true historical figure, is removed from his historical context in the past and placed instead in the timeless world of myth and legend. In each of the other novels of the Albany cycle, however, a protagonist ventures back into his or her past in order to confront and attempt to overcome some past "sin" or failure that still haunts the present: Martin Daugherty in *Billy Phelan's Greatest Game*, Francis Phelan in *Ironweed*, Daniel Quinn in *Quinn's Book*, Molly and Peter Phelan of *Very Old Bones*, and Edward Daugherty and Katrina Taylor from *The Flaming Corsage* each confront their past in an attempt to exorcize its harmful effects in the present.

The movement of these characters from the present into the past is one way in which Kennedy's novels depict his conception of how inextricably connected are the various moments in time—past, present, and future. This connection is also dramatized throughout the cycle, however, in the equally inextricable connection between life and death or, more appropriately, between the worlds of the living and the dead. The world of the dead is, after all, the place that all those from the past must inhabit and the place to which each character must go in the future: in this sense, it is the world in which the past, present, and even the future are all most clearly conflated, in which the conception of time itself is abandoned altogether for the eternal now of the afterworld. *Legs* concludes, for example, by having Jack Diamond witness his own soul leaving his body as he protests to the narrator of the novel that he is not really dead. Billy Phelan is tempted to commit suicide at one point in *Billy Phelan's Greatest Game* when he hears the voices of ghosts who have already killed themselves. Francis Phelan's Albany in *Ironweed* is a literal world of the dead, peopled by ghosts from his past. And Magdalena Colón is resurrected from the dead at the beginning of *Quinn's Book* and celebrates her wake, even though she is alive, at the end of the novel, reversing in both instances the traditional notions of living and dead. Although no living dead actually appear in the present moment of the story in *Very Old Bones*, the narrative itself, as the title implies, explores the past of the Phelan family, including many characters who die throughout the many decades covered in the novel. This past is itself revealed through a series of historical paintings on the day of the reading of Peter Phelan's will, even though Peter himself is still alive. And Katrina Daugherty of *The Flaming Corsage*, a woman who considers the cemetery a most beautiful place to visit, turns her very house into a shrine to death after witnessing a fire in which many die and which eventually leads to the death of several members of her own family. In each of these books, as these examples illustrate, the transformation of "then into now" is evident in the way the timeless world of the dead remains inseparable from the temporal world of the living.

Another "world" which pervades Kennedy's fiction and in which the past is transformed into the eternal present is that of myth or, concomitantly, the world of art. References or allusions to myths, legends, stories, paintings, and fiction abound in the Albany cycle, and they often appear as a means toward or a moment of redemption from the past. In a group of novels intent on dramatizing the transformation of "then" into "now," this world of myth or art, like the world of the dead, is emblematic of that very transformation: myth and story exist in a constant state of the present; they are always the same in the eternal "now" of art, the unchanging world of Keats's urn. This eternal state is in fact the very focus of *Legs*, which attempts both to explore and to enact on its own the mythicization of Jack "Legs" Diamond. In *Billy Phelan's Greatest Game*, Martin Daugherty, himself a writer, is able to resurrect himself from his confused and helpless state in part because he confronts the past by viewing a play about his own life. The entire narrative of *Ironweed* is permeated by mythological descriptions of Francis and the Odyssean-like journey in which he is engaged. In *Quinn's*

Book, Kennedy enacts the transformation of the historical into the mythical himself by transforming actual historical events into grand, mythological disasters at the beginning of the novel. In addition, one of the concluding discoveries by the protagonist of the book is the wisdom of the contemplation of the mysterious that is itself made possible by the powers of the artistic imagination. *Very Old Bones* is in its turn ostensibly the memoir of its narrator, Orson Purcell, a memoir that includes the story of how the artist Peter Phelan transforms events in the shameful Phelan history into paintings that help the family to overcome the shame of that history. And Edward Daugherty of *The Flaming Corsage* attempts to make sense of both his Irish past and of his present marriage through the writing of plays.

Even when the notions of myth or art are not a part of the main thematic or structural presentation of the novel, the ubiquity of their presence in the text confirms the centrality of their place in Kennedy's fiction, a place where past and present, then and now, are inextricably connected: Marion "Kiki" Roberts, Alice Diamond, Martin Daugherty, Edward Daugherty, Melissa Spencer, Helen Archer, Oscar Reo, Magdalena Colón, Maud Fallon, Daniel Quinn, Will Canaday, Orson Purcell, Giselle Marais, and Peter Phelan are characters who are all part of the roll call of artists—novelists, playwrights, journalists, actresses, photographers, singers—who people the Albany cycle. Their roles in resolving the various quests in the novels differ, but they are each emblematic, and usually explicitly so, of the power of art to transform the contingent and transitory in history into the eternally present world of myth and legend and art. Like those Albany cycle heroes who journey into the past or bring the past into the present, and like the intermingling of the world of the living and the dead, the world of myth and of art serves to dramatize in Kennedy's fiction how history can become archetype and how "then" can be transformed into "now."

The purpose of this book will in great part be to explore the various ways in which Kennedy's acknowledged interest in the interpenetration of "then" and "now" is made manifest within the novels of his Albany cycle. But before such a study can be undertaken, one must first consider the question of what exactly constitutes Kennedy's Albany cycle.[1] To answer this question, one must actually first understand some of the complicated publishing history of the books themselves. Kennedy's first three novels, *The Ink Truck* (1969), *Legs* (1975), and *Billy Phelan's Greatest Game* (1978), were not well received, either critically or popularly, and this situation contributed to a series of rejections for his fourth work, *Ironweed* (1983). The book was finally accepted for publication (with the help of Saul Bellow), but only after the publisher decided to involve it in a marketing ploy in which *Legs, Billy Phelan's Greatest Game,* and *Ironweed* itself would together be construed (and sold) as the Albany trilogy. The justification for this was simple if a bit disingenuous: all the novels consider Albany in some way, but although the latter two novels take place in that city, the first one, *Legs,* does not directly involve Albany until the very end. Nonetheless, the conception of a trilogy worked for both Kennedy and the publisher, helped in no small way by the phenomenal reception of *Ironweed* itself (including its winning the Pulitzer Prize and the National Book Critics Circle Award).

Although it might have been a successful marketing strategy, the notion of a trilogy was soon complicated by the publication of Kennedy's next two novels, *Quinn's Book* (1988) and *Very Old Bones* (1992), both related to the previous three books of the Albany "trilogy." What emerged after the publication of these fifth and sixth novels respectively was not a trilogy at all but something more, a "cycle"—the word is Kennedy's own—of interrelated books.[2] In one sense the term "cycle" can simply be understood here to mean a series of related works extending in number beyond the traditional trilogy or tetralogy. In Kennedy's case, the works are related to each other not only by their shared focus on Albany and, less frequently, on a few other cities in New York (such as Saratoga), but also by characters and events that recur in each of the books and that give to them a consistent and shared history from which their respective stories emerge. Francis Phelan, for example, appears as a character in *Billy Phelan's Greatest Game,* *Ironweed, Very Old Bones,* and *The Flaming Corsage.* His seduction at the hands of his neighbor Katrina when he is eighteen years old is an important event for the plots of each of these novels, and Katrina herself is one of the main characters of *The Flaming Corsage* and the mother of Martin Daugherty, a character who is central to *Billy Phelan* and whose ancestors appear in *Quinn's Book.* Marcus Gorman, the narrator of *Legs,* is for his part also referred to in both *Billy Phelan* and *Ironweed.*

This complex web of relationships among the books reveals another possible way to understand the term "cycle" as a description of Kennedy's novels, an understanding that is especially relevant to this study: the relationship between the works in Kennedy's Albany series is dependent upon something more complex than a simple linear narrative which connects the novels and which focuses on the lives of a few protagonists. In the Albany cycle as a whole, major characters in one novel become minor ones in the next; one novel ends in the 1930s, the next goes back to the nineteenth century, and the next one after that begins in 1958 and within its narrative covers the history of the Phelans from 1887 up to the present moment of the book. One novel covers events over three days, another one over seventy-one years: there is, in short, no attempt in the series to progress chronologically from one book to the next, to maintain a consistent focus on a few characters, to be consistent with the pace at which each narrative moves, or to provide similar narrative points of view for each of the novels. As a series, the books spin around each other and within themselves, as the narrative of the cycle as a whole moves forward and backward in history, from now to then and back again, focusing first on this man and then this one (only occasionally is it a woman), moving from the 1930s to the nineteenth century to 1958 as it goes from one book to another and then to another—all like a wheel which spins forward only to roll over the top and come back to where it started from. The ground covered remains consistent and stable, but the method by which it is covered constantly changes. Such a conception reveals how appropriate the term "cycle" is in defining what Kennedy has produced: not only does the term imply an "open-ended and related series of novels," as Kennedy describes it,[3] but it also reveals the nonlinear system of narration of that series as a whole, the way that its shared and consistent history is presented in a roundabout, various, and cyclical way.

Even though Kennedy's term "cycle" not only identifies but even characterizes the series he has written, the complicated publishing history of his work still leaves open the question of which books comprise that cycle. What should one do, for example, with *The Ink Truck*, Kennedy's first book and one which was not included in the publisher's original trilogy? While the city in this novel is not identified as Albany, and while none of the characters reappear in any other Kennedy novel, *The Ink Truck* does share similar themes with those novels (the protagonist Bailey descends into the past of an unnamed city in a hallucinatory tale of his exploits during a strike), and Kennedy has said himself that the city in *The Ink Truck* is based on Albany (McCaffery, 173). Kennedy also claims in an interview to have had the idea for a series of interrelated novels before he wrote *The Ink Truck*, and he says in the same interview, in referring to his collection of novels, "Cycle is my word [for them]. It started with *The Ink Truck.*"[4] In another interview he also claims that he wrote about the nineteenth century in *Quinn's Book* because he had first written about it in *The Ink Truck*, and then he adds: "Even though Albany is never mentioned in *The Ink Truck*, I feel I have the same streets, and the same newspaper as I have in the work-in-progress [*Quinn's Book*], with the same characters running saloons, the same traditional figures existing in the history of this mythic city I'm inhabiting in my imagination" (McCaffery, 173).

In addition to wondering about the inclusion of *The Ink Truck*, one must also ask what should be done with *Legs*. Although *Legs* was one of the publisher's original inclusions in the trilogy, it actually has, as was mentioned above, very little to do with Albany except at the end. And none of the three main Albany families—the Phelans, Daughertys, and Quinns—appears in it. If *Legs* is included in the cycle despite these differences, why not include *The Ink Truck* also? Or if *The Ink Truck* is excluded, should not *Legs* also be? The reasons the publisher had for placing *Legs* in the original trilogy might not be strong enough to sustain its inclusion in the cycle when one is discussing the novel outside of the interests of the publishing world.

While Kennedy's claims about his notion of a related series of novels and about *The Ink Truck* in particular might make one consider counting all of his books, including *The Ink Truck*, as part of the Albany cycle, Kennedy is also on record as saying (in *Fiction International* in 1984) that he "didn't set out consciously to weave a web of novels" (172). Considering the inevitability of the evolution of Kennedy's understanding of his own writing, the uncertainty of memory, and the pressures of trying to get published, it would not be surprising that the author himself would wonder about when he consciously began to write an interrelated series of novels. But instead of relying on this uncertainty, and certainly instead of relying on the opinion of the publishers, one should rely on the books themselves in order to resolve the question of what constitutes the true cycle. In doing so, one can say with no doubt at all that four of Kennedy's novels are a part of that cycle: *Billy Phelan's Greatest Game, Ironweed, Very Old Bones,* and *The Flaming Corsage* not only share characters and a locale but also a common Phelan and Daugherty history, and the novels often allude to events that take place in other of the books. *Billy Phelan* and *Ironweed* even end on the same day and in the same city, and the protagonists from each of those novels appear several times in *Very Old Bones* as relatively minor characters.

A look at the internal evidence of *Quinn's Book* reveals that it too can easily be added to these four novels to become part of the Albany cycle. Not only does *Quinn's Book* take place in Albany from time to time, but Daniel Quinn, the protagonist and often the narrator, is also the ancestor of the George Quinn who marries Francis Phelan's daughter. In fact, Daniel Quinn's ancestor in the twentieth century is himself called Daniel Quinn and appears as a minor character in *Very Old Bones*.[5] In addition, Emmett Daugherty, who appears in *Quinn's Book* in a small role, is a character in *The Flaming Corsage* as well as the father of Edward Daugherty, the main character of that book, and the grandfather of Martin Daugherty, one of the two primary protagonists of *Billy Phelan's Greatest Game*. Such connections between *Quinn's Book* and the other novels allow no doubt at all that it too belongs among the Albany cycle novels.

Of the two remaining works, Kennedy's first novel, *The Ink Truck*, must be excluded. Whatever place it inhabits in Kennedy's imagination, neither the place nor the characters within its text connects it to the other novels. Its locale is not defined as Albany, and its characters never appear again in Kennedy's other books (not yet at least). To include it in the cycle would violate the integrity of the concept of the cycle to the point of destroying the meaningfulness of the conception. Although a study of *The Ink Truck* along with Kennedy's other novels would provide an interesting glimpse into the evolution of a writer as he slowly discovers his artistic interests, the novel itself is not a part of that particular interest Kennedy finally discovered and that is in turn the interest of this study.

The decision about the inclusion of *Legs* in the cycle is more difficult than the decision about *The Ink Truck*, although in the end its similar themes, the (admittedly) slight presence of Albany in the novel, and—most importantly—a key character shared with the other novels argue for its inclusion. Its themes—mythicization, immortality, bringing the past into the present—are ones consistent with other Albany novels, and thus the book naturally fits into any study of the cycle as a whole. *Legs* also takes place in the identifiable New York area, including the city of Albany, where Jack Diamond was murdered as he was attempting to establish his illegal businesses in that city.[6] As J. K. Van Dover writes, "Whoever fired the three bullets into Diamond's head at least assured the gangster's permanent association with Albany, and thus made Legs Diamond an available subject for the imagination of William Kennedy" (42). And as is argued here, the shooters also made him an available subject for the Albany cycle in particular. *Legs* itself ends soon after Diamond's murder, and thus the novel concludes with a character who has literally just arrived in Albany as Kennedy himself seems to have arrived in writing the book at his pronounced and lasting artistic interest in his hometown: all of the novels published after *Legs* revolve around action that occurs in Albany.

Perhaps an even more significant reason for including *Legs* in the Albany cycle than the similar themes and the brief appearance of the city, however, is the appearance in the novel of Marcus Gorman, Diamond's lawyer. Gorman is not only the narrator of *Legs*, but he is also mentioned in *Billy Phelan's Greatest Game* (as the lawyer who defends a kidnapper, Morrie Berman) and in *Ironweed* (as the lawyer who gets Francis out of jail but whose demand for payment requires Francis to work in the cemetery for money). Gorman is also obliquely present toward the end of *Very Old Bones* when Diamond, Berman, and Francis Phelan—all Gorman's clients—are mentioned during a dinner conversation. Gorman is, in effect, a part of the Albany world—including not only the geographical place but also its people and its history—and he plays key roles in the lives of several of its more important inhabitants. Although he is not a significant character himself in the novels after *Legs*, and although he is not a member of one of the three main Albany cycle families, he is the first character to appear who is later reused in another novel, and he thus serves as the first example of Kennedy's conscious attempt to establish a fictionalized city that transcends individual works.

In the end, then, although other critics and maybe even Kennedy himself might dispute the description, the Albany cycle to date can be said to be comprised of *Legs*, *Billy Phelan's Greatest Game*, *Ironweed*, *Quinn's Book*, *Very Old Bones*, and *The Flaming Corsage*. All of these books share not only related themes but also a common imaginary history, including both characters and events. The nature of that relationship is revealed by the term "cycle" itself: the history that the novels of the cycle share, an imaginary history of a place and of people, is revealed to us cyclically, as the series moves back and forth in time, covering one period and then another, revealing a scene or character and then moving on until we glimpse that scene or character again later, in the same book or maybe in another one.

As *Legs* is the first of Kennedy's Albany cycle novels to be published, this study of Kennedy's attention in his fiction to the interpenetrating moments of time—past and present, then and now—begins with *Legs* itself. The novel dramatizes the end of Jack "Legs" Diamond's life as it is narrated by Marcus Gorman, a bored (and fictional) lawyer who adds a little excitement to his own life by accepting Diamond as his client. The book opens as Gorman and some friends get together for drinks several decades after Diamond's death, and the story that Gorman then narrates figuratively brings the historical Diamond into the present moment in the bar. But Diamond lives on in more than just the memory and stories of friends, for the novel focuses on the "mythicization" of Diamond, the way that the public transformed a historical hoodlum into a mythical gangster. Part of this myth includes the belief that Diamond lives on after being murdered, a notion that is not entirely implausible, for during his lifetime Diamond managed to survive several attempts on his life. His immortality, his living in the ever-present "now," is dramatized in the final chapter of the book, in which the dead Jack Diamond comments on his own death. "'Honest to God, Marcus,'" Diamond says in the closing line of the book, "'I really don't think I'm dead'" (317). In depicting this immortal Diamond, the novel thus manages to enact the very theme its narrative has dramatized, the mythicization of Diamond, the transformation of a historical figure into an archetypal and mythological one.

Chapter Three of this study will discuss Kennedy's second Albany novel, *Billy Phelan's Greatest Game*. Billy, a small-time Albany pool hustler and card shark, finds himself at odds with the McCall family, the powerful leaders of the Democratic political machine in Albany. Billy refuses to help the McCalls find one of their relatives who has been kidnapped because such help would go against his own private code of ethics. As Billy wanders the streets during the days of his conflict with the McCalls, newspaperman Martin Daugherty keeps an eye on him and on the events of the kidnapping, attempting, much like Leopold Bloom does with Stephen Dedalus, to protect the young Billy from those out to harm him. Martin's desire to "adopt" Billy, to bring him under his paternal protection, derives from the lack of connection Martin feels with his own family, his break from both his own father and son, his past and his future. Much of the book describes Martin coming to terms with this rupture in his life—specifically by his reenacting a crucial scene from his past—and in the process helping Billy with his predicament with the McCalls.

Chapter Four discusses the story of Billy's father in Kennedy's most famous novel, *Ironweed*. Francis Phelan, the bum-hero of the novel, must struggle with his past and with his family, much as Martin Daugherty does in *Billy Phelan*, when he returns to Albany after twenty-two years away on the run. The three days during which Francis wanders through Albany mirror numerous "myths," most especially those of Dante in the *Purgatorio* and of Odysseus, and the world in which he wanders is a timeless, eschatological moment inhabited by ghosts from his own past. Haunted by these ghosts and visions of other dead he has known, Francis struggles during his journey to atone for his past sins and to forgive himself. In the end the narrative does not so much resolve Francis' situation—the ending is clearly ambiguous —as it attempts to find an appropriate conclusion for its own unique status as a simultaneously mythological, eschato-logical, and existential tale.

Quinn's Book, the only one of Kennedy's novels to deal with Albany (and other cities) exclusively in the nineteenth century, will be discussed in Chapter Five. Perhaps of all of the books, this fourth Albany novel reveals most emphati-cally Kennedy's concern with history. The novel, narrated by Daniel Quinn, begins with the deaths of thousands of Albany citizens in a flood and fire, two natural disasters based on actual historical events. The deaths from these disasters include that of a famous courtesan, Magdalena Colón, a woman Quinn tries to help rescue during the flood. In one of the open eyes of Magdalena's corpse, Quinn is able to read the future before him, although what he does not see is that Magdalena herself will soon be brought back to life by Quinn's necrophilic master, John the Brawn. Magdalena's life after death finds an inverse parallel at the ending of the book, in which Magdalena holds her own wake, a celebration of her death before her life even ends. In between these twin reversals of life and death, Daniel narrates his own adventures as a newspaper correspondent as he attempts to discover the "truth" of history and to conquer the heart of his one true love. In the end Quinn learns to abandon his pursuit for historical truth and instead comes to embrace the mysteries and powers of the imagination, that source of wisdom which can transcend the contingencies of histories and achieve an aesthetically based understanding of truth.

As *Quinn's Book* ends with Magdalena's own wake, *Very Old Bones*, the subject of Chapter Four, ends (and begins) on the day Peter Phelan assembles his family to have his will read even though he is very much alive. The gathering of the family, the bequests Peter presents to each member (especially to his illegitimate son), and the paintings Peter exhibits that portray Phelans of the past all serve as means to understanding and forgiving the shameful or denied Phelan past as well as means to celebrating the present Phelan family. The official adoption of Orson Purcell, the son whom Peter had never claimed as his before, and the proposal that Orson officially remarry his pregnant wife, signify how the Phelan past has been overcome and how the Phelan future, if not guaranteed, is at least offered some hope.

The last book covered in this study, *The Flaming Corsage*, details the troubled and tragic love affair between Edward Daugherty and Katrina Taylor. Daugherty, a playwright, attempts to overcome personally the centuries of mistreatment of his fellow Irishmen through his writing and through his marriage to Katrina Taylor, a daughter of one of the established Anglo-Protestant business barons so despised by the working-class Irish themselves. In his respective artistic concerns for Irish and Albany history and for his wife, Edward struggles to understand himself and make others understand the truth of the public world of history and the private world of the enigmatic Katrina. Curiously, despite his awareness of history, and despite his attempt to use it to help his people, Edward's work and his marriage to Katrina are undermined in part by history itself: Edward's plays are not enough to bridge the great gap between his ancestry and Katrina's, for himself or for his people.

When Loxley Nichols writes that "Kennedy demonstrates" toward the end of *O Albany!* "that nothing is ever past, nothing ever ends" (48), he is identifying a principle as evident in *The Flaming Corsage* and the other Albany novels as in *O Albany!* itself. Each of the books of Kennedy's Albany cycle presents in various ways the transformation of "then" into "now," the way the past lives on in the present. It is an achievement that the cycle itself enacts also: reading the six books in any order is an act in which one goes back and forth in time, from 1938 to 1931 to 1958, from a meandering, three-day journey of a bum (in *Ironweed*) to a romp through nearly seventy-five years and four generations of Phelans and Quinns (in *Very Old Bones*). The novels, as a group and individually, dramatize and enact the cyclical notion of time which Kennedy brings to his fiction, a concept in which the past is always present and in which the historical can also be the archetypal. It is a concept that leads to narratives in which the past can be resurrected, overcome, purified, forgiven, or endured as that past is magically transformed through Kennedy's fiction from "then" into "now." The following chapters will discuss in detail how each of these books enact in their own respective ways this magical, and singular, vision.

Notes

1. William Kennedy has produced in his writing career to date seven novels, two books of nonfiction (the later of which is a collection of previously published work), several short stories, scores of book reviews and interviews, and numerous articles as a journalist and newspaper writer. By Kennedy's Albany cycle one almost always means his novels, all or a portion of them, although J. K. Van Dover discusses some of Kennedy's short stories in his book, *Understanding William Kennedy*, and he also argues that *O Albany!*, Kennedy's first book of nonfiction, "is as much a part of the 'cycle' as *Ironweed* " or any of the other novels (8). While it is true that *O Albany!* is an indispensable resource for understanding Kennedy and his work, and while it is also true that several of the short stories can be better understood in light of the cycle of novels, there is good reason not to include either *O Albany!* or the stories in this present discussion of the cycle: while the nonfiction and the short stories help illuminate the novels—and vice versa—they do not share in the close relationships of character, subject matter, theme, genre, and setting that are themselves the defining criteria of what the cycle is understood here to be.

2. As Kennedy says in *The Paris Review* in 1989, "Trilogy was never my word and I don't want it to be the word. Cycle is my word" (59). In an interview with Peter Quinn, he adds, "I chose the word 'cycle' because it connotes an open-ended and related series of novels" (70).

3. See endnote 2, above.

4. *The Paris Review*, p. 59. In the same 1989 interview, and along the same lines, Kennedy added: " . . . I wanted to write a series of novels that would interrelate. I didn't know how, but this is a very old feeling with me. I came across a note the other day that I wrote to myself about 'the big Albany novel.' This was way back, I can't even remember when—long before I wrote *Legs*, even before *The Ink Truck*" (57).

5. For a genealogy of the Quinns and the Phelans and their joint family history, see Van Dover, p. 130.

6. Diamond was killed at 67 Dove Street in a building eventually bought by Kennedy himself. For more information on Diamond and Albany, see Van Dover, pp. 41-43.

CHAPTER TWO

KEEPING *LEGS* ALIVE: THE MYTHICIZATION OF JACK DIAMOND

*L*egs, William Kennedy's novel dramatizing the last year and a half of the life of the real-life gangster Jack "Legs" Diamond, begins Kennedy's Albany cycle of novels.[1] Although the location of the story in New York state and the use of some characters who reappear in other Albany novels connects *Legs* to the rest of the cycle, the most interesting connection between this novel and the other ones is Kennedy's attention in *Legs* to the ability of history to be transformed into story and myth, to be simultaneously both history and archetype—a condition which characterizes much that is found in the other Albany cycle novels.[2] Kennedy will dramatize the inverse conception—that history is able not only to be transformed but to transform—through characters such as Martin Daugherty in *Billy Phelan's Greatest Game* and Francis Phelan in *Ironweed*; these characters explore their own personal histories in an attempt to redeem their lives and discover some sense of meaning about them. But in *Legs* Kennedy is more concerned with dramatizing how history itself can be transformed, how a story of what happened back "then" might be changed into something that is forever happening "now."

21

Legs explores this ability of history to be transformed by dramatizing the "mythicization" of a historical figure, the process by which a figure from history is changed into an immortal being in myth.[3] Kennedy identifies this process as the central focus of the novel. As he says, the

> notion of myth remained with me and became central to the final version of the book: the idea of how myth is created: an act which becomes a public fascination, and then is blown out of all proportion, so that the doer is given legendary status; then the legend is passed on, and becomes one of the defining myths of the age. (McCaffery, 170)

The myth that Kennedy explores in *Legs* is that of the legendary gangster—in this case, the legendary Jack Diamond. This exploration, in fact, will extend even to the dramatization of the possible immortality of Diamond, a portrayal which makes literal (at least within the narrative) what is already Diamond's figurative immortality as a mythic figure.

In dramatizing Diamond as a mythological and immortal figure, Kennedy still asserts that he "could not be satisfied with designating [his] book as mythic" (McCaffery, 176). He continues:

> The myth had to grow out of the real. . . .[To] talk about gangsters and deal with them *only* as myth seemed absurd to me. So what I did was to go back down to the documentary level in order to understand the history, and to work from some concrete basis on which that reality—which I was about to reinvent and pass on—would have some historical significance. (McCaffery, 176-77)

Legs, then, became an integration between the real and the imagined, the historical and the mythical; it became what

Kennedy himself has called an assimilation and a reinvention: "What I came to eventually," he says, "was a plan to assimilate all the truth, all the lies, all the fudged areas in between, and reinvent Jack . . . as a brand-new fictional character; and so while the novel's historical outline is accurate as to fact, the daily specifics . . . are products of one man's imagination" (*OA*, 200). What Kennedy is revealing in such statements is that through his novel he has actually duplicated the transformation of the historical record into myth that his own novel dramatizes: in enacting its own transformation of the historical Diamond, *Legs* contributes through its storytelling to the same mythicization of Jack "Legs" Diamond that its own fictional narrative explores.

In both dramatizing and enacting in *Legs* the mythicization of a historical figure, Kennedy begins what will be a primary theme of all of his Albany novels, the integral relationship between past, present, and future, the commingling of "then" and "now." It is, as Larry McCaffery has suggested, "an almost mystical view that life is more fluid and interconnected than most people suspect" (167). In *Legs*, Kennedy's reshaping of history into fiction, his dramatization of the mythicization of Diamond, and his portrayal of Diamond living on after his death all work to produce a multilayered exploration of the power of the imagination to transform history into myth, to take what happened back "then" and shape it into what always will be happening "now."

The history Kennedy will turn into myth and legend in *Legs* is based on the life of the real Jack "Legs" Diamond, a gangster who was killed at the age of thirty-four on December 18, 1931, and thus who operated at about the same time as Al Capone, Bonny and Clyde, John Dillinger, and Dutch Schultz, perhaps Diamond's closest rival (Van Dover, 41). Diamond's murderers were never found (nor were those who later killed Diamond's wife, Alice), but Kennedy mentions the belief among many that it was perhaps representatives of Albany law enforcement who killed the gangster. Such officials were themselves possibly prompted by the desires of Democratic political boss Dan O'Connell to keep the trouble-making criminal—and a potential threat to O'Connell's own power base—out of Albany, a city into which Diamond was considering moving his organization at the time of his murder.[4] While Kennedy's novel mythologizes the story of this real-life criminal, it neither simply condones nor condemns the man: "to write about Diamond," Kennedy has said, "I had to respect someone who was a mean, cruel son of a bitch. Yet he fascinated America. My role was to find out why he was so revered. Why people treated him like they treated Lindburgh and Al Jolson" (Agrest, 48). Kennedy's impetus then was to explore how we come to be fascinated by such a cruel and dangerous man, to explore what he has called the "fascination of abomination" (Thomson, 57). Kennedy's epigraph in *Legs*, from Eugene Ionesco, signals this interest in how America could be obsessed by a man as cruel as Diamond: "People like killers," Ionesco says, and "if one feels sympathy for the victims it's by way of thanking them for letting themselves be killed."

Kennedy's exploration of his own particular "killer" is unlike the other five books of the Albany cycle, for *Legs* does not deal with a character who must confront his past or even the present moment to come to some understanding of his life. In fact, not only is Jack Diamond a generally unre-flective person (though not totally so), apathetic or silent about his past, but the story in the novel actually begins four and a half decades after Diamond has died and thus, in a sense, takes place in part in his future. The novel opens with a meeting between Diamond's old lawyer, Marcus Gorman, and several other acquaintances of the dead gangster, and their reminiscences lead Gorman into his role as narrator of the story we read. This story concerns the last part of

Diamond's life, the year and a half in which Gorman got to know Diamond while serving as his attorney.[5]

Gorman is himself a peripheral and generally objective narrator, a reliable source who passes few judgments on Diamond and even less on himself. We do learn that Gorman is not the most noble of people, and by his own admission. He refuses to take charity cases (although he will help Francis Phelan in *Ironweed* for a reduced fee) because he feels that lawyers take such cases only as "whitewash for their chicanery" (230). Gorman has never needed "such washing," he claims, and he builds his legal career on a more honest but nonetheless uninspiring code: "defending not pleasant people, but people who paid my fee. I follow a basic rule of legal practice: establish the price, get the money, then go to work" (230). The work, too, is of a questionable nature ethically. Diamond, in observing Gorman's outright lies in court one day, himself accuses Gorman of being "twice the crook I'll ever be" (239). Gorman says it isn't true, but not out of defensiveness or a desire for innocence: as Gorman says, Diamond's comments "pleased me because it implied prowess in a world alien to me" (239).

Despite these occasional glimpses into Gorman's character, he remains a reserved commentator. He is, as he says himself, a skeptic and a stoic; his first name even derives, he tells us, from his father's "favorite Stoic," presumably Marcus Aurelius (257). His role as narrator is characterized heavily by his position as a lawyer, and specifically a lawyer who is pragmatic rather than one who is concerned with abstract philosophical or ethical issues. Instead of making moral judgments about his and Diamond's behavior, he speculates on more analytical questions concerning the nature of that behavior. What motivated Diamond? From where did he draw his strength and charisma? What was the nature of this strength? Why were others so fascinated by him, and what effect did his life (and death) eventually have on these others? Gorman's role is not to talk about himself or to decide between what is right and what is wrong but, rather, to take what is given and try to define and analyze what that material means about Diamond and the life the man leads.[6]

Despite this rather reserved role for Gorman, occasionally (though rarely) his own condition or nature becomes a consideration in the narrative, though these moments usually focus on how Diamond affected Gorman's own life. In the opening section of the novel, for example, Gorman talks about his life in terms of what it was like before he met Diamond, as if the gangster were the fulcrum upon which Gorman's life swung. Gorman speaks of how his life was "a stupendous bore [that] could use a little Gargantuan dimension" (16) before he met Diamond, and that his "life changed on a summer day in 1930" (15) when he agrees to meet with the man.

Gorman arrives at Diamond's estate with many reservations about accepting Jack's request for him to be the gangster's lawyer, but this hesitancy disappears once Diamond takes Gorman out to his garage to have some fun firing a machine gun. Gorman accepts the chance to shoot at an effigy of Dutch Schultz even though he still thinks of the "powerful Irish Catholic magic at work that prohibits shooting effigies on the side of a barn" (40). The pleasure of shooting the weapon startles Gorman and makes him wonder about working for Diamond, a man for whom such a gun is part of the job:

> What a long distance between Marcus and Jack Diamond. Millenniums of psychology, civilization, experience, turpitude. . . . Would I defend him if some shooters walked through the barn door? What difference from defending him in court? And what of Jack's right to justice, freedom, life? Is the form of defense the only differentiating factor? What a morally confounded fellow Marcus is, perplexed by [the machine gun]. (40)

Though he believes himself "confounded," Gorman quickly loses both his scruples about enjoying firing the gun and about working for Jack. The weapon, in fact, moves him into a feeling of empathy for the gangster. As Gorman begins to accept his pleasure in firing the gun, he becomes a kind of Jack Diamond himself as he plays out the role of an imaginary gangster taking out a rival: "Jack reached for the gun, but I held onto it, facing the ease with which I had become new. Do something new and you are new. How boring it is not to fire a machine gun. I fired again and eliminated the Schultz mouth" (41). Gorman has quickly been seduced by the power and violence of Jack Diamond's weapon, and soon after shooting the effigy he admits in a chilling, understated confession that he will have no trouble not only defending the man but even befriending the criminal. Gorman says, "I smiled at [Diamond's wife] to imply I was her friend, and Jack's, too. And I was then, yes I was. I was intuitively in sympathy with this man and woman who had just introduced me to the rattling, stammering splatter of violent death" (41). To Gorman the machine gun is a taste of a wholly different life for him, one that is both deadly and vital, and it seduces him out of his boring life into one in which he sympathizes with and befriends a killer. If Kennedy's book is in part an exploration of how people become obsessed with an "abomination" such as Jack Diamond, perhaps this scene offers one answer: to taste death is also to taste its other, life, and as reprehensible as violent death may be, to some it offers a better alternative than daily boredom, especially when that alternative can be carried out within the safe confines of the imaginary.

To confirm both Diamond's evil allure and his magical power over others, including Gorman, Kennedy depicts how the lawyer's behavior changes while he is on a cruise with Diamond not long after Gorman has accepted the job as Diamond's attorney. Although Gorman is hesitant to get involved in any illegal activity, he does agree while on the ship to carry some of Diamond's own money, obviously the product of illegal work. And after several days of intimate contact with Diamond, Gorman's own behavior takes on the violence of his client's. His treatment of a woman on the ship soon after he straps on Diamond's money indicates how tempting is this new world of power and wealth. As Gorman says:

> I remember my own excitement, the surge of energy I felt rising in myself from some arcane storage area of the psyche when I strapped on the money belt. No longer the voyeur at the conspiracy, I was now an accessory, and the consequence was intoxicating. I felt a need to drink, to further loosen my control center, and I did.
> At the bar I found a woman I'd flirted with a day or so earlier and coaxed her back to my cabin. I did not wait to strip her, or myself, but raised her dress swiftly, pulled her underclothing off one leg, and entered her as she sat on the bed, ripping her and myself in the process so that we both bled. I never knew her name. I have no recollection of the color of her hair, the shape of her face, or any word she might have said. . . . (106)

What he docs remember, Gorman says, is her "pubic region" at the moment he "assaulted" it (106). Gorman's susceptibility to fall into the violent world of the charismatic gangster for whom he works is confirmed: intoxicated by money, he exercises his own power by "assaulting" a woman who will soon be only an anonymous memory, and all of this is done without any evident remorse on his part.

In addition to his curiosity about how Diamond affects his own moral character, Gorman also considers how Diamond affects other parts of his life too. He worries, for example, about the loss of his political career once he is associated with Diamond (254) and, more poignantly, he wonders what his father would think of his working for Diamond, "a speculation," Gorman says, "which . . . reveals more of me than the old man" (257). Gorman also admits that he—like his own father and even Jack Diamond—is "hounded by religious confusion" (257). Yet despite these reflections, and despite his being changed by Diamond himself, Gorman as narrator remains outside the central focus of the novel, the mythicization of the criminal for whom he works. In a way this is a shame, for no one is in a better position in the novel to reveal how or why Legs Diamond should be honored as a legend when what he does is so reprehensible. But like Nick Carraway, Gorman stands on the outside of the life of a gangster, brooding or commenting occasionally, and marveling too, but not judging the man and for the most part remaining reticent about his own life and the role Diamond plays in it.[7] As Carraway says at the beginning of *The Great Gatsby*, "I'm inclined to reserve all judgments" (1), a description Gorman could have accurately given of himself. Such reticence (and despite Gorman's lies in the courtroom) makes Gorman a reliable narrator for the story that is to be told, a significant notion in light of the nature of that story, the possible immortality of a seemingly magical New York gangster. Without such a skeptical and phlegmatic narrator, the narration might otherwise sound like the fantasies of a Diamond sycophant. Instead, Gorman's stoic, practical, and reserved nature lends reliability to a sometimes outrageous narrative, and his own seduction by Diamond's power, however briefly it is mentioned, lends evidence to how charismatic Diamond is and how magical he just might be.

The stories told by Marcus Gorman and his friends—Flossie, Tipper, and Packy—at the beginning of the novel are a mirror in miniature of the larger mythicization of Jack Diamond by the public. These stories about Diamond, told by admirers or friends of his, are the first, the simplest, and the least questionable way in which Diamond "lives on" in the present: Diamond is immortal in that he is (figuratively) "alive" in the memories of these characters and the stories their memories generate, just as he will be alive in the myths of the public's imagination. But the relationship between subject and object in the storytelling, between the various narrators and Diamond, is one of mutual effect. While Diamond is "brought to life" by the power of his friends telling stories about him, he too seems to have a power over these people: when Tipper says that Diamond's "name had power," for example, Gorman replies, "'It still does. . . . Didn't he bring us together here?'" (15). Thus while Diamond "lives on" in the memories of his friends, he also seems to "live on" on his own, serving as his own active force in the way his name has the "power" to bring his friends together.

Diamond's name also had power immediately after his death, chronologically four decades prior to this opening scene, especially for the lives of his mistress and his wife, both of whom consciously attempted to keep Diamond alive in their own figurative way. Eighteen days after Diamond is killed, Marion "Kiki" Roberts, Diamond's mistress, opened a stage show which fed off of the publicity of her relationship with Jack: "'See Kiki,'" the advertisement for the show read, "'the Gangster's Gal'" (301). Years later, while Kiki is doing another show, Gorman talks to her about Diamond, telling her that she is "'keeping him alive'" (308) by producing shows based on her life with the man. Gorman's statement could also describe with equal accuracy what Diamond's widow, Alice, attempts to do in producing a show of her own after Diamond's death. Gorman tries to dissuade Alice from opening this show, suggesting that she not compete with Kiki over a dead man. But it was, as Gorman says, not only "an absurd suggestion" but also and significantly "the first time I made the mistake of thinking Jack was totally dead" (301).

Attempting to convince Alice not to produce the show was not a mistake, however, for her production is pitiful and unsuccessful. Nonetheless, Gorman can still say after watching it that Diamond is living in Alice: "He was there," Gorman says; he was the "presence within Alice" (304). And Diamond was also there for her, it seems, in a more practical way, in providing Alice with a little bit of money after his death. Although he was almost bankrupt when he was killed, Diamond had told his wife who the people were who owed him money, and she collected what she could of it after he was killed, as if the man were still a threat to these debtors. Gorman says to Alice about these financial concerns that the dead Diamond is "'still taking care of you'" (304). It may be true, but his care does not last long: a year after his death, Alice, like her husband, is mysteriously murdered. She has kept Diamond alive for a while, as has Kiki, but he cannot in the end keep Alice herself alive.

Diamond's power to bring his friends together and to take care of Kiki and Alice is one way in which he remains figuratively immortal, one way in which the historical lives on in the present moment: Legs is alive in story and memory, and in the way that memory affects those who are still alive. But Kennedy's concern in this novel moves beyond these restricted versions of immortality to a more public one, to the way in which Legs Diamond "lived on" after his death in the realm of myth and legend, what one might conceive of as a kind of public story or, as Gorman calls it at one point, a "product of the collective imagination" (89). Diamond's extraordinary and secretive activities as a gangster, and the tendency of the public and of the tabloid press to exaggerate who Diamond was and what he did, left a legacy of contradictions and impossibilities concerning the man and thus made him a perfect model for Kennedy to use in dramatizing the mythicization of a historical figure.

Kennedy writes that "almost every book that carries information about Jack Diamond is contradicted somewhere by another book, or they are both contradicted by accounts in the newspapers, which in turn contradict one another, even on such matters as his age and his name" (*OA*, 199). These contradictions and uncertainties open up space in the historical record that invites itself to be filled by the imagination of friends and enemies, journalists and acquaintances and novelists, so that the historical Diamond slowly becomes a mythical one. Kennedy has said that "one of the important things I was driving at in *Legs* [is] that sense of the gangster as myth, that idea that Legs was moving into mythic status after his life here on earth" (McCaffery, 167). This gangster figure "was a social outlaw and a universal hero" (*OA*, 189), Kennedy says, and prohibition in particular was "notable for . . . making mythic figures out of hoodlums who slaked the public thirst" (*OA*, 198). Kennedy's book is an attempt to explore the mythicization of a man—Jack Diamond—who is this "universal hero" but who is also a social outlaw, a bootlegger, a gangster, and a cold-blooded murderer. Why and how, Kennedy asks, does such a figure become a mythological one? As Kennedy more simply puts it, his book explores the question of why people "relish the memory that they were putting mustard on their hot dog when Legs Diamond walked into the roadside diner" (*OA*, 198).

Although it is Diamond's status as legend and myth that is the focus of *Legs*, this concern with the process of mythicization is occasionally evident in the novel even when the subject is not Diamond. Gorman says, for example, that Kiki, Diamond's mistress, was "personified" in her

> willingness to conform to the hallowed twentieth century chorus-girl stereotype that Ziegfeld, George White, Nils T. Granlund, the Minskys, and so many more men, whose business was flesh, had incarnated, and which Walter Winchell, Ed Sullivan, Odd McIntyre, Damon Runyon, Louis Sobol, and so many

others, whose business was to muse and gossip on the
ways of this incarnated flesh, had mythicized. (70)

Thus Kiki represents for Gorman (and Kennedy) a woman
who has actually been "mythicized" by the great publicity
machine of her time, the men who through "muse and
gossip" and through their insistence on and admiration of a
certain stereotype—what one might perceive as a desacralized
mythical figure—were able to raise a simple human being
(showgirl or gangster) into the mythical creature their
imaginations desired. At one point in *Legs*, Gorman cites the
process by which Diamond's own "mythicization" took
place—a process similar to Kiki's—but he does so with a slight
wink to the reader about what Kennedy and Gorman are
themselves doing: "The magazines never stopped retelling
Jack's story either, and somebody put it out in book form
once, a silly work, and somebody else made a bum movie out
of it" (309-10). Gorman and Kennedy, of course, are only
retelling the story themselves.

As the description of Kiki being "mythicized" reveals, the
most notable source through which Diamond is transformed
into myth in *Legs* is through the media and specifically
through journalism, a process Kennedy himself knew of well
from his career in the newspaper business. Journalistic
records, it will be remembered, were one of the sources of the
contradictory depictions of the real Jack Diamond that
Kennedy discovered while he was writing his novel. Within
Legs, the journalists are often cited as the main vehicle for
the promotion of the myth of Diamond. While in Germany,
for example, Diamond is called "'der Shack,' a mythic
nickname the German press had invented" (107). The attention given to Diamond by the press turned Jack the
individual into a public figure of legendary renown, with
ever more emphasis on the legend than on the reality:

So the newsmen, installing Jack in the same
hierarchy where they placed royalty, heroes, and

movie stars, created him anew as they enshrined him. They invented a version of him with each story they wrote, added to his evil luster by imagining crimes for him to commit, embellishing his history, humanizing him, defining him through their own fantasies and projections. (89)

Diamond became, as Gorman says, a "product of the collective imagination" (89), especially the imagination of the newsmen, rather than a product of his own historical individuality.

Diamond himself comments at least once on this loss of control over who he is, this handing over of his identity to the "collective imagination," although he makes his comment in an attempt to distinguish himself from the criminal that he is portrayed to be in the newspapers. In the *Daily News*, a New York newspaper, Diamond protests that the "stuff" written about him "has created a mythical figure in the public mind. Now I'm Jack Diamond and I've got to defend myself against the mythical crimes of the mythical Legs" (243). Diamond is thus well aware of the phenomenon of his own mythicization, to the point of distinguishing between his historical and his mythological self.

* * *

Although Kennedy has said that "the idea of how myth is created" was "central" to his book, much of *Legs* realistically depicts the life of Jack Diamond the criminal. This life is seen to be outrageous and brutal; it shows Diamond engaged in the torture and murder of both his rivals and those innocents caught up in the rackets he runs. But while Kennedy depicts or informs us of much of this activity—the realistic or even historical facts of the criminal—the novel also presents a Jack Diamond who is in fact mythical, whose powers and status (as they are dramatized in *Legs*, at least) actually validate Legs's status as a mythological figure. The methods of presenting these mythical, often supernatural qualities are various: they include dramatizing Diamond's special powers or merely having a character—most frequently Gorman—assert the special power that he or she senses in Diamond. And the powers themselves too are various, ranging from the magical to the specifically mythological, and culminating in the most startling power of all, Diamond's possible immortality.

Part of depicting Diamond as a specifically "mythological" figure includes portraying him throughout *Legs* as having what one might call generally "magical" powers. The evidence for some of these powers is admittedly questionable in some cases, often coming from the conversation of unreliable characters or being so outlandish as to be silly. One such dubious source is Joe Vignola, a witness to one of the murders Diamond commits. Vignola goes crazy while in protective custody because one night he sees Diamond dressed as a Boy Scout coming through the bars of his cell to kill him (65). Diamond's friend Flossie, for her part, believes that Jack could turn on a light by snapping his fingers, run up a wall and halfway across the ceiling, outrun a rabbit, and tie both his shoes at once. She also believes that his powers extend to his pets. According to her, Diamond had a collie who could count to fifty-two and do subtraction. Tipper seconds this power of Diamond's, saying that the gangster had a dog that knew how to toe dance. And Packy tells a story about Jack's dog taking an elevator up to the gangster's hotel room in order to get a sweater for him. When the dog did not come back, Diamond went upstairs to look for it only to discover that the dog was sewing a missing button on the sweater for him. While each of these anecdotes can be dismissed easily, and while their primary role is to reveal how Diamond's history was distorted and mythicized, they nonetheless indicate in their way the magic that Diamond held over those who knew him; no one would dare to tell such outrageous stories about a less charismatic person.

More interesting and significant than these obviously comic exaggerations are other tales about Diamond that signal his magical power and that are told with no sense of hyperbole and from a more reliable narrative point of view, most notably Gorman's. On the ship cruise to Europe, for example, Jack's presence causes a stir among the passengers, including journalists from European newspapers, and his interaction with all these people leads to some peculiar results, as Gorman himself tells us:

> Just after meeting the British press Jack complained to me of itching hands, small red dots which gave up a clear fluid when squeezed. The broken pustules then burned like dots of acid. A passenger shot off three of his toes at skeet and blamed Jack for hexing the weapon. Then the Minneapolis librarian [who had an affair with Diamond] cut her wrists, but chose against death and summoned help. (90)

Jack, thus, seems to emit a certain mysterious power, and a sinister one at that, causing strange boils, painful accidents, and attempted suicide. As his friend Flossie says more generally of him, "He was magic. He had power. Power over people" (310).

Diamond's power is evident also in his interaction with the animal world, and not just in teaching dogs silly tricks, as Flossie and Tipper might make one think. While Jack is returning from Europe on a ship, he descends into the hold of the boat in order to view some canaries the ship is carrying. As soon as Diamond entered the hold, the "Hartz Mountain birds . . . stopped singing" (111). Startled by this, Jack goes up to look at the birds and asks the sailor who is feeding them if he can help, but the sailor says the birds wouldn't like Diamond, that they quit singing when he entered the room because they know who he is. "They love people," the sailor says, but "they're afraid of you" (112). Unconvinced, Diamond attempts to help feed the birds anyway, but the results reveal his strange power:

> Jack opened a cage to gentle one of the birds. It pecked once at his knuckle. He lifted the bird out and saw it was dead. He put it in his pocket and opened another cage. That bird flew out, silently, and perched on top of the highest stack of cages, beyond Jack's reach unless he used the sailor's ladder. The bird twisted its tail and shat on the floor in front of Jack. (112)

The instinctive fear and disgust the birds have for Jack is in some ways more convincing evidence for Diamond's powers than are the stories from the human beings with whom he interacts. The power that the human mind has to imagine what it wants and to delude itself cannot be blamed for what happens with the canaries.

Diamond's special nature—usually not a positive force, as these stories show—is one that is even apparent to the skeptical Marcus Gorman: "I noticed that Jack had a luminous quality at certain moments, when he stood in shadow," Gorman writes at one point (105). And even though Gorman says that he suspects "a derangement of [his] vision," he adds, "I remember that the luminosity intensified when Jack said that I should carry a pistol to protect myself. . . ." (105). This "luminosity" or "energy" (106) eventually leads the less-than-gullible lawyer to believe not only in Jack's special powers but in a whole "world run not by a hierarchy of talents but by a hierarchy of shining energetics" (106). Like a prophet, Diamond introduces the stoical and practical lawyer to a mysterious, improbable world.

Gorman praises Diamond's luminosity—what he calls elsewhere Jack's "vital current" (48)—numerous times throughout *Legs*. He describes Diamond in a toast late in the book as someone whose energy is ubiquitous, and he even attributes to Diamond powers of illumination, talents usually reserved for God: "You are the undercurrent of our lives," Gorman says, "You turn on our light. . . ." (289). And after being surprised at seeing Jack use a rosary, Gorman says that the gangster was offering up the "cheapjack stuff of his ragged optimism to the only mystical being he truly understood," and that being was Diamond "Himself" (243). "No one else," Gorman insists, "had the power to change the life at hand" (243). A few pages after he is found using the rosary, Diamond, this "mystical being," to the great pleasure of an audience, dances with both his wife and his mistress simultaneously in a scene that is the apotheosis of this magical gangster and that seems to confirm Gorman's praises: Jack and the two women "twirled on their own axis and spun around the room to the waltz like a perfect circle as the slowly growing applause of the entire room carried them up, up, and up into the ethereal sphere where people truly know how to be happy" (248).

Diamond's ability to ascend into an "ethereal sphere" endows him with the kind of magical powers that make his mythicization by his public understandable, though not necessarily laudable, within the context of the narrative. But to reinforce that these powers are truly "mythical" and not merely magical or vaguely supernatural, to validate even more Legs's mythicization, there are throughout the novel numerous references to the specifically mythical nature of the gangster or of places where he spent his time. The Rain-Bo room, where Diamond often went for a drink and music, is one such mythological locale, though it is a place, Gorman says, "whose mythology has not been handed on" (235). Also of a mythological nature are a mountain where Diamond often travels and a car he owns, as Gorman lets us know in one of his numerous anecdotes about the gangster. After he has left Diamond in a New York mountaintop restaurant, Gorman almost finds himself in an accident on his way down the mountain while riding with one of Diamond's henchmen. Gorman must then give "traffic directions to a bleeding, one-eyed psychopath who was, with one hand, trying to drive a mythic vehicle backwards up an enchanted mountain" (78). It is, of course, the fact that Diamond owns the car that makes it "mythic" and also the fact that he, as the ruling gangster in the area, in effect "owns" the mountain that makes it "enchanted." Gorman, despite his serious and skeptical nature, can still believe in Diamond's mythical nature to such an extent that he humorously muses over the predicaments that Diamond's mythological status might cause: as Gorman asks at one point, "How does a mythical figure ask a lady to dance?" (243). As we have seen, such a figure might solve the problem by asking both his wife and his mistress to dance at once, and in a perfect three-step be apotheosized before an adoring audience.

As narrator, Gorman is the most important source of these impressions of Diamond as myth, and in this role he makes numerous other references and allusions to that mythological nature, references that are all the more believable considering Gorman's skeptical personality. Gorman states in one instance, for example, that the artist Thomas Cole's painting, *Prometheus Bound*, reminds him of Jack (167), and later, in reflecting back on Diamond's life, he states that he believes that Diamond was "an ancestral paradigm for modern urban political gangsters" (215). Gorman goes on to explain the difference between the mythological Diamond and another "crook" who, Gorman believes, does not share that special mysterious quality that can transform a person into myth:

> . . . I don't want to trivialize Jack's achievement by linking him to lesser latter-day figures such as Richard Nixon, who left significant history in his wake, but no legend; whose corruption, over- whelmingly venal and invariably hypocritical, lacked the admirably white core fantasy that can give evil a

mythical dimension.   Only boobs and shitheads
rooted for Nixon in his troubled time, but heroes and
poets followed Jack's tribulations with curiosity,
ambivalent benevolence, and a sense of mystery at
the meaning of their own response. (216)

Villains may abound, Gorman implies, but not villains with
a "white core fantasy" that enables them to become legend.

Of all Diamond's magical and mythological powers, the
most outrageous one dramatized in the narrative is his
immortality. While Diamond has been described as figuratively immortal in the memory of friends and in the
"collective imagination" of the public, within *Legs* itself he
is also described as being literally immortal: he is a character who seems unable to die and who in the end survives
his own death.[8] The mythicization of Diamond in *Legs* is
thus presented through a combination of the public's
exaggeration and imaginative rewriting of the historical
Diamond; the impressions of Diamond's magical and mythic
nature by other characters, especially Gorman; and the
dramatized manifestations of Diamond's powers, the most
stunning of which is his immortality.

The importance of Diamond's immortality in *Legs* is
evident in the way that the novel both opens and closes on
an insistence on this immortality. Marcus Gorman opens the
book by saying in reference to Diamond, "'I really don't
think he's dead'" (11).   Gorman is sitting in a bar remi-
niscing with the three other old friends of Diamond's, at least
two of whom agree with the lawyer about the gangster's not
being dead. Gorman listens to them talk about Diamond's
death and the possibility of his still being alive, thinks about
what he knows of the topic himself, and then announces his
own conclusion about the gangster's fate to his three friends:

"Say what you will," I told them, . . . remembering
[the] autopsy myself, remembering Jack's face intact

but the back of his head blown away by . . . three soft-nosed .38-caliber bullets: one through his right jaw, tearing the neck muscle, cutting the spinal cord, and coming out through the neck and falling on the bed; another entering his skull near the right ear and moving upward through his brain, fracturing his skull, and remaining in the fracture; and the third, entering the left temple, taking a straight course across the brain and stopping just above the right ear.

"I still don't think he's dead." (12–13)

The possibility of accepting the startling juxtaposition between such graphic evidence of death and such an insistence on Diamond's not being dead will find supporting evidence throughout the tale Gorman is about to tell, including testimony from the most important witness of all, the "dead" Jack Diamond. It is his voice that concludes the novel, though he himself has been shot and killed, in an echo of Gorman's own introductory words: "'Honest to God, Marcus,'" the dead Diamond says, "'I really don't think I'm dead'" (317).

Kennedy has said that his initial inspiration for dramatizing the gangster's immortality was his desire to "suggest something very aligned to the sense of transmutation that is one of the most striking things in the *Tibetan Book of the Dead*—the notion that people are born again into this life or they transcend it, cease to exist, enter Nirvana" (McCaffery, 167). Although the final version of the novel moved some distance from this original conception,[9] the inspiration of *The Tibetan Book of the Dead* is still apparent in the exploration of Diamond's immortality in the book, a possibility that is not as outrageous as it might first seem in light of the fact that Diamond lived through at least four attacks on his life. In the novel, this ability to survive endows him with an aura of invincibility and makes his immortality a more probable conclusion than one might otherwise think.

As he is with Diamond's other though less impressive magical powers—his luminosity or vital current, for example—Marcus Gorman is also the important commentator on Diamond's immortality. Gorman often implies, as he makes clear from the opening line of the novel, that Diamond just might be able to live forever. As he says of one of the first attacks on Diamond, which was an attempt to kill the gangster and his then partner, Augie Orgen, "Jack took the gang over after he and Augie were both shot in a labor racketeering feud. Augie died, but you can't kill Legs Diamond" (66). Much later in the novel, Gorman toasts the gangster by repeating his admiration for Diamond's ability to endure what seems impossible: "I toast . . . to his uncanny ability to bloom in hostile seasons," Gorman says, "and to survive the blasts of doom" (289).

Gorman's belief and his consequent admiration are not mere bravado, as the various attempts on Diamond's life that are dramatized within the novel attest. After one such attempt, the comic understatement of Kiki's discovery of the injured Diamond announces the matter-of-fact nature of the gangster's miraculous ability to survive: Kiki "saw the door open and Jack on the floor with his eyes open but not moving, looking up at her. And she said, 'Oh, Jackie, you're dead,' but he said, 'No I'm not, help me up . . .'" (157). Kiki's and Diamond's simple and comically understated declarations belie the seriousness of the gangster's injuries. Kiki discovers that Diamond was shot in "two places in the chest and once in the stomach and once in the thigh and once in the forehead," and the doctor that works on him says that Diamond "was certainly not going to be able to go on living with all those holes in himself" (158). Diamond, however, certainly does survive to continue his illegal activities and, eventually, to subject himself to yet another attempt on his life. His survival confirms what Kiki herself believes, that Diamond "'didn't die easy'" (72). As she says,

"'Some people could cut their little toe and give up and bleed to death. Jack never gave up, not his body, not anything'" (73).

After yet another shooting, the wounded Jack is discovered by one of his gang members, who found "Jack on his stomach, blood bubbling out of holes in his back" (227). Diamond's reaction to this attempt is the same understated bravado he had when Kiki found him: "'Bum shooting,' Jack said, 'Better luck next time'" (227). While Diamond is not as seriously injured this time as during the previous attempt, his surviving the attack again attests to his unusual ability to avoid death. Gorman writes:

> They'd hit him with four half-ounce pellets. They'd fired ten double-ought shells with nine pellets to a shell. Somebody counted eighty some holes in the windows, the siding, and the inside porch walls. Ninety pellets out of two shot guns, and they only hit him with four, part of one shell. It really *was* bum shooting, Jack. You ought to be dead, and then some. (228)

But Jack is neither dead nor "then some." Ironically he is removed from the scene of this shooting in the hearse of an undertaker friend, for Diamond does not want any police involved. The only role of a hearse in Diamond's life, it seems, is to take him to the hospital where death will once again be evaded. Like a mythic figure invulnerable to the futile attempts of lesser men to destroy him, Diamond inexplicably survives numerous attacks, any one of which ought to have ended his life.

Although after the first two attacks on his life Diamond expresses a certain awareness of his own mortality, and although he is a notably unreflective character, Diamond's odd ability to survive makes even him wonder about his ability to keep on living. When Gorman finds a prayer book by Diamond's hospital bed after one of the shootings, for example, Diamond confesses that he's been "dreaming," that he's been "talking to God," and then he asks Gorman, "Why the hell is it I'm not dead?" (163). But Diamond answers the question himself before Gorman can reply: it's "because I'm in God's grace," he says, and "because God wants me to live" (163). Though Gorman remains impressed with Jack's ability to survive, he scoffs at these ideas, at the gangster's unexpected return to what the lawyer calls the "holy smoke" of religion (164). But Jack's reply to Gorman is quick and indicative of his attitude toward his own inability to die: "What the hell am I supposed to do after people keep shooting me and I don't die? I'm beginning to think I'm being saved" (164). So strong is this belief that the possibility of his own death slowly begins to seem either unlikely or even insulting to Diamond. Here Gorman describes Jack's reaction to one of the shootings: "'Jesus, they really almost got me, almost wiped me out,' [Diamond] said one night and shook his head as if this were an incredible possibility, some wild fancy that had nothing to do with the real life and potential of John Thomas Diamond" (182).

Ironically, more threatening than the attempts on Jack's life is the simultaneous attack by the judicial system against Diamond's criminal power. In Gorman's mind, the tedious machinations of the legal system, and the difficulty Diamond increasingly has in extricating himself from prosecution and sentencing, are a far worse fate for Diamond than the shootings. Gorman even describes Diamond during one summer in which the gangster undergoes several state and federal prosecutions as a wolf "who was learning the hard way how to die" (253).

Despite Gorman's ability to get Diamond acquitted against overwhelming evidence (and obvious guilt), the legal system and its trials eventually take their toll on Jack, undermining his pride, his identity, his self-confidence, and his magical powers alike. After a trial over Diamond's kidnapping and torture of the driver of a truck of cider, Legs feels an impulse to toss rotten eggs at the newspapermen following him; as he says of himself when he thinks of such a juvenile and pathetic act, "this was the Jack Diamond who once hired a press agent to get his name around" (287). While he's undressing after the trial, he discovers a card to get into a speakeasy, and he realizes that once his name alone opened any door for him, but that now others were imitating him and no one believed that he was himself. He seems to have lost control over himself, over his own identity, the Jack giving way to Legs giving way to numerous Diamonds. He uses the cards now to get into the bars "because he no longer even looked like his own pictures" (288). Diamond's collapsing self-confidence is also reflected in his worries about further prosecution as he considers the "no end of other charges pending" (288). And when he leaves the party celebrating his acquittal in order to visit Kiki (Marion Roberts) for a while, he has "no climax" despite their attempt at sex: "Jack erected, Marion lubricious, they could've danced all night. But Jack wearied of the effort, and Marion ran out of her capacity to groan with pleasure. They rolled away from each other and let the sweat slowly cool, the breathing return to normal, the artifacts dry" (297). This fatigued and exasperated figure is a far cry from the mythic angel who ascended into the heavens with both Kiki and his wife on his arms.

After the failed sex, Diamond returns to the rooming house where he is staying during the trial and marvels at the "giddiness" he feels over his acquittal (287). It's a natural reaction, despite the signs of his unraveling, but he also wonders why he jeopardized everything he worked for over the pointless kidnapping and torture of a driver of one truck of cider. Diamond's doubts about himself hint again at his personal disintegration, one that is overtly symbolized once he reaches his room by the odd inability of his clothes to follow the laws of physical reality. As Diamond begins to undress, he finds that these clothes, beginning with his hat and coat, are tossed into a chaotic or entropic world of disorder and uncertainty that his previously legendary nature had been able to overcome: "When he'd tossed his forty-dollar brown velour hat onto the bed, it had hit the threadbare spread and rolled off. He folded his brown chinchilla coat . . . over the footboard, and it too slipped to the floor" (287). With each item Diamond takes off, the disintegration continues: "Jack took off the coat of his lucky blue suit and hung it on the back of the chair. . . . The suit coat fell to the floor in a pile" (289); "Jack undid his tie, blue with diagonal white stripes, and hung it on the upright pole of the dresser mirror. It slid off" (290); "Jack . . . took off the blue pants" and hung them "on the open drawer of the tawdry dresser, and they stayed there a few seconds before they fell to the floor" (295); and Jack took off his shoes, dropping them to the floor, and then tried but failed to drop his socks into them (297, 298).

This sartorial disintegration—what Loxley Nichols calls a "sartorial mutation" (46)—mirrors the simultaneous disintegration of Diamond's personal vital force that had separated him from his common—and mortal—fellow human beings. The numerous trials have affected the man (and the myth) more severely than any attempt on his life. After he undresses, Diamond wonders what will happen next for him now that he has been acquitted and now that his organization has also been broken up:

> Jack would not begin life again in the same way. Adirondacks? Vermont? Maybe. But Coll was in jail, his mob busted up after a shoot-out in Averill Park and a roundup in Manhattan. Jack would have to recruit from scratch, and the prospect was wearying. So many dead and gone. Mike Sullivan, Fatty Walsh, Eddie. He [remembered] all the old boys, friends and enemies. Brocco. Babe. Frenchy.

Shorty. Pretty. Mattie. Hymie. Fogarty. Dead, gone off, or in jail. And he seemed to himself, for the first time, a curiously perishable item among many such items, a thing of just so many seasons. When does the season end? (298)

Despite numerous attacks on his life, it is the weariness of going to trial that at last has Diamond considering his own mortality, the end of his "season." His vital current has been replaced with resignation. The system rather than the machine gun seems to have discovered and attacked the man's vulnerability.

Yet even amid these doubts and failings—his own inner consternation, the exhaustion of his undressing, his failed sexual powers—the night after Diamond's acquittal nonetheless seems to hold for the gangster also some mysterious revelation and it signals in its own way the mythical nature of this criminal. At one point Jack feels a "new surge of giddiness": "it was bringing him a breakthrough perception. I am on the verge of getting it all wrapped up, he said to the steam heat that hissed at him from the radiator. I hear it coming. I have been true to everything in life" (289). And even as Diamond begins to doubt himself, he also still believes that he will be able to solve the problems affecting his gang and his livelihood, a belief that indicates that he will indeed be true to himself until the end: "something would come up," he says to himself (298) at one point, and he also believed that "he would solve it," whatever the problems facing him might be (299). Diamond feels, in fact, that he has been "designed," and he is "so happy with his perception of being what was designed, so released from the struggle to change, that he begins with a low rumble that rises from the sewers of madness; and yet he is not mad, only enlightened" (299). Eventually from this low rumble, "his whole being . . . is convulsed with an ecstasy of recognition" (299). Out of the chaos and disintegration of his night, some mysterious ecstasy or "Nirvana"—as the influence of *The Tibetan Book of the Dead* should make us consider calling it—some sense of his purpose or place in the world, has begun to overtake Diamond.

What this gangster discovers or recognizes, other than his own unchanging nature, his being true to his own life, is never explored or defined further in the novel. Diamond says little more to explain his revelation, and soon after it he is finally murdered—as if the weariness of his trial permitted an opening in his invincibility—and the myth of the gangster's immortality is momentarily punctured. But even though the ramifications of Diamond's self-discovery are never explained, his assertion of his mystical self-awareness makes less surprising the curious final chapter of *Legs*, which begins when "Jack (Legs) Diamond, aged thirty-four years, five months, seven days, and several hours, sat up in bed in his underwear and stared into the mirror at his new condition: incipiently dead" (315). Such a description is the most startling assertion in the book of Diamond's immortality, rendering literal what heretofore has been figurative or hyperbolic. No longer described in merely metaphorical terms—as the subject of a conversation, as an inspiring memory, as a mythicized celebrity, as a shooting victim bragging of his survival—the "incipiently dead" Diamond sits up and surveys his wounds, realizing that someone has finally succeeded in killing him.

In death, Diamond has attained a moment "outside time" (315) and has several improbable visitors, including Damon Runyon and, it seems, the still-living Gorman, who is (impossibly) narrating the scene. Eventually Diamond finds that he is "completely dead," his soul having escaped from the top of his injured head. It is then that he knows his "last human feeling: his body being blown to atoms, the feeling of fire sinking into air" (317). He is dead though he seems to possess in death as he did in life superhuman quali-

ties and his own special luminosity. As the narrator, presumably Gorman, says,

> [Diamond] looked around the room, but could see no
> one any longer, though we were all there, watching.
> He felt his absent pupils dilate to receive the light,
> which was his own light as well as everyone else's.
> When the light came, it was not the brilliant
> whiteness Jack expected, but a yellowish, grayish light
> that made no one blink. The motion of the light was
> perceptible. It swirled around Jack's neck like a
> muffler, rose up past his eyes and hairline like a
> tornado in crescendo, spun round his entire head
> with what was obviously a potentially dazzling
> ferocity, reduced in effect now by the horrendous life-
> tone of Jack Diamond. It was obvious to everyone
> that given propitious conditions it could centripetally
> slurp the entire spirit of Jack into the vortex and
> make off with it forever; but now it moved only like a
> bit of fog on a sunny morning, coiled by a frolicsome
> breeze, then gone, with not enough force to slurp up
> a toupee. (317)

Diamond, ever the mythical figure, seems strong enough
somehow to survive this mysterious wind, but he is nonetheless soon "falling backward" and after that "twisting and
flailing against this ignominious new development" (317).
But before he "disappeared into the void, into the darkness
where the white was still elusive," he yells out: "'Honest to
God, Marcus, . . . I really don't think I'm dead'" (317). And
thus as the novel began, so does it end: with the insistence
(this time by the dead Jack Diamond himself) that the
gangster is not, in fact, dead after all.

What this imagery and this highly imaginative scene adds
up to ultimately is debatable. Larry McCaffery feels that the
ending "seems to suggest that Jack has, in some sense, failed
to make that final leap into transcendence, that he's doomed

to be reborn into other incarnations . . ." (167, McCaffery).
For his part, Loxley Nichols believes that in "death Diamond
does not stop being, he merely undergoes a 'sartorial
mutation' of sorts and 'goes away,' pulled sluggishly by an
oversoul" (Nichols, 46-47). However one might read this
final, curious chapter—as Diamond's transcendence or as the
impossibility of his transcendence; as Diamond's soul swirled
into heaven or down to hell or back to earth—what is
significant is that the soul itself seems to survive Diamond's
death. Diamond's immortality has previously been primarily
hyperbole or metaphor, but in this final chapter it is
depicted as a literal condition: Diamond observes his own
death and, though murdered, asserts that he does not think
he is dead. Kennedy attests to both the uncertainty and the
power of this image by insisting that the scene is "utter
metaphor" while also admitting the undeniably mystical
element of the ending and even wondering aloud in an
interview in what form Diamond might be reincarnated
(McCaffery, 167).[10]

Such questions of reincarnation are beyond the scope of
the novel, but within the text Diamond has still stepped
"outside time" altogether in the final chapter to become the
mythical figure that his friends and the journalists had all
along imagined him to be. By this ending, as Jack Diamond
witnesses his own death, he has also moved out of the
tangled history that Kennedy studied in writing the novel
into a mythical, eternal state in the story. Through this
process, the novel itself thus promotes the transformation of
a historical figure into a mythic one, so that this transformation becomes both the focus of *Legs* and the phenomenon
that the novel itself helps to accomplish. In *Legs*, Kennedy
dramatizes the myth of Jack Diamond; and through *Legs* he
is passing on that myth, the legend of a universal hero and
sadistic criminal. Although Kennedy claims that his final
chapter is "utter metaphor," his method of dramatizing a
magical, mythical, and ultimately immortal Diamond allows

one to read the novel not only as depicting but also enacting Diamond's mythicization. No one would claim that Kennedy feels Diamond actually could kill canaries on touch or observe his own death, but in dramatizing such possibilities, Kennedy has nonetheless contributed to the mythicization of a celebrity. He has shown how Legs Diamond could be considered figuratively immortal in memory and in legend; while showing this figurative immortality he has dramatized a literally immortal figure within his narrative; and in the process of dramatizing this immortal figure he has contributed to the initial figurative immortality of the legend of Legs himself.

Kennedy reveals and sustains this legend of Diamond by mixing in his novel—in the style of the magical realists—the real and the surreal, the actual and the imagined, a mixture which echoes the work of the journalists who wrote about the gangster and who Kennedy studied in writing his book. Susan Agrest has noted that in Kennedy's fiction in general he "is neither reined in by the [newsworthy] event nor burdened by the duty of getting all the facts" and that he is instead "able to give his characters the mythic dimensions he loves" (Agrest, 48). This is exactly what happens in *Legs* in particular as Kennedy combines actual historical fact with the "products of one man's imagination" to "reinvent" Jack "Legs" Diamond. This reinvention leads to a novel that depicts how the legend of Diamond was passed on and that also becomes a participant in that endeavor. As Kennedy has said, Diamond "was destined to be reborn, . . . perpetuated in this society by people like Marcus [Gorman], and me, who have retold the legends that grew up around him" (McCaffery, 167). Kennedy admits that he sustains the myth of Legs Diamond in the same way that the narrator of his own novel does. It is an admirable if disturbing accomplishment: as the Ionesco epigraph to the book notes, "People like killers," and this book reveals and embodies the seductive powers of such killers.

Legs, thus, embodies the theme its narrative pursues: the ability of the imagination to transform the history it observes. Both the story within the narrative and the book itself reveal the important conception within Kennedy's work of the ability of history to be transformed by the artist's imagination. It is a conception founded on a belief in the fluidity of traditionally distinct moments of time, as what is historical moves "outside time" into myth, as what happened (or who lived) back "then" still lives on "now" in memory, myth, fiction or—possibly—actuality. In *Legs* in particular, this belief is revealed in how the history of Jack Diamond is transformed within the narrative of the novel and through the novel itself into the (immortal) myth of the possibly immortal Legs Diamond.

Notes

1. See "Introduction," pp. 8–15, for a discussion of which books constitute Kennedy's Albany cycle.

2. The transformation of the historical into a timeless myth or archetype occurs especially through art in Kennedy's fiction. The playwright Emmett Daugherty transforms Francis Phelan's actions during a trolley strike and his own affair with the actress Melissa Spencer into well-known dramatic productions in the narratives of *Ironweed*, *Billy Phelan's Greatest Game*, and *The Flaming Corsage*. Such a transformation is also the phenomenon Kennedy will both write about and practice himself in *Quinn's Book*, a novel in which the character Daniel Quinn attempts to reconcile his artistic impulses with the history he observes as a journalist and in which actual natural disasters are described by Kennedy in mythological terms in the opening scenes of that novel. In addition, this kind of transformation will be the crucial means of the redemption of the entire Phelan family in *Very Old Bones* as Peter Phelan recaptures much of his family's history in a series of paintings and in the process purges the family of many of its skeletons.

3. The word "myth" in talking about Legs Diamond is used throughout this chapter and this study in general to mean what Kennedy seems to mean by it, a "popular belief or tradition that has grown up around something or someone" (*Webster's Ninth New Collegiate Dictionary*). It does not mean either of two other popular connotations of myth as supplied by *Webster's*: a "traditional story of ostensibly

historical events that serves to unfold part of the world view of a people or explain a practice, belief, or natural phenomenon"; or "an unfounded or false notion." Because of the definition used here, "myth" is occasionally used interchangeably with "legend" and, less frequently, with "archetype." The terms "mythical" and "mythological" are likewise used in their general connotations of having qualities pertaining to myth, and they are thus also used interchangeably, as are the verbs "to mythicize" and "to mythologize."

4. For a discussion of some of the historical background concerning Jack Diamond and his murder, see "Prohibition: It Can't Happen Here;" "The Death of Legs Diamond;" and "They Bury the Boss: Dan Ex-Machina" in Kennedy's *O Albany!* See also Van Dover, 41-42.

5. Gorman is based in part on the real-life attorney for Jack Diamond, Daniel H. Prior. In *Billy Phelan's Greatest Game*, Gorman offers to defend one of the culprits in the McCall kidnapping case just as Prior actually defended one of the culprits in the famous O'Connell kidnapping case upon which the story in *Billy Phelan* is based (see *OA*, 92-93). Gorman also plays a small role in *Ironweed*, for he agrees to represent the jailed Francis Phelan for a reduced fee. His demand for this fee forces Francis to find work and leads him to his important journey to St. Agnes Cemetery in Albany at the beginning of that novel.

6. Stephen Whittaker believes that Gorman's point of view as a lawyer is one of the defining characteristics of *Legs*. Whittaker writes that " . . . Kennedy makes the reader's dependence upon the lawyer as narrator a predominant characteristic of the book and the reader's problem becomes, like a juror's, the problem of choosing among competing stories, or narrations, built out of more or less the same facts" (158).

7. The comparison to Carraway is itself encouraged by both Gorman and Kennedy. Gorman refers to *The Great Gatsby* in saying that Diamond had met F. Scott Fitzgerald and that Diamond's car "was a facsimile of the Gatsby machine" (73-74). And in an interview, Kennedy responded to a question about the similarities between *Legs* and *Gatsby* by saying that these similarities are "deliberate" (Quinn, 71). Kennedy adds: "*Gatsby's* a great book, I think. . . . I wouldn't want anybody to think I was cavalierly using the narration of Marcus Gorman about a gangster without understanding the precedent. But I also feel that the narrator in *Gatsby* was boring as a character, and I don't think Marcus is" (Quinn, 71). Kennedy also says that he feels that the biggest difference between Gatsby and Legs Diamond is that Gatsby was not a killer, only a thief (Quinn, 71).

8. The ability of a celebrity like Diamond not to die is, of course, a phenomenon not unlike that attributed to other celebrities such as

Elvis Presley, a man sighted throughout the world many years after his death.

9. See Kennedy's comments in his interview with Larry McCaffery and Sinda Gregory: "At one point in its trajectory through many, many forms, the novel was going to be structured as a totally surreal work, based in part on the *Tibetan Book of the Dead*, from which [the] last chapter [of *Legs*] derives. There is very little left of that original conception except that last chapter" (167).

10. Despite Kennedy's claim that the depiction of Diamond's immortality is figurative ("utter metaphor"), the combination of the realistic and surreal, the historical and the imaginative, is an important characteristic of Kennedy's approach to fiction and one that will reappear in various but significant ways throughout every book within the Albany cycle (as well as *The Ink Truck*). Such an approach, in offering an equally valid ontological status to both the figurative and literal, places Kennedy well within the category defined as magical realism. For a discussion of Kennedy as a magical realist, see Robert Gibb's dissertation, *The Life of the Soul: William Kennedy, Magical Realist.*

CHAPTER THREE

THE PRESENCE OF THE ABSENCE OF FATHERS IN
BILLY PHELAN'S GREATEST GAME

The title of *Billy Phelan's Greatest Game*, the second book of William Kennedy's Albany cycle, refers on the one hand to a simple bowling game, at which the good-natured hustler and gambler Billy Phelan rolls a 299. But the "greatest game" of the title also refers to life itself and how Billy Phelan plays it—specifically, how he handles himself when an acquaintance is kidnapped, a much more serious and complex affair than a bowling match. The victim of this kidnapping, Charlie Boy McCall, is the adult son of the McCall family who controls Albany politics and, consequently, the life of thirty-year-old Billy Phelan, who as a small-time gambler must abide by the McCall rules if he is to work in Albany.[1] One of the primary suspects, as it turns out, is also an acquaintance of Billy's (and Charlie Boy's) named Morrie Berman. Yet despite Billy's acquaintance with Morrie and with Charlie Boy, and despite the fact that the McCalls control Billy's business, Billy himself is hesitant to try to uncover what Morrie knows about the kidnapping, a task the McCalls ask him to do. Billy feels that such spying, despite the many arguments justifying it, violates his personal code of behavior, a code which includes his refusal to be a "squealer" and to cheat: like any game, relationships have rules too, and for Billy these rules cannot be broken.

Even though the plot of *Billy Phelan's Greatest Game* pursues this conflict between Billy's desire to remain true to his code and the McCalls' growing pressure on Billy to find out what he can about the kidnapping, and despite the implication of the title of the novel that we are to focus on Billy, another of Billy's acquaintances, Martin Daugherty, actually surfaces by novel's end to be as responsible for the outcome of the "game" Billy is playing as Billy himself. Martin, a writer twenty years Billy's senior and a former neighbor of Billy's father, is the only other character in the novel through whose point of view the story is told. He follows Billy around town, worrying about him, much as Leopold Bloom does for Stephen Dedalus. Billy has no one else to look after him because his father, the Francis Phelan of *Ironweed*, left Billy and the family over twenty years before the start of the action in *Billy Phelan's Greatest Game*. Martin's desire to help the fatherless Billy is motivated by his obsession throughout the novel with the fractured relationships between fathers and sons that he observes everywhere, an obsession brought on by Martin's alienation from both his own son (who wants to join a seminary) and his father (Edward Daugherty, the main character of *The Flaming Corsage*).

But while Martin may be concerned for Billy as a son without a father, this concern is not alone sufficient to get Martin to act on Billy's behalf against the McCalls. First Martin must heal himself, specifically his own relationships with his father and as a father. This healing comes through Martin's reunion with Melissa Spencer, an actress and the former mistress of both himself and his father, Edward.[2] In deciding to meet Melissa again when she returns to Albany after many years, Martin forces a troubling part of his own past to resurface as he reenacts in their lovemaking his own former affair, his father's former affair, and—because Melissa is now playing Katrina Daugherty, Martin's mother, on stage—even his father's lovemaking with his mother that leads to Martin's own conception.[3] Through this confusing, complex, and (for Martin) painful exploration and re-enactment of the past, of what happened back "then," Martin not only re-sees himself as the son of Edward Daugherty again but he is also being Edward for a moment, living through events, however perverse and complex, that Edward himself did. This heightened sense of who he and his father were indirectly helps Martin better appreciate the complicated relationship between fathers and sons every-where and thus appreciate and forgive both his own father and son. Eventually this struggle with his past also leads Martin to help two other sons who have a predicament right now in the present moment, Charlie Boy and Billy Phelan himself, as each plays the greatest, or at least the most important, game of their lives.

While the significance of Martin Daugherty's role in Billy's game is certainly evident by the end of *Billy Phelan's Greatest Game*, there is little evidence of that significance from the title or the opening scene of the novel. The story begins in a bowling alley at which Billy is in the middle of rolling a perfect game (although he will end up with a 299), on one level the "greatest game" of the book's title. Martin Daugherty, who is one of many watching the action, is impressed with what he is seeing. As he watched,

> Martin was already thinking of writing his next column about this game, provided Billy carried it off. He would point out how some men moved through the daily sludge and transformed themselves. Yet what they became was not the result of a sudden act, but the culmination of all they had ever done: a triumph for self-development, the end of something general, the beginning of something specific. (2)

To Martin, Billy is exactly that kind of person who is able to transform himself into something specific and special: as Martin believes, Billy is among those who are able to "send, in the time of their splendor, telegraphic statements of mission: I, you bums, am a winner" (8).

Despite Billy's performance and Martin's own conception of the young man's "winning" position in the world, Martin also cannot help wondering why he is so obsessed with someone whom he admits is a "low-level maestro unlikely to transcend, either as gambler, card dealer, dice or pool shooter" (6). It is a question many might ask of Kennedy himself—first a novel about a brutal gangster, and then one about a hustler. Martin Daugherty can supply at least some part of an answer, and that is simply that these are the people, like them or not, who make up Albany. In their compromised, human, maybe violent ways, they are the major players in the drama of this city, but players who you would also know as your neighbors, your boss, maybe your own family, those with whom you share a history. Why, Martin asks himself, "are you so obsessed with Billy Phelan? Why make a heroic *picaro* out of a simple chump?" (7). Martin answers his own question and in the process reveals what will be an important motivation for protecting Billy throughout the story:

> Well, says Martin, haven't I known him since he was a sausage? Haven't I seen him grow stridently into young manhood while I slip and slide softly into moribund middle age? Why, I knew him when he had a father, knew his father too, knew him when that father abdicated, and I ached for the boy then and have ever since, for I know how it is to live in the inescapable presence of the absence of the father. (7)

Martin's obsession for Billy thus derives from his and Billy's shared condition in the "inescapable presence of the absence of the father." Martin feels that even though his father, a playwright, was physically present during Martin's youth, the man was nonetheless emotionally absent, wrapped up in his artistic passions and adulterous affairs: Martin concedes that he had "too much father" but he also adds that he had "too much absence as the great man pursued his greatness" (44). Billy's absent father, on the other hand, is literally gone—Francis Phelan, the hobo whose brief appearance in *Billy Phelan* is expanded on and portrayed in the third book of the Albany cycle, *Ironweed*. Francis ran away from Billy and the rest of the Phelan family in 1916, over twenty years prior to the events in *Billy Phelan*, when Billy was a young boy. The reason for this flight was the guilt Francis felt over accidentally causing the death of his thirteen-day-old son (and Billy's brother), Gerald. Significantly, Billy does not know his father's reason for fleeing; Billy's mother, Annie, has never explained Francis' role in Gerald's death. While this secret attests on the one hand to Annie's kindness to Francis, it leaves the motivation for Francis' departure and absence much less clear to Billy.

Billy's relationship with Francis receives little more emphasis in *Billy Phelan* than other father-son relationships in the novel, and it receives far less attention than Martin's relationship with his father. But this does not mean that the significance of Francis' absence in Billy's life is not apparent in the narrative. Billy meets his father during the days around the McCall kidnapping, asking him to come home to visit the family, and at one point Billy tells Martin how disappointed he is in the advice Francis gave him on how to handle the McCall affair. Billy also often looks at the old Phelan home where Francis grew up with disgust because he feels the family has always rejected and despised the errant Francis.[4] And when Billy thinks about the separation of Charlie Boy McCall from his father after Charlie is abducted, his very next thought is about his own "fatherless" life. Billy considers that the kidnappers "took Charlie Boy's world away from him and maybe they'll even kill him," and then he

immediately thinks about when his own "father was gone for
a year," specifically how

> his Uncle Chick told him he might never come back
> and that Billy would pretty soon forget his father and
> develop all sorts of substitutes, because that was how
> it went in life. Chick was trying to be kind to Billy
> with that advice. Chick wasn't as bad as the rest of
> them. And did Billy develop substitutes for his father?
> Well, he learned how to gamble. He got to know
> Broadway [the main Albany street]. (243)

Although Martin does not realize it, his admiration for Billy's
style as a gambler is in part an admiration for the one and
obviously inadequate substitute Billy has found for his own
absent father.

Although Billy's separation from Francis has made him
sensitive to the separated McCall father and son, he decides
that he wants nothing to do with the attempts to find Charlie
and catch the kidnappers, despite his close acquaintance
with one of the primary suspects (and, eventually, the proven
culprit), Morrie Berman. Billy's decision on the way he plays
this game of life, the true "greatest game" of the title, is in
part pragmatic:

> All anybody on Broadway needed to hear was that
> Billy was finking on Morrie. . . . Who'd trust him after
> that? Who'd tell him a secret? Who'd lend him a
> quarter? He wouldn't have a friend on the whole
> fucking street. It'd be the dead end of Billy's world,
> all he ever lived for, and the McCalls were asking him
> to risk that. Asking hell, telling him. (156)

Despite these legitimate worries on Billy's part, one suspects
that these pragmatic issues are not the real consideration, for
the McCalls, the "Irish-American potentates of the night and
the day" (3), have, after all, their own highly effective threat
against Billy, one far worse than the rejection he would get

from friends if he "finked." In their control of the Albany gambling joints, the McCalls can easily prohibit Billy from working at all. Kennedy's description of the reach of the actual O'Connell political machine, upon which the fictional McCalls were based, gives a clear picture of how Billy Phelan's own life would have been affected by the McCalls:

> Your identity was fixed by both religion and politics, but from the political hierarchy came the way of life: the job, the perpetuation of the job, the dole when there was no job, the loan when there was no dole, the security of the neighborhood, the new streetlight, the new sidewalk, the right to run your bar after hours or to open a card game on the sneak. These things came to you not by right of citizenship. Republicans had no such rights. They came to you because you gave allegiance to Dan O'Connell and his party. The power he held was so pervasive that you often didn't even know it existed until you contravened it. Then God help you, poor soul. Cast into outer darkness. (*OA*, 43–44)

Eventually the McCalls use their fictional version of this ubiquitous power and mark Billy "lousy" (239), casting him into "outer darkness"; no bar will serve him or pool hall allow him to play. Otherwise, as the owners well know, they would have their taxes raised by the McCall-controlled political system.

The obvious threat of the McCalls to Billy's livelihood indicates that there is a more important consideration than pragmatism affecting Billy's decision not to "fink" or spy on Morrie. This consideration is his desire to remain true to his private ethical code, one of the tenets of which says he cannot go behind someone's back—cannot, in effect, cheat at the game of life by betraying someone. "'I ain't cut out to be a squealer,'" he says to Bindy McCall, Charlie's father, when Bindy asks for his help (198). That Billy is not merely rationalizing his own cowardice or pragmatism is evident from the fact that he refuses to go against his established code of conduct—to be honest, to pay his debts, to meet his obligations to others—several times throughout the novel during events other than the McCall kidnapping. The most notable of these instances is his insistence on paying a large debt he accrues in losing a bet to Martin Daugherty in which Martin is absurdly lucky. Part of Billy's code is to play by the rules, and paying debts such as Martin's is one of those rules. As he tells George Quinn, his brother-in-law, who is complaining about his own gambling situation, "Don't cry the blues to them. Don't beg for anything. If they say pay, just pay and shut up about it" (160).[5] The code, though simple to grasp in such situations as Martin's or George's, sometimes seems complex in how it is applied. Billy, for example, is willing to accept the services of a prostitute, but then beats up the pimp when he discovers the man is the prostitute's brother. Billy also attempts to lose a pool match intentionally—an event that will favor Morrie Berman—so that he will no longer feel obligated to Morrie and then might be free to "fink" on him.[6]

Although Billy's ethics declare that he must play by the rules and be willing to take a loss by them, he finds that his refusal to break the rules in the "game" of Charlie's kidnapping results in the loss of his entire livelihood. Though a good pool hustler, Billy is a man unprepared for the game of life: the kidnapping is a much bigger and more serious game, and one in which Billy is far removed from his natural environment of the pool and poker table and one that may, indeed, need different rules than the ones Billy plays by. The simple ethics of a regulated card game are far different than a situation in which human greed threatens a human life. When he first meets with the McCalls in their house after Charlie Boy's kidnapping, Billy senses the difference between his world and theirs, the world of the poker table and the world of power politics:

There was a world of behavior in this room Billy did
not grasp with the clarity he had in pool and poker,
or at the crap table. Billy knew jazz and betting and
booking horses and baseball. He knew how to stay at
arm's length from the family and how to make out.
He resisted knowing more than these things. If you
knew what the McCalls knew, you'd be a politician.
. . . They had their rewards but Billy did not covet
them. Tie you up in knots, pin you down, put you in
the box. He could learn anything, study it. He could
have been in politics years ago. . . . But he chose
other ways of staying alive. There never was a
politician Billy could really talk to, and never a
hustler he couldn't. (154)

Realizing that he is out of his element, Billy tries simply to
evade the issue of his possible role in solving the kidnapping,
ignoring the McCalls as long as he can, and then later telling
them only hunches of his which do not violate his personal
code. He is so confused by the affair that he admits himself
he doesn't know what to do; when a cop tells him to keep his
nose clean, he confesses that he was "not at all sure [that] he
knew how to do that" (156). In the end, what he says and
does is not enough, and when he draws the line and refuses
to help anymore, the McCalls shut down Albany to him.

Throughout Billy's ordeal with the McCalls, Martin
Daugherty keeps a careful eye on the younger man who so
inspired him at the bowling alley, a man with whom he
shares a notable "presence of the absence of the father" but
who also is as different from Martin as one can imagine. As
J. K. Van Dover has written,

Billy seems to exist in the moment, focusing his
energies on the game at hand, relying on his
"sassiness" to carry him through. He shows little
foresight, the most obvious example being his crucial

failure as a small-time bookie to lay off part of
Martin Daugherty's wager, and he seems to take little
account of the past. He is not consciously searching
for his father. He is naively surprised when his girlfriend presents him with the prospect of fatherhood.
Martin, by contrast, is all too aware of his place in
time. Even as he watches Billy bowl, he dwells upon
the future of his own errant son. With his reflections
on his own and Billy's pasts and his perpetual
thoughts about his father and his son, Martin
represents an intelligence preoccupied with time past
and time future. That he proves to be endowed with
a peculiar form of precognition emphasizes this
orientation. The action of the novel is filtered
through these two minds, one reactive, the other
meditative. (67)

Martin is himself fully aware of these differences, as he
reveals in an article he eventually writes about Billy:

[Martin] viewed Billy as a strong man, indifferent to
luck, a gamester who accepted the rules and played
by them, but who also played above them. He wrote
of Billy's disdain of money and viewed Billy as a
healthy man without need for artifice or mysticism,
a serious fellow who put play in its proper place: an
adjunct to breathing and eating.
        By comparison, Martin wrote, I find myself an
embarrassed ecclesiarch, a foolish believer in luck,
fate, magicians, and divine animals. It would serve
me right if I died and went to heaven and found out
it was a storefront run by Hungarian palm readers.
In the meantime, he concluded, I aspire to the condition of Billy Phelan, and will try to be done
mollycoddling my personal spooks. (200)

The hyperbolic tone, the Old Testament language
("ecclesiarch"), the harsh self-criticism are all characteristic

of Martin Daugherty and antithetical to whom Billy is. Martin is the "meditative" one, someone with a "preoccupied" intelligence and a heightened sense of perception and the ability to articulate both, all characteristics that mark how different he is from the instinctual, hustling Billy Phelan. Ironically, it is Martin Daugherty, despite his intelligence and perceptiveness, who aspires to be his opposite, Billy Phelan, and not the other way around.

The differences Martin sees between himself and Billy also extend to their shared "absence of the father," the primary reason for which Martin finds himself in sympathy with Billy. Billy was fatherless "from age nine, when Francis Phelan left home, left wife, son and daughter . . ." (44). Martin sees his problem as "similar, but turned inside out" (44):

> too much father, too much influence, too much fame, too much scandal, but also too much absence as the great man pursued his greatness. And these, my friends, are forces that deprived a young man of self-possession and defined his life as a question mark, unlike Billy Phelan's forces, which defined *his* life as an exclamation point. (44, emphasis Kennedy's)

Martin's lack of "self-possession"—his question mark to Billy's exclamation point—surfaces throughout the story in his constant berating of himself for his behavior and in his uncertain relationships with his father and with his son, two signs of uncertainty for which there is no real comparison in Billy's life. While thinking about his father and Melissa Spencer, the actress/mistress who so upset the family's life, Martin says, "*Mea maxima culpa*," taking upon himself all the guilt of the family (171, emphasis Kennedy's). This extreme self-incrimination and lack of confidence also appears in what Martin sees as the inadequacy of his work as a writer in comparison to Billy's life as a "winner" on the streets of Albany. When certain "editors regarded Martin as a writer of notable talent and encouraged him to challenge it," all he could do was write "two-thirds of a novel about reincarnation" (234). Martin's own father feels this novel is "foolish and will be judged the work of a silly dilettante" (235), a criticism Martin partially agrees with in admitting to himself his own inadequacies as a writer:

> He . . . wrote endlessly on a novel, a work he hoped would convey his version of the meaning of his father's scandalous life. He had written twelve hundred pages, aspiring to perhaps two hundred or less, and could not finish it. At age fifty he viewed himself, after the publication of two books of nonfiction, one on the war, the other a personal account of the Irish troubles, plus the short story collection and innumerable articles for national magazines, as a conundrum, a man unable to define his commitment or understand the secret of his own navel, a literary gnome. He seriously valued almost nothing he wrote, except for the unfinished novel. (25)

Martin's playing of his own game, a literary one, is, to him and his father at least, a failure. Whereas Billy is a "serious" fellow who knows the rules, lives by them, and stakes his honor on them—to the point of threatening his very livelihood—Martin "wasn't quite serious about himself" (25). In the end, his readers saw him as he saw himself, "a mundane poet, a penny-whistle philosopher, a provocative half-radical man" (25).

Martin does have one notable talent, a "gift of foresight" (25), an ability to catch glimpses of mystical connections and to see the future. Yet this gift is one that Martin himself downplays despite his own decided pleasure in possessing it and one that is also, like his writing, essentially flawed. It is this talent, for example, that causes Martin to write in his article on Billy that he will stop "mollycoddling [his] personal spooks" (200), and Martin always insists to everyone, including himself, that "he did not seriously believe in ghosts, miracles, resurrection, heaven, or hell" even though he considered himself a "mystical naturalist" (24). The first time he felt his power, in October of 1913, Martin was inexplicably drawn to North Pearl Street in Albany, where he just happened to witness the suicide of his cousin, but after this time his ability to use his power is always compromised in some way. The many other coincidences, visions, and predictions that follow the witnessing of the suicide are usually vague, their meanings are uncertain, and their accuracy is questionable, as when Martin "was off by only one day in his prediction of when his father would win [a] libel suit" (24). Such inaccuracies do not bother Martin much, for his gift was important to him, if for nothing else for the way it allowed him to distinguish himself from his father. Throughout his life, Martin

> dwelled on his visions and found them comforting, even when they were false and led him nowhere and revealed nothing. He felt they put him in touch with life in a way he had never experienced it before, possessor of a power which not even his famous and notorious father, in whose humiliating shadow he had lived all his years, understood. (24)

Unable to outdo his father at literary games, Martin embraces the only thing that he does better than the older man—has visions—even if he does not do it that well himself.

Significantly, Martin's visionary power is one that, until Billy's 299 bowling game and the kidnapping, he has lost in part because of his father, specifically because of the guilt Martin feels over a three-day "debauch" he had in 1928 with Melissa Spencer, his father's mistress. This guilt is also perhaps the most important reason for Martin's lack of self-

possession.   The shame of the affair haunts his days,
although Martin's sexual escapade with Melissa is only one
event in a bizarre series of sexual and artistic betrayals in the
combined Daugherty-Spencer history.   Edward Daugherty,
Martin's father, not only had an affair with Melissa
(complete with lesbian rivalry and marital discord) but then
wrote a play about it, *The Flaming Corsage* (which of course
serves as the title of the sixth book of the Albany cycle).
Edward wrote the play in order to "transform his melo-
dramatic scandal with Melissa and her jealous lesbian lover,
and the consequent destruction of his career and his wife,
into anguished theatrical harmony" (48).[7] But the relationships between all the lovers, as well as the relationship
between the real world and the artistic world, grow even
more complex than this translation of life into art.

At first Melissa "yearned to incarnate the role she had
inspired in life" (48)—in short, yearned to play herself on
stage—but the scandalous nature of the play never lets it
reach Broadway or, despite Melissa's efforts, the movies.   It
is not until twenty-five years after it was supposed to reach
the stage that it finally does so in Albany, and this time
Melissa, twisting the relationship even more, does not play
herself but Katrina, Edward's wife and the very woman
scorned by Melissa's own affair with Edward.   Complicating
the scenario further is that between the original attempt at
the play and its appearance on stage, Martin engaged in his
"debauch" with Melissa, a gift he got (along with eight
hundred dollars) for selling her the volume of his father's
journals which detailed the events about the play.   Martin
thus not only sold out on his father but he also repeated his
father's affair with Melissa, perhaps in part to avenge his
father's betrayal of his mother.

The complexity of such a situation is boggling, of course,
especially to Martin himself.   He even wonders at one point
while he is watching Melissa acting on stage from which
"mating" he himself is an offspring: "Your father's with your

mother? Your father's with Melissa? Your own with Melissa?" (176). In the course of *Billy Phelan* Martin ends up returning to Melissa for a second debauch and subsequently imagines himself as his own father, thus complicating the situation even more and creating an unbelievably complex and protean transformation of identities: Martin simultaneously plays both himself recreating his own affair *and* his father recreating his in an off-stage and real-life redramatization of Edward's betrayal of Martin's own mother, which has itself been recaptured by Melissa on stage over the years in her roles as both herself and Katrina—an almost incomprehensibly complex situation which leads in turn to the Oedipal coupling of Martin with the figure of his own mother in the form of the actress Melissa Spencer, his and his father's former mistress. No wonder Martin is confused.

It is, thus, an insecure and uneasy Martin Daugherty —haunted by the bizarre family saga of *The Flaming Corsage*—who witnesses Billy Phelan's greatest bowling game and the young man's attempt to handle himself during Charlie Boy McCall's kidnapping. Martin is impressed with Billy as a man who can know and play by the rules in a way that Martin, a psychically wounded man, cannot himself do. Martin is also sympathetic toward Billy as a young man who has grown up without a father as Martin has figuratively done himself, and he sees Billy as the kind of son he would like to have rather than the seminary-bound son he does have. Because of this admiration, sympathy, envy, and possessiveness, Martin takes an active interest in Billy as the events of the kidnapping unfold, although this concern will only circuitously lead to Martin acting on Billy's behalf: Martin's concern for Billy becomes part of his larger worries about fathers and sons everywhere, a concern itself prompted by his own problems with his father and son, and it is only after attempting to resolve his own personal problems that Martin finds a way to help Billy in any meaningful way. The effect is circular: Billy's condition helps prompt Martin into acting for himself (in returning to see Melissa), and this action in turn encourages Martin to help Billy.

The significance of Billy and his affairs for Martin's own crises is evident right from the bowling match that opens the novel. Scotty, Billy's opponent, is accused of hexing the perfect game Billy had going when he asked Billy about the score in the middle of the match. Unlike Billy, Scotty does not live by a strict code of behavior, and some of the other bowlers accuse him of "cheating" by asking Billy the unlucky question. Immediately after the match, while Scotty is defending what he did, he dies of a heart attack or stroke, perhaps, as Martin thinks, out of shame and anger at his behavior during the game. All of these events lead Martin to try to communicate "across the miles of the city to his senile father in the nursing home bed," to tell the man how Scotty's behavior was inappropriate and that somewhere in such inappropriateness was the "secret" of Scotty's death (14). In his own mind, Martin speaks into the "microphone of the filial network" as he tries to reach out to the father from whom he is estranged and who is himself estranged through his senility from the entire world: "Do you hear me? Can you understand?" Martin asks (14).

Martin attempts to heal the broken "filial network" in part by watching out for Billy and adopting him as a kind of substitute son, but this adoption reveals more of what Martin needs at this point than Billy. Martin's son, Peter, wants to become a priest, an idea that Martin abhors. Billy, on the other hand, is the kind of son Martin never had: if Martin had his way, "he would infuse a little of Billy's scarred sassiness into his own son's manner, a boy too tame, too subservient to the priests" (8). Martin reveals that he has already served in a kind of paternal role for Billy during the younger man's life at least once: while watching Billy bowl, Martin recalls that when Billy was fourteen, the exact age that Peter is in the novel, he injured his finger at a bowling alley and Martin took him to the hospital (7).

The night after the 299 bowling match and Scotty's death, Martin has a dream about both Peter and Billy which reveals his impressions of each of them:

> The boy, Peter, had been sitting in a web of ropes, suspended beyond the edge of the flat roof of home. Billy Phelan, in another suspended web, sat beside Peter, both of them looking at Martin as they lounged in the ropes, which were all that lay between them and the earth. Martin marveled at the construction of the webs, which defied gravity. And then Peter leaped off the web, face forward, and plummeted two stories. His body hit, then his head, two separate impacts, and he lay still. Two priests in sackcloth scooped him into a wheelbarrow with their shovels and one of them pushed him off into the crowded street. Billy Phelan never moved from his web. (16)

Billy is able to keep himself magically aloft on the tangled web of his young life; Peter, on the other hand, gives his life over to the "priests in sackcloth." These priests had "stolen" Peter away, Martin believed, "seduced" him into entering a "twig-bending pre-seminary-school," this son who is the "center-piece of his life, the only child he would have" (17). During the morning after the dream, Martin thinks to himself, "In the name of the Father, in the name of the Son, who will savor the Father when the Son is gone?" (15). His disdain for religion makes Martin leery of his boy's involvement with the priests, but he also has a very traditional selfishness motivating him to keep his son at home: as Martin says to his wife, "I always wanted Peter to . . . grow up and beget. I don't want to see the end of the Daughertys after the trouble of centuries took us this far" (19).

Just as his son leaves him for the seminary, and just as
Melissa Spencer returns to Albany to force Martin to think
back about his severed relationship with his father, in walks
Billy Phelan—a son separated from his father as Martin is
from his and as Peter is from Martin—to bowl his greatest
game ever.   Right after this game, Charlie Boy McCall is
kidnapped, and the coincidence that Charlie is yet another
boy separated from his father is not lost on Martin, who is
beginning to feel again the "mystical" sense he had long lost.
After Chick Phelan (Billy's uncle) calls Martin to tell him
about the kidnapping, and after Martin recognizes Francis
Phelan on the street, Martin begins to wonder about the
significance of the convergehce of the many strange events:

> Martin . . . recognized Francis Phelan, Billy's father,
> and he knew his own presence here had a purpose.
> Forced confluence of Martin and the Phelans: Billy
> and Chick, now Francis, and yet more than that.
> The McCalls were part of it. And Martin's father,
> too, in his bed of senility; and Melissa, in town in the
> old man's play. A labyrinth. (37)

Martin's ability to perceive mystical connections seems to be
returning, as his visionary dream about Billy and Peter
signaled, and this power now senses the convergence of the
many strange events after the bowling match as a
"labyrinth," a classical puzzle waiting for Martin's solution.
    This labyrinth Martin perceives taking shape will be the
"game" he will have to learn to play, much as Billy is
learning to play at kidnapping and power politics: what
Martin must do, he realizes, is "grasp the significance of so
many people suddenly webbed in the same small compass of
events" (211). He must work his way through the confusion—the web, the labyrinth—of the relationships he sees
around him, specifically those in the Daugherty-Spencer
affair and all the severed father-son relationships he has
noticed. Martin must right the great error of his and his

family's past—the scandal of *The Flaming Corsage*—and also try to reconnect those broken family lines, including and especially his own, that should connect the past to the future, the fathers to their sons.

Martin's quest to solve and escape the labyrinth is challenged not only by the expected diachronic complications of time passing but also by synchronic ones. The relationship between past, present, and future is of course always changing when viewed diachronically: present becomes past, future becomes the present, sons become fathers whose own sons become fathers in turn, and this unavoidable change complicates the identities of those people whose labyrinthine relationships Martin is trying to unravel. Martin's synchronic problems, on the other hand, occur with moments "outside" of time as they are staged in the world of art, where the confusion of conflated moments of time is replicated in the confusion of persons: Katrina and Melissa are transformed from themselves in real life to themselves in art, an impure transformation resulting in the hybrid name of Marina (for Katrina) on stage; Melissa is an actress who is of course herself but who is also associated with both the character of herself and with that of Katrina; Melissa's lovers are both Martin and Martin's father; Martin, in taking on his father's mistress, symbolically becomes his father; Martin sees his own, real-life mistress become his mother on the stage; and Martin's second "debauch" with Melissa can be read variously as a reenactment of his first debauch, as an Oedipal coupling with his mother, as Martin replacing his father with Melissa, or as a reenactment of Edward and Katrina conceiving Martin.

The incredible complexity engendered by these labyrinthine relationships—both diachronic and synchronic —is captured in the appearance throughout *Billy Phelan's Greatest Game* of the important image and story of Abraham and Isaac. The image of this prototypical father and son is

significant in the novel for its intimations about the latent
violence in even the most loving of father-son relationships.
In an interview with Kay Bonetti, Kennedy has said that "we
are all in conspiracy against the next man, against the next
generation" (76), an idea that Martin Daugherty echoes
exactly in revealing what he has written in his Bible above
the picture of Abraham and the bound Isaac: "We are all,"
Martin writes, "in conspiracy against the next man" (17).
This idea of conspiracy against the next generation, Kennedy
has said, was "one of the motivating principles of building
[the] father/son complexity" throughout *Billy Phelan* (Bonetti, 76), and the frequently cited image of Abraham and
Isaac in the book begins to reveal this principle and this
complexity from its first appearance in the novel.

After Martin returns from the bowling alley where Scotty
has died, he compulsively leafs through the Old Testament
and then goes to bed with the picture of Abraham and Isaac
and the sacrificial ram on his mind. The reason for his
preoccupation is Peter's similarity to Isaac: Martin "had
equated Isaac with his son, Peter, sacrificed to someone else's
faith: first communion, confirmation, thrust into the hands
of nuns and priests, then smothered by the fears of a mother
who still believed making love standing up damned you
forever" (17). But the generational conflict that the Old
Testament scene symbolizes is complicated by the fact that
it is not Peter's actual father but the priests, nuns, and
Peter's mother who are sacrificing him. This complication
over the image is in turn reinforced with a vision Martin has
himself the next morning. After his dream about Billy and
Peter in their suspended nets, Martin awakens to find some
kind of sweatered figure, perhaps animal, perhaps human,
sitting on a chair beside his bed. Martin considers that it
might be a fox, or a fawn, or a lamb, but later he asks
himself: "Had Martin's fuzzy, half-animal bedside visitor
been the ram that saved Isaac from the knife?" (17). Martin
thinks this improbable: "In a ski sweater? What did it have

to do with Peter? . . . The sweatered animal at bedside bore no resemblance to the ram of salvation" (17). Such an inaccuracy parallels the fact that Martin as the father bears no real resemblance to Abraham either: it is not he who is willing to sacrifice his son, as the figure is not really the ram.

Later in the day, the vision of Abraham and Isaac reappears again to Martin—this time in an even more confused state—when Martin visits Jake Berman, the father of Morrie Berman, Billy's friend and a suspect in the kidnapping. As he talks to Jake, Martin discovers that the man considers Morrie, his own son, to be a troublemaker, and thus Martin discovers yet another separated father and son. While thinking about this discovery, Martin at first tells Jake he looks "very much like [the] engraving of Abraham" that he has in his Bible. After saying this, however, Martin quickly changes his mind, thinking that Jake looks nothing like the picture, and then he finally has a vision of the image of the sacrifice changing protean-like before him, an uncertain vision indicative of Martin's own confusion:

> [He] now had a clear memory of the biblical engraving . . . Abraham's was a face of weakness, a face full of faith and anguish, but no bitterness, no defiance. And the knife did not touch Isaac. Abraham's beard then disappeared in the vision. Where he gripped the sacrificial knife, part of a finger was missing. Isaac bore the face of a goat. The vision changed. The goat became a bawling infant, then a bleating lamb. Martin shut his eyes to stop the pictures. (115)

The transformations in the image represent the confusion engendered by the many overlapping and inadequate father-son relationships in the story, even more numerous now that Martin has discovered Jake's separation from his son. At first Abraham, like Jake, has a beard, but then this disappears in the vision, as does a finger too, a deformity shared by Francis

Phelan, Billy's father. And as Daniel M. Murtaugh tells us, in this scene the "sacrificial ram of the Hebrew tradition . . . becomes the satyr of the Greek tradition, the goat-child whose anarchic lust negates all authority," just as Martin's lust for Edward's mistress negates the authority of the father in their relationship (300). The goat-child in turn becomes a "bleating lamb," an image applicable to Peter, a boy led by the shepherd-priests into the fold of the Catholic Church.

As Martin gets more involved in his various concerns with Melissa, Billy, and Charlie Boy, he continues to consider the image of Abraham's sacrifice as one indicative of the vulnerability of children that he perceives everywhere—of himself many years before, of Billy and Charlie and even Peter now. The power of Abraham over the vulnerable Isaac, and the father's willingness to sacrifice his son, sickens Martin:

> We are all in conspiracy against the children. Fathers, mothers, teachers, priests, bankers, politicians, gods, and prophets. For Abraham of the upraised knife, prototypical fascist father, Isaac was only a means to an enhanced status as a believer. Go fuck yourself with your knife, Abe. (267)

Martin cannot think such thoughts, of course, without soon turning them close to home, and ultimately he becomes both implicating and self-implicating: his father is an Abraham to him as is Martin a "prototypical fascist father" to his own son. Martin's desire to help Billy Phelan is in part brought on by his empathy with the vulnerable Isaacs of the world and by his guilt for being an Abraham himself.

The theological explanations and interpretations of the story of Abraham and Isaac reveal the troubling issues that promote Martin's disgust for Abraham. Daniel M. Murtaugh has written that Abraham's God, the God of the Jews, is a more humanized father figure than the pagan deity that characterized earlier conceptions of god; but, Murtaugh adds, "a religion of filial piety must eventually deal with the fact that a father's authority can be the most arbitrary of all" (300). The story of Abraham and Isaac, he argues, presents this dilemma in a "palliative disguise," separating the figure of the "father's love," Abraham, from the figure of his "arbitrary power," God (300). But the agnostic Martin does not have time for such fine distinctions between Abraham and God, love and authority. The fathers in the story, including Martin, cannot separate their love and their power so neatly.

For Martin, the image is an all-too-accurate symbol of the real-life fathers and sons he observes in their confused and painful struggles with each other, a "labyrinth" of generational feuds. And Martin's feuds may be the most complex of all: as their roles change through time—as diachronic changes take place—Edward, Martin, and Peter become a confusing disorder of fathers and sons, a "labyrinth" of identities: the priests are Peter's new fathers; Peter desires to be a son-less "father" as a priest himself; and Martin is now "the functioning father of the senile Edward" (214). Synchronically, the familial line is equally confused by Melissa's restaging of the confusing Daugherty scandal that began thirty years before. From such disorder, it is no wonder that Martin cannot clearly see who is God, Abraham, and Isaac in his own family tableau. Not only is the "palliative disguise" irrelevant to Martin, but the role of each player in the masque has been thrown into uncertainty. All that Martin can really see in the biblical image is Abraham's willingness to sacrifice, a willingness for which Martin curses him, whoever the many Abrahams may be.

Understanding the meaning of the image of Abraham and Isaac will eventually provide Martin with part of an understanding of his own family, but he first must try to unravel the equally complex "web" of relationships between and among the figures involved in the scandal of *The*

Flaming Corsage. The transformations, conflations, and exchanges of the identities of the individuals involved in the affair are dizzying and outrageous, especially when one considers the explicitly Oedipal nature of Martin's desires. Not only does Martin witness the chaos and scandal on the stage as he watches his mistress/mother in Melissa pretending to be Katrina, but Martin also decides that he might find Melissa later and make love to her, thinking that he "might ask her to wear the blond wig" that she wears to play Katrina and that he "might even call her Katrina" and she "could call him Edward" (177). Together they "would pretend it was 1887" and that the offspring of "their fierce and fraudulent love" would be Martin Daugherty himself (177). In such a bizarre reenactment, Martin becomes his father as the lover of Melissa or Katrina and plays the role of his own original progenitor; Melissa herself is already the actress on stage playing the woman she once betrayed and also watching her self of many years before played on stage by some other actress; Melissa is Martin's lover in real life and his mother in the drama; and Martin, when he is in the audience during the play, is watching himself dramatized on stage as he once was: father, son, lover(s), husband, wife, and actress blend in a confused and Oedipally charged series of real and enacted moments of betrayal, sex, and love.

Ironically for Martin, returning to Melissa and reenacting his (and his father's) "debauch" with her will be his way of curing himself of the guilt that he has felt all along for his various and confused roles in the affair. Martin believes that he should "find a way to make love to Melissa again, in the way a one-legged man carves a crutch from the fallen tree that crushed his leg" (172), thus identifying the source of his pain and anguish as also the cure for that pain. Martin wishes to travel from "now" back into "then," a moment in his history, in an attempt to repair the wrong in that history. Martin has, after all, a strong interest in the possibility of the power of life to regenerate itself, as his novel attests to in its

story about the reincarnation of the "soul of the Roman
soldier who diced for Christ's cloak" into its most recent
manifestation as a "twentieth century Mexican trollop"
(234–35).

Making love to Melissa, a literal reenactment of his sinful
debauch, would replace Martin's earlier fraudulent attempt
to rid himself of guilt when he figuratively reenacted his sins
through the Catholic sacrament of confession—an attempt
that failed, perhaps because of Martin's hypocrisy, insin-
cerity, and lies. After his first debauch, Martin

> sensed that his mystical talent was gone. He
> recuperated from the ensuing depression after a
> week, but rid himself of the simoniacal stink only
> when he acceded to his wife's suggestion, and, after
> a decade of considering himself not only not a
> Catholic but not even a Christian, he sought out the
> priest in the Lithuanian church who spoke and
> understood English only primitively, uttered a
> confession of absurd sins (I burned my wife's toenail
> parings three times) and then made his Easter Duty
> at Sacred Heart Church, driving out the odor of
> simony with ritual sacrilege. (26)

The odor leaves him but not the sin or its consequent guilt,
and Charlie Boy's kidnapping, Billy Phelan's troubles,
Melissa's return, and the return of Martin's visionary powers
all finally combine to force upon Martin the realization that
he has been carrying these problems around with him for
years. Pressing even more guilt upon him is the sad fact that
now his father, at the very moment of his play's triumphant
staging, has in his senility "forgotten that he had ever written
that play, or any other" (174). Martin's revenge on his father
ten years earlier in sleeping with the man's mistress looks
only pathetic now that that man no longer knows who he
himself is.

Martin's guilt that he hopes to purge from himself has

already been the source of several troubling visions during the days of the kidnapping and Melissa's return to town. During a visit to a whorehouse, for example (the one in which Billy beats up the pimp), Martin opens a broom closet and thinks he sees the notebook for *The Flaming Corsage* that he sold to Melissa hanging inside from a nail. On the cover of the book is written: *"To my beloved son, who played a whore's trick on his father"* (189, italics Kennedy). In another vision, while thinking of Charlie Boy, Martin sees himself as Ham before a naked Noah, as a man who has taken advantage of his vulnerable father:

> Martin shaped the picture of Charlie Boy again in his mind but saw not Charlie but Edward Daugherty, tied to a bed by four towels, spread-eagled, his genitals uncovered. Why such a vision now? Martin had never seen his father in such a condition, nor was he in such a state even now at the nursing home. The old man was healthy, docile, no need to tie him to the bed. Naked prisoner. Naked father. It was Ham who saw Noah, his father, naked and drunk on wine, and Noah cursed Ham, while Shem and Japheth covered their father's nakedness and were blessed for it. Cursed for peering into his father's soul through the pores. (105)

Martin's visionary power, lost after the debauch, has returned, but now it has become tainted by the equally strong sense of guilt he feels over that debauch: Martin is both a guilty Ham-like figure and a kind of Abraham to his own vulnerable father, a vulnerability symbolized in the image of the naked and senile man strapped to a bed.

Such visions while watching his and the others' troubled father-son relationships are what push Martin toward going to see Melissa's play, to return again to the source of his own "psychic downfall" (207). As Martin watches the drama, his guilt grows even more intense than it has been: the "corruption he felt after his time with Melissa came back now with full power: the simoniac being paid off with venereal gifts" (176). This newly intensified guilt promotes in turn even more self-incrimination on Martin's part than he has been practicing. He accuses himself of cannibalizing his father's own love, in the form of Melissa, in a sacrilegious metaphor brought on by Martin's other crisis with his son and the priests: "What son eats the body of his father in the womb of his mother? The priest, of course, devouring the host in the Holy Church. But what son is it that eats the body of his father's sin in the womb of his father's mistress? Suggested answer: the plenary self-indulger" (201). Self-indulger, cursed son, simoniac, a man living in corruption: this is the Martin Daugherty that Martin himself perceives, the one that he feels must be cured.

Martin going to the play and searching out Melissa for this cure is a "fellow out for redemption" (174), a man, like Francis Phelan, looking to be reborn. Martin imagines himself and Melissa reenacting Edward's and Katrina's lovemaking and thinks that both he and Melissa "would know that a new Martin Daugherty would be the offspring of this divine mating" (177). It would be a "new Martin" in the sense that the Martin and Melissa of 1938 are recreating or reenacting the original biological conception of Martin by Edward and Katrina in 1887; but it would also be a "new Martin Daugherty" of 1938, a Martin cleansed now of his guilt and made new, reborn and redeemed. Martin feels that in returning to Melissa to conquer his own guilt, in carving a crutch from the tree that crushed him, he has at last discovered the game that he is playing in his life and the rules that accompany it, an important hope in light of his respect for Billy Phelan's ability to know and even play above the rules of his games: after Martin conceives of the possibility of a "new Martin Daugherty," he decides that the "quest to love yourself is a moral quest," and then concludes with relief, "How simple this psychic game is, once you know the rules" (177). Thus Martin feels that his "game" is not social, like Billy's, but "psychic," and now he believes that at last he knows its rules.

Martin's reunion with Melissa leaves little doubt that his game is indeed "psychic": it is a game in which he attempts to seek redemption in Oedipally reenacting sex with the woman who plays his mother on stage and in which he both attempts to reconcile himself with his father and also avenge the man again for the sins he has committed against the family. At first, Martin seems to understand the rules of this outrageous game and succeed at it. Because he manages to have sex with Melissa, it's evident that he overcomes physically any potential obstacles from the obviously Oedipal nature of his lovemaking. Martin is able to make love to Melissa, for example, even as he "studied the portion of her neck and breast where his mother had been scarred by the point of a flaming, flying stick" in a fire (209). And after Martin accuses Melissa of being a "crazy bitch" and a woman "as crazy as [his] mother" (213), he pins her arms down and drags her to the floor and makes love to her a second time.[8]

In addition to overcoming these psychic challenges, Martin also seems to handle his dual objectives in seeking both vengeance against and forgiveness from his father during the sex. As he is making love to Melissa, he observes in the room the goat-child figure he had imagined earlier while thinking of the sacrificed Isaac, the same goat-child who is a symbol of his lustfilled vengeance against his father (210). As Daniel M. Murtaugh has pointed out, Martin seems paradoxically able both to avenge his mother (in having sex with Melissa and cheating thus on his father) and to separate himself from the goat-child that represents his vengeance (since Martin and the goat-figure are distinct—one acting, the other watching) (300). Even more convincing of Martin's seeming success is the fact that this goat-child, astounded by Martin's passion, suddenly turns to "ashes, a spume of sooty flakes flying upward" (210). On "behalf of mother,"

Murtaugh writes of the scene, "Martin's passion, like Abraham uninterrupted by the angel, consumes the goat-child" (300) of his own vengeance and lust, and thus Martin seems both to have avenged his mother and destroyed the anger that has prompted this vengeance against his father in the first place.

The destruction of the vengeful goat symbol is only one of numerous clues during Martin's reenacted debauch to signal the possible healing that is taking place. Melissa, for example, in a literal act of helping Martin retrieve what he has lost, returns as a gift to him Edward Daugherty's ledger that Martin had sold her years before. Martin, in turn, discovers that he shares some things with his father, a belief in luck, for example, and sexual "exuberance" (208), as Melissa describes it. As he studies Melissa for marks of his mother, Martin also feels the sex to be a "cleansing siege of the taboo," and, when he climaxes, he "ejaculated with an onrush of benediction" (210), further signs each of the healing nature of the sex despite its perverse nature and the convoluted and uncertain roles of the two participants.

Martin's second time having sex with Melissa during his reenacted debauch elicits from him a flow of thoughts that reveal even more clues to the seemingly redemptive nature of the sexual encounter. As Martin ponders how he uses Melissa, he thinks:

How do I use thee? Let me count the ways. As a sacred vessel to be violated. As a thief of Holy Writ. As the transcendent trinity: Melissa-Katrina-Marina, which my father discovered and loved; which I now love. As my father immortalized them all, like the figures on the Grecian urn, so do I now perceive them in all their lambent lunacy. Seeing with my father's eyes and knowing how he was victimized by glory and self-absorption, I now forgive the man his exorbitant expectations, his indifference, his absence. Once forgiven, it is a short walk to forgive myself for

failing to penetrate such passionate complexity as his.
Forgiving myself, I can again begin to love myself.
All this, thanks to the use of the fair Melissa. (213)

As he thinks all this, Martin also imagines his parents in the
room

> holding hands and watching him do diddle with
> Melissa for them, just as he had once done proud
> piddle for them in his personal pot. Clearly, they saw
> him as the redeemer of all their misalliances, the
> conqueror of incoherence, the spirit of synthesis in an
> anarchic family. Martin, in the consanguineous
> saddle, was their link with love past and future, a
> figure of generational communion, the father of a son
> en route to the priesthood, the functioning father of
> the senile Edward. More than that he had, here,
> obviously become his own father. He was Edward,
> son of Emmett Daugherty, father of Martin
> Daugherty, grandfather of Peter Daugherty, and
> progenitor of the unchartable Daugherty line to
> come. Lost son of a lost father, he was now father-
> hood incarnate.
>
> Perceiving this, he spent himself in Melissa's
> ravine of purification. (213-214).

Thus sex with Melissa is fraught with thoughts by Martin of
healing and renewal. Melissa is a "sacred vessel" and the
"transcendent trinity." He sees with his "father's eyes" and
forgives both him and himself. The parents are holding
hands, and Martin becomes the "redeemer," the
"conqueror," the "spirit of synthesis," the "link with love past
and future, a figure of generational communion." As
"fatherhood incarnate," he becomes the cure for the gap
between the past and the future, the possible healer of the
rifts between all the Abrahams and Isaacs, including and
especially the rift between himself and his own father and

son. At last, as he spills his seed in Melissa's "ravine of purification," Martin's psychic game is over and won.

Or so it would seem—for Martin quickly wonders about all he has just done and thought. As soon as he has spent himself, physically as well as psychically, he witnesses Melissa insert her finger into her vagina and then lick the finger, an act that triggers in Martin a "ten-year-old memory of the same act" (214) from their first "debauch" together; and as he thinks about Melissa's identical acts of sensuality, all the illumination and healing we have witnessed are deflated in Martin's painful but honest commentary: "Moved profoundly both by the act and the memory, he loathed himself for his own psychic mendacity, for trying to persuade himself he had other than venereal reasons for jingling everybody's favorite triangle" (214). It seems, after all, that Martin has invented both the game and its rules, both creating and then manipulating those rules like a child would so that he can cheat and still convince himself he won. But as an adult, assisted by his memory, he realizes that he has indeed lied in order to win—that he is a practitioner of "psychic mendacity"—and that such methods mean the prize is only sex, not union, forgiveness, and rebirth.

Despite the disappointment of this discovery, the failure of Martin's "game" and of his attempt at redemption, Martin nonetheless does not continue to act simply as the "penny-whistle philosopher" (25) he has been during the prior events of the novel. In part this change may derive from his admission that he used Melissa simply to "jingle her triangle," a moment of self-honesty that has at last led him to discover the source of his self-loathing: his attempt to lie to himself about his motivations, his attempt to make his debauchery into some significant psychic enterprise when it was primarily an act of sexual desire. More importantly, in abandoning his concerns about Melissa and the accompanying psychic game he played with her and still plays in 1938, his attention is turned from his inwardly directed thoughts of himself and the affair to more important outward concerns, including the life of Charlie McCall, the happiness of Peter, the livelihood of Billy Phelan, and the state of his senile father. Aware of the truth about himself, shameful as it may be, and no longer obsessed with himself as the child of Edward, Martin instead worries about how other present-day "children" are doing right now—worries that in turn lead to resolutions and action. "Free the children," Martin thinks at one point after his affair with Melissa, and of these children, "Charlie McCall was the child uppermost in his thought," though Martin also "kept receiving images of Peter as a priest in a long, black cassock, blessing the world. He'd be good at that. Free Peter. Let him bless anybody he wants to bless" (265). It is thus to the future, not the past, that Martin seems to be turning, and in a spirit of concern and benevolence that he has not had before: the discovery of his "psychic mendacity" has also led to a certain spiritual generosity.

Martin will soon have a chance to act upon his new-found perspective, for the McCalls ask him to help deliver the ransom money for Charlie Boy and pick him up from the kidnappers. His decision to do so not only confirms the strength of his new beliefs, but it also leads him to even more honesty about himself. As Martin helps deliver the money and drives away with Charlie safely in his charge, he thinks about his own problems in light of the "new fact" of Charlie's kidnapping and release, and he berates the torturous logic he always uses in obsessively studying and condemning himself:

> Martin's vision of his own life was at times hateful. Then a new fact would enter and he would see that it was not his life itself that was hateful but only his temporary vision of it. The problem rests in being freed from the omnipotence of thought, he decided. The avenue of my liberation may well lie in the overthrow of my logic (270).

The way out of the labyrinth, it seems, is simply to destroy its walls. As Martin says to himself, in using another classical metaphor, when "we free the children we also drown Narcissus in his pool" (270). He has looked in the pool of the past for years, hoping to find there the reflection of himself, the boy on the stage, the victim of Edward's "absence," the predecessor of who he now is. But now, it seems, he has found a way to escape that obsessive self-interest and look toward the future, to his own child and the children of others.

Such concern for the future leads Martin to two important acts beyond helping with Charlie Boy's release. The first is to stake his own reputation and livelihood in Albany on Billy Phelan by sending an article defending Billy's actions during the kidnapping to Damon Runyon, who publishes the article in the *Times-Union*.[9] Martin argues that Billy could not have gone behind Morrie Berman's back during the kidnapping since Morrie had saved Billy's life in a brawl, and he says that Billy had actually helped the investigation by telling the police to look in Newark where several of the criminals were actually caught. The suggestion about Newark was the questionable (and, as it turned out, inaccurate) information Billy had told to the McCalls, but by a quirk of fate the criminals showed up there by chance and were arrested. To the mystically minded Martin, such coincidences are of course more than chance: they are a sign of "insight as much touched with magic, or spiritual penetration of the future, as was any utterance of the biblical prophets which time has proved true" (272). Although few people agree with Martin's argument in defending Billy, the publicity the article receives, and the respect in which Martin is held for his role in helping Charlie get freed, are impressive enough for the McCalls to change their minds. Eventually from the McCall camp the "word went out to Broadway: Billy Phelan is all right. Don't give him any more grief" (275). Thus Martin, despite his failed attempt to be reborn with Melissa, not only ends up helping Charlie Boy, but he also helps Billy out too. Such an action signals not only that Martin is healed after all—albeit through a process he was not expecting—but it also shows that it is he, not Billy himself, who gets Billy back into the action of the Albany nightlife and thus actually ensures that Billy will survive his "greatest game."

The last significant step Martin takes after his time with Melissa is to visit his father in the nursing home and to read to him a letter from Peter, to thus be a symbolic conduit between the past and the future, a connection in the "filial network" extending from grandson to grandfather. The conversation between Martin and Edward is the most tender exchange in the book, devoid of all but the briefest of Martin's psychic wanderings. Martin has abandoned his introspection and his disgust for his father as he attempts to read him a brief letter from his son Peter, a boy whom Martin mentions four times but that each time the elder Daugherty cannot recall. "Daugherty," Edward says after he is told his grandson's name for the fourth time, "That's the same name as mine" (278).

While J. K. Van Dover writes perceptively that "Martin still cannot communicate with either his senile father or his alienated, Catholic son" (78), one should also recognize the sympathy implicit in the conversation between Edward and Martin and see the letter Martin reads from Peter as an important attempt by Martin to repair the broken filial network and to establish the previously absent "generational communion" (214). Though the letter is steeped in excessive sentiment and what Edward calls "medieval bullshit," it is still a "nice letter" (according to Edward) and the "sentiment is real" (according to Martin) (278). Moved by this letter and the pitiful sight of his own father, and fresh from his saving of Charlie and Billy, Martin at last is able to understand the father-son relationship, an understanding that is captured in the end in the image of Abraham and Isaac: "all sons are

Isaac," Martin thinks, "all fathers are Abraham, and . . . all Isaacs become Abrahams if they work at it long enough" (278).   Martin has learned to accept the inevitably fluid nature of time, that "now" always becomes "then" and that "then" was once "now": he has learned thus to empathize, to understand that an Isaac today will grow up to be an Abraham tomorrow and that Abraham was once a child as vulnerable as Isaac.   Martin learns to see in the man his father once was the man Martin is now himself, a father with a son—each an Abraham, each with an Isaac, each an Isaac once himself.   He accepts who his father is much as he has accepted that his son Peter should be "free" to be a priest: Martin has, at last, freed himself from the disgust he once felt toward his father as he has already freed his own child from himself.

As the title of *Billy Phelan's Greatest Game* suggests, Martin Daugherty is not the only or, according to many critics, even the primary, protagonist of the novel.[10]   Scenes of Billy Phelan gambling and hustling open and close the novel, as if he were the first and last concern of the narrative. And there are occasions in the story when Billy must make important decisions for himself, the most notable of which is his refusal not to commit suicide on the night he finds himself isolated in Albany by the McCalls' edict.   On that night, Billy can find company only with the derelict Slopie, and after Slopie leaves him, Billy becomes "aware that [now] nothing and no one would save him from the coldness of the moon and the October river" (258).   He hears "whisperings on the water and thought they might be the spirits of all the poor bastards who had jumped off the bridge, calling him to make the leap" (258).   Though tempted by the voices, as his father will be haunted by other voices and visions in *Ironweed*, Billy runs away, refusing to kill himself (259).   In addition to this important decision, Billy also briefly makes contact with his own father, an act which thus places him in a long line of sons who reconcile with or rejoin their fathers in the novel (a line including Martin, Peter, Charlie Boy, and even Morrie Berman, whose father, Jake, promises to pay Morrie's legal fees). Billy helps to bail Francis out of jail (he's been arrested for voting twenty-one times) and, as we have seen, invites him to come visit the family. This invitation becomes part of the reasoning Francis will use in deciding to return to his old home, an act that is dramatized in full in *Ironweed*.

Despite this generosity on Billy's part, however, and despite the courage of his decision not to kill himself, neither attribute and neither action leads to anything within the narrative of *Billy Phelan's Greatest Game*. Billy's decision not to commit suicide is done while he is alone and is never discussed directly with any character in the story. Its impact on Billy himself is unclear: after escaping the suicide and hearing that he is allowed to return to the Albany nightlife, Billy "knew he'd lost something he didn't quite understand, but the onset of mystery thrilled him . . ." (259). The best that Billy can muster, it seems, is an admission of ignorance and a thrill of some mystery, one that is itself never explored or elaborated upon and that serves no function in the closing action of the book.

For its part, the consequences of Billy's interaction with his father are reserved for another book in the Albany cycle altogether. Even there, while Billy's invitation encourages Francis, it is the actions and decisions of Francis himself that lead him to come home. And as Anya Taylor points out, the "theme of [*Billy Phelan*] is less Billy's own personal purgation than the reunion of fathers and sons in several families, Daughertys, Bermans, and Phelans, miracles that bring renewed life" (116). Billy's reunion with his father, then, is not only limited but one of many other (and more successful) reunions between fathers and sons. Overall, Billy remains a surprisingly ineffectual character throughout the novel despite the focus on him encouraged by the title. During the events surrounding the kidnapping, he simply does what he always has—survive as a gambler and live by his rules—until the McCalls mark him "lousy" and he can no longer play. Nothing changes for him until the McCalls change his circumstances, and it is Martin's intervention that gets those circumstances changed.

The most that can be said for Billy is that he sticks to his rules, but since these rules affect no one but Billy, and since Billy himself does not change or grow from what he endures in sticking to his rules, the greatest game Billy plays could actually be considered Martin's. Despite his overly meditative nature, Martin acts on his desires to see Melissa, and although at first it seems Martin's reunion with her is a failure, his admission that his desire for her is purely sexual seems to free him from playing psychic games and enables him both to help Charlie and Billy and to understand better both his son and his father. His awareness of his own overly meditative life, flawed as it is with his "psychic mendacity," frees him "from the omnipotence of thought." And because of this new found freedom, we see him in the closing pages helping to "free the children"—his own, Bindy McCall's, and Francis Phelan's—and we see him in sympathetic conversation with his senile father, reading a letter from his own son, Peter, and fully aware of the complexity of his relationships with each. Martin, as a more meditative and articulate person than Billy, also provides the insight into the story that we otherwise would not have. Daniel M. Murtaugh writes that "Billy's world is a world without grace, but it takes Martin Daugherty's more highly developed sensibility to reflect on this absence of grace . . ." (300). While this is true, Martin's "more highly developed sensibility" also adds a little grace of its own to the lives of those sons and fathers around him.[11]

Kennedy may come under some criticism for Billy's oddly passive role in the novel, but that Martin Daugherty may be a more effective and dynamic character than Billy himself should not surprise readers of Kennedy's work since Martin is the one who is more fully "aware of his place in time" (Van Dover, 67) and thus in history, the medium through which so many of Kennedy's characters struggle for understanding. In addition to Martin, these characters include not only Billy's father, Francis, in *Ironweed*, but also Daniel Quinn of *Quinn's Book*, Orson Purcell and Peter Phelan of *Very Old Bones*, and Edward Daugherty himself in *The Flaming Corsage*. Billy lives for the moment, hustling up what he can out of the present situation and focusing on "immediate, real problems" (Murtaugh, 300). He is, as Murtaugh says, "unencumbered by the ghosts that haunt the fathers and sons around him" (300). Martin, however, is obsessed with history—in fact, that's part of his problem—especially his and his father's personal history with Melissa, but also the history of Albany itself, including Henry James's visits, Francis Phelan's exploits, and Martin's own childhood with the McCalls and Phelans. By the end of the novel, Martin is fully aware of the transformative power of time as this power reveals itself in the inevitable transformation of Isaacs into Abrahams. And it is through his oddly successful return to the past in his second debauch with Melissa, and in his even more successful work for the future in trying to "free the children," especially Charlie and Billy, that Martin at last comes to a reconciliation with his own father and son. He returns to what happened back "then," his and his father's affair with Melissa, and discovers in the process that he was and is venal, that he has been a psychic liar, and that his father (and all other fathers, including himself) suffers as both Isaacs and Abrahams: out of this return and discovery Martin accepts who he, his father and his son now all are. Martin's return to what happened back "then" provides him in the end with the means to achieve a more generous, less narcissistic way of living and playing "now."

Notes

1. The kidnapping in *Billy Phelan* is based on the real-life 1933 Albany kidnapping of John O'Connell, Jr., nephew to Boss Dan O'Connell, who controlled Albany politics for decades. For Kennedy's discussion of this real kidnapping, see "Shanties, Mansions, and Murder" in *O Albany!*, pp. 91–95. In the history Kennedy provides of the incident and the consequent arrests, one can discover a collection of figures offering real-life antecedents to the McCalls (including Charlie Boy) and to other important characters in *Billy Phelan*, namely the newspaperman Martin Daugherty; Morrie Berman, one of the suspects in the kidnapping; and Marcus Gorman, who eventually, we are told, serves as Berman's attorney. See also Kennedy's interview with Kay Bonetti, p. 84, and Van Dover, pp. 63–66.

2. Edward Daugherty's affair with Melissa Spencer becomes one of the main concerns of the last novel in this study, *The Flaming Corsage*.

3. Such a reenactment prefigures Francis Phelan's witnessing of his own conception in *Ironweed*, pp. 98–99.

4. A feeling which is partially true, but also significantly false in many ways. Billy's disgust with the Phelan home, and a clearer picture of Francis' ambiguous relationship with his parents and siblings, will be a concern of *Very Old Bones*, a novel in which, among other things, Orson Purcell must convince the embittered Billy to enter the Phelan house in order to hear the reading of Peter Phelan's will.

5. The George Quinn example is cited in Reilly, 65.

6. See Van Dover, 69–70.

7. Edward Daugherty is also the author of *The Car Barns*, another (fictional) play. Its significance, as Anya Taylor points out, is that it presents a fictionalized Francis Phelan as the sole culprit in the killing of a scab during a trolley strike, an event which prompted one of Francis' flights from Albany. This depiction, slightly inaccurate as it is (there were other violent protesters that day too), exacerbates Francis' sense of guilt over the murder and encourages his sense of self-loathing (see Taylor, 118, and *Ironweed*, especially pp. 205–207). The example of *The Car Barns* is curious for the way it offers an example of a fictional character rewriting history (albeit history which is itself fiction-alized—Francis' committing murder during the strike), much as Kennedy himself rewrites history into fiction. And as Taylor points out, Edward's fictionalizing of Francis is similar to Martin's near-fictionalizing of Billy Phelan in the article Martin eventually writes to encourage the McCalls to lift their ban on Billy (118).

One should also note here that, even though the play *The Flaming Corsage* was written to achieve "theatrical harmony," Kennedy's novel of the same title reveals anything but harmony—the disturbing uncertainties of *The Flaming Corsage* (the novel) reflect in their own way the stupefying complexities of the Daugherty-Spencer affair that we see in *Billy Phelan's Greatest Game.*

8. Martin Daugherty is not exaggerating in calling his mother "crazy." Part of the scandal of the Daugherty past includes episodes involving Katrina's insanity, the most notable of which concern her walking naked outside her house and her related attempt to seduce Francis Phelan when he was eighteen years old. Some of these episodes are referred to in *Ironweed* and in *Very Old Bones* as playing a significant part in Francis' alienation from his own family, especially from his mother, who thought Francis' concern for Katrina shameful and scandalous. Katrina's behavior receives its fullest depiction in *The Flaming Corsage,* a novel in which she is one of the main characters.

9. In *Ironweed,* Helen finds Martin Daugherty's story about Billy in the paper and cries when she reads it. She senses from Martin's description of Billy that it is inevitable that Billy and the rest of the Phelan family are going to take Francis away from her (see *Ironweed,* 129).

10. Edward C. Reilly, for example, argues that *Billy Phelan* "focuses on Billy, to whom most of the chapters are devoted" and also writes that a "major portion of the action occurs in Nighttown, Billy Phelan's world . . ." (64). For his part, Daniel M. Murtaugh calls Billy and Francis Phelan the "heroes" of *Billy Phelan* and *Ironweed* respectively. And J. K. Van Dover says "*Billy Phelan's Greatest Game* covers a crucial week in the life of Billy Phelan," not, significantly, a week in the life of Martin Daugherty (63).

11. J. K. Van Dover is not incorrect to say that both Billy's and Martin's "victories are marginal ones" (78), though one could legitimately argue that Billy's is more marginal than Martin's, a perspective that one can adopt more readily by turning away from the focus on Billy that the title of the novel encourages.

CHAPTER FOUR

EXISTENTIAL STRUGGLES IN AN ESCHATOLOGICAL WORLD: THE MYTH OF FRANCIS PHELAN

*T*oward the end of *Billy Phelan's Greatest Game*, Annie Phelan asks that her children not hate their father (and her husband) but mourn him: "when a good man dies," she says, "it's reason to weep" (250). The man she is talking about, Francis Phelan, is not literally dead but only metaphorically and spiritually so, to both himself and his family. The details of this figurative death and its effects on Francis are revealed in full in *Ironweed*, the third and most famous novel in the Albany cycle, and also the one that most emphatically and imaginatively captures the commingling of "then" and "now." As *Ironweed* reveals, Francis' "death" is the result of the guilt and self-hate he feels because of his long and frequent absences from Albany and his family and because of the violence and death in his life for which he has been responsible. For many years of his marriage to Annie he abandoned the family for months at a time so that he could pursue his dream of playing baseball, and in 1901, at the age of twenty-one, he fled the city after murdering a scab during a trolley strike. When *Ironweed* opens, Francis has been gone from Albany for twenty-two years (since 1916), all the while living the life of a hobo after

95

he accidentally killed his thirteen-day-old son when he dropped the boy while trying to change his diaper. As we learn in both *Ironweed* and *Billy Phelan's Greatest Game*, for many years Annie did not say anything about Francis' role in their son's death. And, as *Billy Phelan* reveals, when Annie finally does speak up, in 1938—and only then after Francis has already told the truth to Billy—she says to her children that after the tragedy of Gerald's death Francis "went away and buried himself and he's dead now, dead and can't be resurrected" (*BP*, 250).

In many ways *Ironweed* is a test of the legitimacy of Annie's belief as she presents it in *Billy Phelan*, a test of whether Francis really is spiritually dead and "can't be resurrected." *Ironweed* covers three days of Francis' return to his hometown of Albany, a journey which begins on Halloween Monday, October 31, 1938, the day before Billy Phelan is restored to his livelihood as a gambler in Albany (an event which occurs in *Billy Phelan's Greatest Game*).[1] What we learn of Francis during these three days confirms the accuracy of Annie's description of a man who is "dead." Francis is seen to be a violent and often drunk hobo, yet another of Kennedy's curiously compromised heroes. He is alienated from his past and his family, dead to everything that has ever mattered in his life. And while this condition may be only a figurative (or spiritual) death, the world in which Francis lives is defined by numerous actual deaths, both past and present: not only do several people Francis knows die during the course of the novel, but he is also haunted throughout his stay in the city by ghosts and visions of the dead from his past, including several men he has killed himself. The pervasiveness of these deaths not only legitimates and emphasizes the spiritual death and despair which characterizes Francis' life, but it also emphasizes how his life is itself a frail and vulnerable affair, how Francis' actual physical death is always an immediate possibility.

Yet despite the way that both spiritual and physical death

pervade Francis' life and his days in Albany in particular, he may not be, as Annie claims, a man who "can't be resurrected." Ultimately the ability to verify or refute her claim may reside in interpreting the complex and ambiguous conclusion of *Ironweed*, in which Francis seems to return to his house and his wife, although what happens exactly in the closing scenes depends on how one reads the conditional mode in which these sections are written.[2] Prior to this ambiguous ending, however, we are given numerous clues as to how we might read that ending, clues that themselves hint at the possibility of Francis' redemption, at the chance that Francis just might be able to be "resurrected." *Ironweed*, after all, describes Francis' return home, and even though it might be a temporary or provisional return, it is a startling change from the twenty-two years of running that have preceded it since Francis accidentally dropped his son Gerald. And according to William Kennedy himself, *Iron-weed* is, like Dante's *Divine Comedy*, "a journey through planes of escalation into a moment of redemption out of sin" (Quinn, 74). "Redemption is the key word," Kennedy says, adding that it is what the novel is "all about" (Quinn, 74). If one wonders how a novel as bleak as *Ironweed* can in any way be concerned with redemption, Dante may provide an answer: has a story about an ascent to God ever been so horrifyingly vivid as *The Divine Comedy*?

Kennedy's reference to Dante and the related theme of redemption signals, in fact, one of several clues provided by the narrative that are integral to considering whether Francis can be "resurrected" or not, for the meaning of Francis' journey through the Albany of *Ironweed* must be read in part through the numerous allusions to myth in the narrative of that journey, including the "myth" told in *The Divine Comedy*. One need think only of the length of Francis' stay in Albany, three days paralleling Christ's days in the tomb, and the nature of Francis' trip in general, a struggle to get home similar to Odysseus', to begin to see the multilayered,

mythological structure of the novel. Although the characteristics and lives of the mythic figures to whom Francis is
comparable vary, the shared characteristic of the heroism of
these figures and the stories of their successful journeys imply
that Francis Phelan may actually be a redeemable hero
himself, a Dante able to reach heaven.

Many mythological figures—Aeneas, Odysseus, Christ,
Orpheus, even Dante, to name several—confront the dead or
the world of the dead as part of a defining moment of their
respective lives, and Francis' confrontation with such a
world, perhaps the most startling aspect of the narrative of
Ironweed, signals another way through which one must
approach the question of Francis' redemption. During his
journey through Albany, Francis descends into his own
version of the world of the dead when ghosts of people from
his past observe him and when he observes and meets several
of these dead himself. The presence of these dead transforms
Francis' Albany into an "eschatological" world, a universe
inhabited by those living forever at the end of time, although
it is a world only Francis can see: no one in Albany but he
communes with the ghosts.[3] In descending into this world
inhabited by his own personal dead, Francis is really
descending into his own history and, in the process, moving
his past into the present, moving what happened back "then"
into what's happening "now." And as with many other heroes
of the Albany cycle—Martin Daugherty, Daniel Quinn, and
Peter Phelan, for example—Francis' journey into his own
history will afford him a chance to confront his past and the
sins of that past, and that confrontation allows him at least
an opportunity to redeem or forgive himself.

Although Francis' journey is similar to those of other
Albany cycle heroes and of various mythic figures, the
"private" nature of his hell, the fact that he alone confronts
the ghosts, also differentiates him from many of these other
heroes. Hell is another world for Odysseus and Dante and
Christ, and they go there to save or observe the souls of

others; hell for Francis, however, is his own past, his own personal history, and he must descend into this private hell in order to save himself. It is a conflict over Francis' soul itself, taking place in his private universe and, as we shall see, resolvable by him alone: Francis' struggle is, in other words, an existential one. Francis Phelan may be a mythological figure, as the allusions in the text make undeniable, and he may be living in an eschatological universe, as his confrontations with the dead make clear, but the battle that this mythological hero joins in this magical world is in the end an existential one: *Ironweed* tells the story of a mythological hero enduring existential challenges in an eschatological world. Borrowing the modernist's love of myth and the magical realist's penchant for magical worlds, adding the existentialist's struggle for self-created meaning, Kennedy has constructed in the late twentieth century a remarkable work that does more than simply put these literary styles and concerns together in one narrative: as we shall see, he uses the very fabric of that narrative—the English language itself—to weave them into a singular, startling tapestry.

The Mythological Francis

The conflation of various moments of time and even of "being"—of various "planes" of reality, to borrow one of Kennedy's own terms—is a standard practice in Kennedy's Albany cycle. But this conflation is itself duplicated in the text in one of the important considerations in defining and interpreting those "planes," the mythological allusions within *Ironweed*: as the "past and the present and the future merge and mingle,"[4] so too do various mythological stories describing Francis. Peter P. Clarke has described this mingling of myths as the "protean mythological background" of *Ironweed* (167), a phrase which seems appropriate considering the variety of mythological interpretations, from Christian to Celtic, that *Ironweed* has received since its publication. Almost all of the criticism concerning the novel, and indeed much of the criticism about Kennedy's work in general, has been about the mythological strains in *Ironweed*. One of the more impressive studies, completed by Michael Tierce, discusses Francis' wanderings in Albany as a "monomythic" journey in general and as an Odysseyan voyage in particular. To explain how Francis' trip mirrors the "basic pattern of what James Joyce labels the 'monomyth'" (247), Tierce quotes from Joseph Campbell:

> The standard path of the mythological adventure of the hero is a magnification of the formula represented in the rites of passage: *separation—initiation—return: which might be named the nuclear unity of the monomyth. A hero ventures forth from the world of common day into a region of supernatural wonder: fabulous forces are there encountered and a decisive victory is won: the hero comes back from this mysterious adventure with the power to bestow boons on his fellow man.*[5]

As Tierce accurately observes, Kennedy's story of Francis Phelan adheres closely to Campbell's pattern of "separation—initiation—return" and a journey from "common day" into a "region of supernatural wonder." One should add, however, that this classical pattern in *Ironweed* is shaped also by the existential vision of the novel: the regions of common day and supernatural wonder exist in *Ironweed*, as Tierce implies, but both reside specifically within Francis Phelan himself.

Although Tierce describes *Ironweed* in terms of a generalized monomythic narrative, he specifically analyzes how Francis' journey through Albany parallels to a startling degree the story of Odysseus, much like the story told by one of Kennedy's own important literary influences, James Joyce.[6] Tierce argues, in fact, that "Kennedy was much more concerned than Joyce with the actual chronology of Odysseus' adventure" (249). As proof of this close relationship, Tierce produces a chart, similar to Stuart Gilbert's analysis of *Ulysses*, in which Francis' actions and events in *Ironweed* are paralleled to events in *The Odyssey*.[7] Tierce argues that this chart reveals that, "with the exception of the Calypso episode, Francis' ordeal follows almost exactly the chronological pattern of Homer's narrative" (249). Although the parallels are too numerous to list here, a small sampling will provide some evidence for the kinds of associations between *Ironweed* and *The Odyssey* that Kennedy develops and that Tierce unveils: *Ironweed* begins in St. Agnes Cemetery, the Hades or world of the dead of Albany; there is a trip to The Gilded Cage, a bar in Albany in which Helen Archer, Francis' girlfriend, is tempted into delusion by the songs of the bartender and from her own memory as a singer, much as the Sirens might tempt someone by their song; and Francis' wife, Annie, has been waiting for many years for the return of her husband, much as Penelope awaits Odysseus. These examples are only three of dozens of parallels, both major and minor, that Tierce cites in his detailed study.

Although Tierce's analysis may be the most thorough of the mythological studies of *Ironweed*, he is hardly the only scholar to have noted these parallels to the story of Odysseus or to have argued for its central role in reading Kennedy's novel. Daniel M. Murtaugh, for example, though arguing that *Ironweed* follows a "carefully limited pattern of allusions to the *Odyssey*," mentions how Odysseus, like Francis, returns in the "guise of a beggar" (301). He also believes that Helen Archer is a "hapless derelict Calypso whose failed musical career makes her something of a siren as well," and he identifies Katrina Daugherty, Martin Daugherty's mother, as a Circe figure because of her sexual tempting of Francis when he was eighteen years old. Critic Loxley Nichols, for his part, draws attention to the "names Helen and the Ulysses-sounding Aloysius (Francis' middle name)" and remarks that, after a "twenty(-two)-year absence, Francis returns home to find a grown son, a faithful wife, and a friendly dog," just as Ulysses did (47).

As significant as these parallels are between *Ironweed* and *The Odyssey*, it is hardly the only myth to which the novel alludes. The epigraph to the book derives not from Homer, after all, but from the opening lines of Dante's *Purgatorio*: "To course o'er better waters now hoists sail / the little bark of my wit, leaving behind her a / sea so cruel." Kennedy's own claim that his novel parallels Dante's second book of *The Divine Comedy* of course cannot be ignored (see Quinn, [1985] 74), though the parallels are perhaps more evident on the surface than they are exact in their depth: both heroes go on a journey, both have a love interest waiting for them, and both must endure (or observe) a purgatorial series of challenges and punishments. Edward C. Reilly notes numerous other and more specific parallels, including among them Francis' three-day journey and Dante's Easter journey; the similar ages of the two heroes; the conversations with the souls of the dead;[8] and the similarity between Francis' constant desire to "wash" his body and Dante's desire for a spiritual cleansing.

While *The Odyssey* and *The Divine Comedy* are the two myths most frequently alluded to in *Ironweed*, other scholars have noted allusions and similarities to other mythological systems and stories as well. Sean de Hora calls Francis Phelan "an Irish version of the Wandering Jew" (472), for example, and Peter P. Clarke writes that "Francis' roots seem to reach to Menelaus and perhaps even to Agamemnon" (167). George W. Hunt cites parallels between events in *Ironweed* and the Catholic liturgical cycle for Halloween, All Saints' Day, and All Souls Day, the three days covered in the narrative of the book (374). Anya Taylor, in seeing Francis as a shaman or magician, curiously challenges Hunt's reading by arguing that, in the first three Albany novels, including *Ironweed*, "Phelan's violence and refusal to submit, his wavering belief in himself as a warrior . . . , suggest that Kennedy seeks to place his hero in a different, perhaps pre-Christian, culture, before the Church broke men with guilt and the requirements of goodness" (114). Even though she acknowledges that "Christian themes of atonement suffuse" the first three Albany books, she also writes that the "novels give as a whole a picture of a Celtic, male, tribal group, whose lives, violent and vengeful, are governed by a code of shame, and whose laws are self-generated" (114). In explaining her assertions, Taylor identifies Francis Phelan as a kind of contemporary Cuchulain and argues that in Francis' life there is a certain male pride in a dominant chieftain, much like the Celts. She adds too that within the book women "appear as goddesses," a depiction suggestive of a pre-Christian mythological interpretation (114).

The variety of these mythological allusions may seem surprising considering the relatively small length of *Ironweed*, but they also might raise serious questions about the possibility of interpreting both the novel and the actions of its protagonist or even about whether Kennedy is in control of his narrative. Is Francis Phelan a sinful Catholic penitent enacting the Catholic liturgy or a Celtic warrior not yet "broken" by guilt and goodness? Ultimately, these competing questions are not as important as the similar conclusions they all eventually provide: that the mythologizing of Francis in *Ironweed* makes him a hero despite his antiheroic life as a murderer and alcoholic, and that this heroic nature leads one to read *Ironweed* as a story of possible redemption. What is important about these various myths, in other words, is not what is different about them but what draws them all together—not Clarke's "protean mythological background" so much as Campbell's and Joyce's monomyth, the basic pattern of the myth and its consequent sense of Francis as a hero worthy of redemption. Whether Francis' salvation is described as a return home, redemption, forgiveness, or success in battle is not as significant as the similarities between each of these, the sense

they give of Francis' heroic nature and ultimate success. As
Peter P. Clarke writes, "Kennedy's use of myth serves . . . to
elevate apparently degraded bums to heroic stature . . . "
(168), and it is this elevation which is the contribution of the
mythological allusions, no matter the origin or plot of those
myths. It is this elevation which is also one of the more
remarkable achievements of the novel: What better way to
make a hero out of a bum than to compare him to Odysseus
(a pirate and murderer), to Dante (a sinner) or to Jesus (a
lowly carpenter after all)?

Other critics echo these sentiments of Clarke's, each
analyzing *Ironweed* according to a particular myth but citing
what is overall most important about such mythological
interpretations, namely the understanding of Francis as hero.
As Anya Taylor writes:

> Kennedy glorifies the simple, ordinary, ruined man,
> by connecting him with mythic undercurrents. . . . In
> suggesting that this homeless man with shoes tied by
> a string, sleeping under the cold stars, is a hero,
> Kennedy also suggests, as Joseph Campbell does, that
> inside each of us glimmers a heroic nature and that
> each of us momentarily possesses ancient power.
> Even a criminal vagrant is swathed in dignifying
> myths if he invents his life in a heroic mode, defying
> his temporary circumstance. (118-19)

Thus while Kennedy's numerous and various mythological
allusions have led to numerous and various readings of the
book, all of these allusions, despite their many differences,
manage to bestow meaning on Francis and his universe. The
particulars of that meaning may vary, but the importance of
Francis' life does not once each myth identifies him as a
heroic figure. As the deluded salesman Willy Loman represents Arthur Miller's democratic reinterpretation of the
classic tragic character, Francis Phelan represents Kennedy's

reinterpretation of the classical or mythological hero, here in the guise of a Depression-era bum.

This sense of Francis as a mythological hero is significant, of course, for the way it affects our reading of the novel as a whole and particularly our reading of whether Francis is a character capable of being redeemed or "resurrected." In arguing for the importance of under-standing *The Divine Comedy* in reading Kennedy's book, for example, Edward C. Reilly argues that the quotation from Dante at the beginning of *Ironweed* "not only relates to the novel's plot, but it also underscores its major theme—Francis Phelan's journey to redemption" (5). Without this notion of an intricate relationship between the mythological structure and the meaning of the narrative, the use of so much myth in the book would merely be a structural convenience, a kind of postmodern literary game of using the architecture of a classic to support the edifice of a contemporary novel. Instead, the use of the mythological allusions in the novel, as Reilly argues, is integral to an interpretation of the key question of the possibility of Francis' salvation. To read Francis as Dante, for example, is to see him on a quest for redemption, as Reilly and Kennedy himself have argued, and even as Anya Taylor believes despite her sense of a pre-Christian myth behind Kennedy's work. Taylor cites as important evidence for her reading of *Ironweed* the lines from the *Purgatorio* that follow the lines quoted in the epigraph to Kennedy's book but that Kennedy does not include: "and what I sing will be that second kingdom, in which the human soul is cleansed of sin, becoming worthy of ascent to heaven" (115). To be aware of this allusion to cleansing and ascent cannot help but influence how we read the outcome of Francis' own struggles during his stay in Albany.

The other allusions in the novel serve a similar function as those to *The Divine Comedy* in leading toward an interpretation of the book as a journey toward redemption.

Allusions to *The Odyssey*, for example, suggest Francis'
possible rebirth by evoking a sense of the long-awaited return
of a hero to his home and loving wife. And George W. Hunt,
in arguing for the importance of the Catholic liturgy in
interpreting the book, writes that throughout *Ironweed*,
"Kennedy artfully exploits dramatically what this liturgical
cycle enacts: the Catholic belief in the communion of saints,
the conviction that the living are linked spiritually and truly
with all the dead, with those suffering still and those
successful, and that their mysterious unity and mutuality
transcend the limits of heaven and earth" (374). With such
an interpretation behind a reading of the book, one cannot
help envisioning Francis, though he is suffering, as a man
who can be "successful," who can transcend his earthly
limitations, and who might one day be able to rejoin a
communion of his own.

The use of myth in *Ironweed*, then, signals an important
consideration in interpreting the book itself. The myths are
not a decorative image or metaphor imposed on the
narrative; instead, they help to define that narrative itself by
identifying Francis as a contemporary (though certainly
compromised) mythological hero and consequently revealing
at least the possibility of his redemption, whether that
redemption be described in Dantean, Odyssean, Catholic, or
Celtic terms. The appearances of these myths are various
and complex, generating more critical attention than any
other aspect of the novel and yet also resulting in little
agreement. What the critics almost universally do agree on,
however, is the prevalence of mythological allusion in the
story and the fact that these myths, these worlds outside of
time, when imposed on the world of Francis Phelan in
Albany around Halloween in 1938, raise him out of his
status as inconsequential bum and vagrant and into the
realm of classical hero, Depression-era American style. It is
a noteworthy achievement in late twentieth century American fiction, made all the more so when one considers in turn

the eschatological and existential nature of the struggle this "bum" endures.

The World of the Dead: Into the Past, Outside of Time

While the mythological background in *Ironweed* provides a strong argument for reading the book as the story of the redemption of Francis Phelan, the journey toward that redemption is one that is played out, despite the mythological man that Francis is, in Francis' own private universe and on the streets of Albany itself. In a way both of these places are the same, for Francis' private world—specifically the world of his past—is intricately dependent on the city of Albany, the scene of that past. Francis' return to Albany is the geographical equivalent of his temporal return to an earlier time, to those years he spent in the city as a child and young man. But the city to which Francis returns is also his alone, for in this city only he encounters numerous ghosts and has visions of people from his past, people who include his mother, his father, his dead son, Katrina Daugherty, dozens of unnamed friends and relatives, and the men he has killed in his life.

Francis' frequent encounters with these ghosts and visions reveal that Francis is, as Anya Taylor puts it, a man "drenched in death" (109). On the one hand, of course, such a phrase refers to Francis' spiritual death as a self-exiled alcoholic and murderer. But it also describes the prevalence of physical death in Francis' life and the death-drenched time of the year covered in the novel itself. The physically dead include those who haunt Francis during his days in Albany, family and friends who have died by natural causes as well as those men who have died at Francis' own hands—strikebreakers and bums that he killed in his youth and during his days on the road.[9] But these dead also include those who actually die during the time covered within the narrative itself: in the three days that pass in *Ironweed*, Francis unsuccessfully attempts to help one dying bum, Sandra, when he finds her freezing outside a mission for the homeless; his road companion, Rudy, is dying of cancer and gets murdered at the end of the book; and his "wife" on the road for the past nine years, Helen Archer, dies alone in her Albany hotel room. In *Ironweed*, Kennedy emphasizes how these and other deaths pervade Francis' life: "Bodies in alleys, bodies in gutters, bodies anywhere, were part of his eternal landscape: a physical litany of the dead" (29). Over the years, Kennedy writes, Francis "had watched two dozen people suspire into death, all of them bums except for his father, and Gerald" (45). Francis has actually been responsible for several of these deaths himself, and at the end of the novel, as he seems close to settling down at last, to escaping the death that haunts him, he is the cause of even more death: he kills yet another man when he and his fellow hoboes are attacked by a band of legionnaires.

The physical deaths that occur during the time of the novel seem almost a natural result of even the season of *Ironweed*: the three days covered in the narrative not only occur in autumn, the season of decay, but they cover specifically Halloween, All Souls' Day, and All Saints' Day, feasts that acknowledge the living dead, the anonymously dead, and the holy dead respectively, all terms which could describe Francis Phelan himself. Halloween is even described within the novel as the day "when spooks made house calls and the dead walked around" (23) and the night when the "old and the new dead walk abroad in this land" (29), a description as apt for Francis' own time in Albany as it is for Halloween in general. For its part, All Souls' Day, as Anya Taylor explains, "celebrates the dead and their continued presence among the living" (111), again a description as appropriate for Francis and his ghosts as it is for the holiday itself. The whole three days covered in the narrative are times in which the world at large, and not only the often drunk Francis, acknowledge—prayerfully or playfully—the interrelationship between the living and the dead, between life and death.

Francis' journey through Albany is thus a trip defined by death, whether it is his own spiritual one, the physical ones of his friends and acquaintances, or the season of the year. But in no way is this sense of death made more emphatic than in the ghosts of the dead whom Francis sees throughout the city during his stay there. The appearance of these ghosts in 1938 Albany represents the familiar concern in Kennedy's fiction with the ability of the past to move into and affect the present—with the way the past, in effect, becomes part of the present. What is different about this past in *Ironweed*, as Kennedy makes clear, and as opposed to the past as it is evoked in much of the rest of the Albany cycle, is its essentially private nature: the past that Francis sees is seen by him alone.

Francis' confrontation with the dead and thus with the past begins, appropriately enough, on Halloween and in the Albany cemetery, where he rides up a "winding road" (1) in a truck much as he has taken a figurative winding road back to Albany and, as Reilly remarks, much as Dante wound his way up through the various "planes of escalation" until reaching heaven.[10] Francis is working at the cemetery in an attempt to earn money to pay attorney's fees to Marcus Gorman (the narrator of *Legs*), who represented Francis when he was arrested for accepting money for voting over twenty times in a recent election (an event discussed in *Billy Phelan's Greatest Game*).[11] Once in the cemetery, we meet the first of the numerous dead who will appear during Francis' days in Albany, but the way these dead are described signals that they are not merely hallucinations of an alcoholic or a spiritually damaged man. While later in the narrative Francis will see ghosts and hold conversations with them (ghosts that no one else sees), in these opening pages it is the ghosts who perceive Francis and, unknown to him, react to his presence.

As Michael Yetman points out, the "reader's ability to witness ghostly presences that the protagonist himself is not always aware of makes it difficult to dismiss Francis' visions as mere hallucinations, chimeras of a whiskied brain" (87). Two young Phelan men killed in 1884, for example, are lying in their graves in the cemetery, and they see in "Francis' face the familiar scars of alcoholic desolation, which both had developed in their graves" (3); the narrative does not pause or qualify itself in its description of these two dead men as if they were still alive—they see Francis; they develop the scars of alcoholism—nor does it say that Francis himself saw or talked to them. Like these two Phelan ancestors, Daddy Big Dugan, the late manager of a pool hall whose death is described in *Billy Phelan*, also goes unobserved by Francis as Dugan lies in his grave and tries "futilely to memorize anew the fading memories of how he used to apply topspin and reverse English to the cue ball" (4-5). Just as if he were alive, Dugan recognizes Francis "even though he had not seen him in twenty years" (5).

Eventually Francis does see the dead himself and interacts with them, but even these encounters are described in such a way that one cannot attribute their presence to hallucination or dream. The actual appearance of a "ghost" (one hesitates to use the word) in the story is as natural in the narrative as some character recalling that person through memory or as flashback. When Francis travels by the old carbarns in Albany, for example, he remembers the strike he was involved in there in 1901, and the narrative then turns to describing the strikebreaker Francis killed in that strike and, without calling attention to itself, adds that the dead man is present right now in the Albany of 1938:

> That scab was the first man Francis Phelan ever killed. His name was Harold Allen and he was a single man from Worcester, Massachusetts, a member of the IOOF, of Scotch-Irish stock, twenty-nine years old, two years of college, veteran of the Spanish-

American War who had seen no combat, an itinerant house painter who found work in Albany as a strikebreaker and who was now sitting across the aisle of the bus from Francis, dressed in a long black coat and a motorman's cap. (25)

Harold Allen *was* a certain person—the scab Francis killed in 1901 during a violent strike—and still *is* a certain person, even though he is dead—the ex-scab sitting across from Francis on the bus: what happened back then in 1901 is as real as what is happening now in 1938. Harold of 1938, thirty-seven years dead, has the same ontological status within *Ironweed* as Harold the living scab of 1901. Kennedy's style in this novel, a form elsewhere and accurately defined as magical realist,[12] is such that language grants to both the dead and the living equal validity and reality. It is true that the ghosts serve a figurative function, for throughout *Ironweed*, as Michael Yetman writes, these ghosts help to "dramatize as they help to explain the character's abidingly harsh self-assessment" (87); but beyond this dramatic and figurative function lies the important ontological condition of the ghosts being *literally* present within the narrative, for there is no distinction in Francis' mind or, more importantly, within the narrative itself between the nature of the ghosts and visions and that of any of the "real," living characters, between those from the past and those from the present.

Harold Allen, though one of the more important ghosts, is only the first of many dead Francis encounters. Not long after spotting Allen, Francis also sees Aldo Campione, an Italian immigrant and horse thief whom Francis once tried to help onto a boxcar in which Francis himself was riding as Campione was running from the police. Francis grabbed Campione's hand but could not hold on and the man fell to his death. In *Ironweed*, Campione, though long dead, boards the same bus that Harold Allen is riding and gives Francis an ambiguous gesture with his hand, what might be a "simple

Abruzzian greeting," a "threat," a "warning," an "offer of belated gratitude," or a "show of compassion" (29). Francis considers that the greeting might be "a gesture of grace, urging, or even welcoming Francis into the next [world]" (29), an option to which Francis is not attracted and which leads him to refuse to take Aldo's hand. This confusion over the gesture reappears when Francis sees Aldo later in The Golden Cage, a bar where Francis and Helen and Francis' friend Rudy go for some fun on Halloween night. "What are you telling me, dead man," Francis thinks to himself in watching Aldo and his gesture, and then he asks him, "and who's that with you?" (52). Who's sitting with him is Rowdy Dick Doolan, a man Francis had killed years ago when Doolan tried to cut off Francis' feet with a meat cleaver in order to get his shoes, and now another ghost Francis encounters.

In addition to these ghosts of men for whose deaths Francis is responsible, two other significant ghosts in *Ironweed* are those of Francis' parents. As with the Phelan brothers and Daddy Big Dugan, Michael and Kathryn Phelan see Francis in St. Agnes Cemetery (while he is working there and thus before he meets Harold Allen and the others). Since Francis at first does not see his parents, they too confirm the magical rather than the hallucinatory nature of the universe in which Francis moves. Kathryn, Francis' iron-willed mother and also the bane of his life, is in her grave weaving crosses from dead dandelions and other weeds and eating them with an "insatiable revulsion" (2), an attitude with which she attacked life in general, unable to be satisfied in her intense distaste for anything physical. Her eating of the weeds of course makes one think of her as attempting to devour Francis himself, the "Ironweed" of the title. As Yetman writes, Kathryn "continues to haunt her aging son's imagination as a punishing, devouring specter" (89), although the "toughness of the stem" of an ironweed, a toughness that Kennedy tells us gives the plant its name,[13] makes Kathryn's efforts seem futile and, like her life, primarily self-punitive. Michael Phelan, Francis' father who died after a train accident at work, is also in the cemetery watching his son, and like Kathryn, he too observes Francis without Francis observing him. As he watches his son on the cemetery lawn above him, Michael lies both bemused by his wife's displeasure at seeing Francis and curious at the condition of his son after all these years.

Certainly the most important grave and ghost that Francis encounters is that of Gerald, the infant son for whose death Francis is responsible, even though Gerald, like Francis' parents, is not seen by Francis himself. Although at first Francis tries to ignore Gerald's burial plot, he eventually moves toward the grave without knowing it, so that Michael Phelan grows "amazed . . . that the living could move instinctually toward dead kin without foreknowledge of their location" (16). Francis does not have the knowledge of this location himself because he did not attend the funeral of his son, an act that scandalized not Albany so much as the "resident population of Saint Agnes's"(16), a description which, in attributing emotions to the dead, once again reinforces the legitimacy of the appearance and nature of the ghosts within the narrative. Despite the disapproval the dead felt at Francis' absence from Gerald's funeral, they now join in with Michael in rooting for Francis as he moves toward his "instinctual" discovery of the grave of his infant son.

As Francis approaches this grave, he is both literally and symbolically "closing the gap between father and son, between sudden death and enduring guilt" (16), the first clear hint that this entrance into the world of the dead might also be the beginning of Francis' possible redemption. Aware of the significance of this moment, Michael Phelan immediately signals "to his neighbors that an act of regeneration seemed to be in process" (16). In visiting Gerald, Francis is returning to a figure from a key moment in his past, just as Martin Daugherty returned to confront Melissa

Spencer. In writing of this similarity, Loxley Nichols argues that while "Martin attempts to expiate past sin by physically repeating the transgression, Francis re-enacts his past by communing with ghosts who lead him on a Dantean tour of his own underworld" (47). While this description is accurate, the "communing" is more complex than Nichols implies, for as we have seen Francis himself is at first unaware of the dead communicating with him.

In addition, Francis' confrontation, unlike Martin's, is not one that he enters entirely willingly, as his own ignorance of the ghosts in the graveyard and his attempt to ignore or escape the other ghosts (such as happens with Aldo Campione and his gesture) make evident. And the regeneration itself, although Francis does not realize it, is not needed to correct or expiate the dropping of the baby, the error in the past for which one might expect Francis needs to be forgiven or redeemed (and for which Francis himself probably expects some required expiation also); rather, Francis' redemption, whether he realizes it or not, must be from his *reaction* to that tragedy, his flight from Albany and from his family, a fact Gerald himself makes clear as he watches his father standing above his grave: "should he absolve the man of all guilt," Gerald wonders, "not for the dropping, for that was accidental, but for the abandonment of the family, for craven flight when the steadfast virtues were called for?" (17). What must occur for Francis to be redeemed, then, is not the correction of a historical accident, or a return such as Martin's to a specific moment in the past, but the absolution of Francis' continuing sin of abandonment and the removal of the guilt that accompanies that sin and that still haunts Francis today.

When Francis discovers he is at Gerald's grave, he begins to recall and acknowledge what happened twenty-two years before when he dropped Gerald and accidentally killed him. Francis' return to this past, however, is more than just simple remembering, more than a going back in his mind to that moment before his guilt propelled him into an endless journey of self-hate and self-recrimination. While standing above Gerald's grave, Francis is able to re-see that past not merely in simple memory but in a "panoramic memory" (18) that endows him with an extraordinary sense of the exact nature of the past: "Twenty-two years gone, and Francis could now, in panoramic memory, see, hear, and feel every detail of that day," including a drop of urine that fell on Francis' shoetop as he was changing the baby's diaper (18). The memory is so exact, in fact, that it actually becomes another means of present-day perception, for now "memory was as vivid as eyesight" for Francis (18). Memory becomes, in short, a means of seeing as valid as actual vision, so that what Francis sees in his memory and what he sees in actuality are of equal validity. That the two types of vision share the same status is emphasized when Francis is said to have not remembered but "*reconstructed* the moment when the child was slipping through his fingers into death" (18, emphasis mine), as if the events from the past of 1916 are available for their reconstruction in the Albany of 1938.

Francis' "reconstruction" of the past, his use of memory as a means of perception, and his encounters with the dead are all part of Francis' larger return to his own history and his own past, a return that is paralleled by his more mundane reappearance in the city of Albany, where his walks along its streets are both a mechanism for his encountering the ghosts of his past and a return to the literal location of that past. This return could be described as both a literal and a figurative one for Francis, except that within the narrative of *Ironweed* there is no distinction between the literal and the figurative when it comes to describing the details of Francis' journey: the living hobo is as real as the dead scab on the trolley, memory is as accurate and vivid as eyesight, and Albany is the city of 1901, 1916, 1938, and all the years in between. "The present Albany of the novel," Anya Taylor writes, "is doubled or tripled by an overlay of time schemes" (110), and the vehicle for revealing these many Albanies is Francis himself. Kennedy has said that we "might think of Francis Phelan as always being aware of where he is, and yet also always aware of all his history" (McCaffery, 177), and through this heightened awareness on Francis' part of both here and there, now and then, Albany is transformed from the city of 1938 into a quasi-mythological city of all-time. As J. K. Van Dover writes of Francis and his city, "All his Albanies are present in this Albany" (85).

What Francis sees in the present city and what he remembers of previous Albanies begin to intermingle as he wanders through the city (on his way to working at the cemetery):

> At Shaker Road [Francis and Rudy] walked up to North Pearl Street and headed north on Pearl. Where [his family] live now. They'd painted Sacred Heart Church since he last saw it, and across the street School 20 had new tennis courts. Whole lot of houses here he never saw, new since '16. This is the block they live in. What Billy said. When Francis last walked this street it wasn't much more than a cow pasture. Old man Rooney's cows would break the fence and roam loose, dirtyin' the streets and sidewalks. You got to put a stop to this, Judge Ronan told Rooney. What is it you want me to do, Rooney asked the judge, put diapers on 'em? (10)

This intermingling of perceiving and remembering continues as Francis moves through the streets toward the cemetery where he will work. He observes a tavern where he remembers a fight occurring once and a stadium that replaced the park where Francis played baseball when he was young. "Perceptions dovetailing into memories," Robert Gibb writes of this phenomenon, "Francis walks in both the past and the present" (61), the Albany (or Albanies) of then and now.

All this that Francis sees and remembers of his old hometown could easily be dismissed as just a stroll down a very sad memory lane did we not know both the important status of memory in *Ironweed* and the fact that many of these memories are strolling about themselves as ghosts. And as we soon read, these memories are not moments simply separable from the present. After Francis finishes his work at the cemetery, he walks again along the city streets, a journey that is a stepping through time itself and not just memory. Francis does not go backwards so much as he goes in a "series of overlapping circles,"[14] a spiraling into and out of the past:

> Francis saw the street that lay before him: Pearl Street, the central vessel of this city, city once his, city lost. The commerce along with its walls jarred him: so much new, stores gone out of business he never even heard of. Some things remained: Whitney's, Myers', the old First Church, which rose over Clinton Square, the Pruyn Library. As he walked, the cobblestones turned to granite, houses became stores, life aged, died, renewed itself, and a vision of what had been and what might have been intersected in an eye that could not really remember one or interpret the other. (64)

Throughout his journey, as in this scene, Francis is able to see "what had been and what might have been" even though he could not really "remember or interpret" those visions himself. The vision of a changing history, "histories" from various times all present now, is ironically made legitimate by Francis' own inability to use what is fallible memory or perception to conjure up these histories: something else other than Francis is joining the past and present, then and now. The visions of time past, including the Albany of the past, do not derive from memory or delirium but are themselves magically reconstituted, providing legitimacy to moments such as the one in which Francis looks down a street and impossibly sees someone coming toward him "looking not unlike himself at twenty-one" (153). The past appears again in the present, so that there might even be two of Francis, at two different ages, walking along the same street.

At one point in observing this many-layered city, Francis considers how extensively his old hometown has changed since he last left. Yet there is one important item that is not yet "gone": "What the hell ain't gone?" Francis thinks to himself. "Well, me. Yeah, me. Ain't a whole hell of a lot of me left, but I ain't gone entirely. Be god-diddley-damned if I'm gonna roll over and die" (88). Francis is a man who has not only seen death everywhere and who confronts the dead in Albany, but one who has almost died several times himself, a man who even "stanched death its very self" (75) by escaping the murderous Dick Doolan. And yet in such defiant statements as his refusing to "roll over and die," we see that Francis asks for no pity and has no desire to join those already dead, as was evident from his refusal to accept Aldo Campione's ambiguously outstretched hand. Francis' defiance of time and death, his stand against becoming a mere memory or a ghost himself, will serve him well during his "monomythical" journey through Albany: the past can be a means toward redemption for Francis because he refuses to become a part of it.

How the past penetrates and actually affects the present action of the narrative begins to be apparent when Francis and several of his friends, including his girlfriend Helen Archer, enter The Golden Cage for a drink on Halloween night. This bar is the scene in which the behavior of characters in the present moment begins to change decidedly in light of the past resurfacing before them. Up until this point, Francis has been either oblivious to the dead (those who watched him in the cemetery) or he has only watched in passive curiosity the ghosts that he sees following him

(Harold Allen, Aldo Campione, Rowdy Dick Doolan). But even though the bar is a magical place where the past resurfaces in the present, how Francis will act on his own encroaching past is withheld for the moment, for it is Helen, not Francis, who experiences most intensely a return to the past while they are in The Golden Cage. And this return of hers, while it accentuates the thematic concern in the novel with the intermingling of the past and present, is more significant for its differences from Francis' own return than for its similarities: Helen's reliving of the past, unlike Francis', is ultimately revealed to be an illusion.

Helen's return to the past, the single most important one that does not involve Francis, begins when Francis meets an old acquaintance of his tending bar at The Golden Cage. Oscar Reo is both an ex-drunk and an ex-lounge singer, his career ruined by the drinking. Yet despite the tragic waste of his talents, Oscar has not lost the talent itself, a skill that is magical in perhaps more than a figurative way: at one point, Oscar "sang into the bar microphone and, with great resonance and no discernible loss of control from his years with the drink, he turned time back to the age of the village green" (49). With time effectively "turned . . . back" by Oscar's singing, Helen, a former student of the piano, decides that she too wants to sing a song in the bar. Her stepping up to the stage microphone is a stepping out of time, a collapsing of many past moments into one undifferentiated one:

> . . . Helen smiled and stood and walked to the stage with an aplomb and grace befitting her reentry into the world of music, the world she should never have left, oh why ever did you leave it, Helen? She climbed the three steps to the platform, drawn upward by familiar chords that now seemed to her to have always evoked joy, chords not from this one song but from an era of songs, thirty, forty years of songs that

celebrated the splendors of love, and loyalty, and friendship, and family, and country, and the natural world. (54)

Carried away by the strength of these memories, Helen becomes a "living explosion of unbearable memory and indomitable joy" (55).

As Helen begins to sing, the narrative describes a return to a moment far different from Helen's current painful life as a dying hobo: she sings with a voice that left her audience "hanging on her every note" and hears applause that was "full and long" (56). Her talent is as appreciated as it was decades before when she sang on the radio. On the stage now Helen is defiant and proud at the microphone and realizes how much Francis loves her, and then she hears the "thunder! Thunderous applause! And the elegant people are standing for Helen, when last did that happen? More, more, more, they yell . . ." (57). When she is finished, Helen descends the three steps of the stage, receiving praise from Francis and a job offer from Oscar. And then we hear from the narrative voice that

> Helen closed her eyes and felt tears beginning to force their way out and could not say whether she was blissfully happy or devastatingly sad. Some odd-looking people were applauding politely, but others were staring at her with sullen faces. If they're sullen, then obviously they didn't think much of your renditions, Helen. Helen steps delicately back down the three steps . . . (57)

Finishing her singing has meant for Helen stepping back into the reality of the present moment: the collapsing of past into present has occurred only in Helen's mind, as we learn when Helen descends the steps again, this time for real, not as she imagined it earlier with the applause sounding around her. Her singing over, she is left to face the reality of her poor performance and the "sullen" audience that watched her.

Her return to the past, perhaps because it is only an illusion, has not helped to redeem her from her own present sad state.

In addition to this moment in The Golden Cage, there is at least one other significant scene in which Helen again enacts Kennedy's magical transposition of time, another of those moments, to borrow Robert Gibb's phrase, in which "time gives way to timelessness" (2). After spending the night in a car with a fellow bum in order to keep warm—at the cost of her having sex with him—Helen realizes that even in her despair she is "joyous" because she "had mastered the trick of escaping into music and the pleasures of memory," exactly the trick she had mastered temporarily on the stage at The Golden Cage (120). Helen, still a believing Catholic, goes to Mass the next morning and eventually retires by herself to a room in a run-down hotel. Hanging on the back of the door in the room is a sign, a blue cardboard clock above which is written "WAKE ME AT:" (124). Always set at ten minutes to eleven, the clock symbolically has "frozen" time in Helen's hotel room, removing that time from the contingent nature of its own passing.

In this room Helen thinks back on her own tragic life, one in which her mother hid her father's will and denied Helen her share of the inheritance, and one in which a music teacher used and betrayed Helen, claiming to love her while really only wanting her for the sex. Helen thinks back to that affair on "that continuing Tuesday and Thursday and unchanging Friday," moments in her history that are now removed from history and time and occur repeatedly in memory, "continuing" and "unchanging" (126–27). These moments are like the blue cardboard clock, itself outside the normal pattern of changing time, forever set at ten minutes to eleven. Significantly, the hotel clerk looking after Helen knocks on the door of her room at eleven o'clock, only moments before she dies. Time has stopped at ten to eleven, but eventually for Helen eleven o'clock comes: for her, time's up.

* * *

Although Helen's singing in The Golden Cage and her death in the hotel room introduce in their compromised way the vital interaction between past and present that is possible in *Ironweed*, the truly significant effects of such interaction are reserved for Francis. His trips out of the present are far more numerous and complex than Helen's. In addition, his ghosts are never proven to be illusions: the intersection of the past and the present occurs not merely in his memory or imagination—as it seems to with Helen—but in Albany itself, that unlikely place of archetype and history, as Kennedy might describe it, a city where Francis sees "what had been and what might have been" (64).

One of the important visions composed partially of what "might have been" includes Francis witnessing the arrival of his parents after their honeymoon at the Colonie Street house where the Phelan family lived. In having Francis witness an episode he obviously never could have seen himself, Kennedy again asks us (as he did in the scenes with the ghosts) to take the narrative at its word that what is happening in the vision is as real or legitimate as what is happening in the present moment of Francis' life. The vision itself occurs while Francis is helping Rosskam, the neighborhood junk collector. As he sits on Rosskam's wagon, Francis sees his father in his "trainman's overalls" and his mother wearing her wedding dress and looking "as she had when she hit Francis with an open hand and sent him sprawling backward into the china closet" (97), a reference to what Kathryn Phelan did when she discovered that the then eighteen-year-old Francis had been embracing the naked Katrina Daugherty. The way Kathryn looks after her honeymoon thus connotes not connubial bliss but sexual disgust, for her appearance is the same as the one she had while punishing Francis for what she perceived to be his sexual transgressions.

More significant than the actual events and characters this vision reveals is its "plane of escalation," as Kennedy might say, its ontological status within the narrative and its eschatological nature as a world beyond time. The description of the vision reveals it to be one that transcends the limitations of the linear nature of "chronological" time and to be instead a moment outside of time altogether. It is a vision in which distinct moments of history are collapsed, in which "then" is the same as "now":

> The newlyweds . . . climbed the front stairs to the bedroom they would share for all the years of their marriage, the room that now was also their shared grave, a spatial duality as reasonable to Francis as the concurrence of this moment both in the immediate present of his fifty-eighth year of life and in the year before he was born: that year of sacramental consummation, 1879. (98)

Anya Taylor has described this scene as one of "telescoped memory" (113), but it is really much more than that, for the narrative does not ask us to read the vision in terms of its being filtered through Francis' remembering, even if telescopic. Perhaps it would be more accurate to describe this scene in terms similar to David Black's understanding of the concept of time in general in *Ironweed*. Black argues that the treatment of time in Kennedy's novel is similar to the Greek notion that the future is what is behind us rather than what is in front of us; in this way, the Greeks see the past, as does *Ironweed*, "as lying in front of us, before our eyes" (177). Such is certainly and literally the case for Francis here, for the past is right before him as he sits on Rosskam's cart, but Black is slightly inaccurate, as was Taylor in her way, in arguing that this "Greek concept of time" is "at work in the mind of Francis Phelan" (177). What is significant about *Ironweed* is that the concept of nonlinear time is at work in *VG* the narrative itself, not in the mind of the characters in that narrative, just as the ghosts and the living past are products of the narrative point of view and not ones of a character's imagination.

The rest of the scene that Francis witnesses from the wagon is of Michael and Kathryn's first act of intercourse, another episode that Francis obviously could not have witnessed and one that further reveals Kathryn's disgust with sex. But this vision is again most significant for the way in which Kennedy describes it and how that description reveals once more the concept of time as it is treated in the novel: "In their room," Kennedy writes in beginning the scene, "Michael Phelan embraced his new wife of fifty-nine years and ran a finger down the crevice of her breasts" (98). The unqualified paradox of a "new wife of fifty-nine years," like Francis seeing as "reasonable" the "spatial duality" of 1879 and 1938, exemplifies the way in which Kennedy unapologetically demands that the expected distinctions of history—various moments of time; past and present and future—be disregarded in reading this mythological journey of a hobo-hero. And as Francis (the Francis Phelan of 1938, that is) continues to witness the Michael and Kathryn Phelan of 1879, the various moments of Phelan history in particular mix and merge and blur: past and present, life and death, memory and perceived act, first time and always, new and old come together in a tour de force of the conflation of traditionally distinct moments of time:

> Now, as her husband lifted her chemise over her head, the virginal mother of six recoiled with what Francis recognized for the first time to be spiritually induced terror, as visible in her eyes in 1879 as it was in the grave. Her skin was as fresh and pink as the taffeta lining of her coffin, but she was, in her youthfully rosy bloom, as lifeless as the spun silk of her magenta burial dress. She has been dead all her life, Francis thought. . . . As she yielded her fresh body to her new husband out of obligation, Francis

felt the iron maiden of induced chastity piercing her everywhere, tightening with the years until all sensuality was strangulated and her body was as bloodless and cold as a granite angel.

She closed her eyes and fell back on the wedding bed like a corpse . . . and the old man's impeccable blood shot into her aged vessel with a passionate burst that set her writhing with the life of newly conceived death. Francis watched this primal pool of his own soulish body squirm into burgeoning matter. . . . The body sprouted to wildly mature growth and stood fully clad at last in the very clothes Francis was now wearing. He recognized the toothless mouth, the absent finger joints, the bump on the nose, the mortal slouch of this newborn shade, and he knew then that he would be this decayed self he had been so long in becoming, through all the endless years of his death. (98–99)

The ability of history to be more than linear, to exist at all times simultaneously, means that in Kennedy's fiction we accept a "virginal mother of six," the equally terrified eyes of a bride and a corpse, a woman "dead all her life," the "aged vessel" of a young virgin, and "the life of newly conceived death." Most remarkably, we watch these moments in the past give life to matter which changes and grows until it shapes a Francis that the Francis of the present moment sees to be himself as he is becoming and, in fact, will be forever.

This vision of Francis' parents, and eventually even of Francis himself, though remarkable for the way it captures the concept of time in *Ironweed*, is hardly the only moment in which the past is described in such a way. A few moments after seeing his own conception and growth—a scene reminiscent of Martin Daugherty's reenactment of his own conception in *Billy Phelan*—Francis sees his mother again, this time pouring salt on the roots of a tree that belonged to the Daugherty family who once lived next door to the Phelans.

Kathryn's act of vengeance against the Daughertys, whose tree, she claimed, was "insinuating" itself into the Phelan yard, seems to have been fruitless, for Francis on the junk wagon "saw the tree now, twice its old size, a giant thing in the world" (101). As he watches, the tree changes, and with it the time, so that again we are transported back into the past, much as Helen was on stage, but again with no qualifying comments to identify the vision as memory or delusion: "On this high noon in 1938, under the sun's full brilliance, the tree restored itself to its half size of forty-one years past, a July morning in 1897 when Francis was sitting on a middle branch, sawing the end of a branch above him" (101). This picture of Francis in the tree is a vision of a crucial moment in his life, when, at age eighteen, he sees the crazy Katrina Daugherty walk naked from her house. Francis helps her back in, and in the weeks that follow Katrina introduces him into the mysteries of eroticism and the female body. Although the narrative does not make clear all that Katrina did with the young Francis, enough is revealed of her behavior—such as her asking Francis to touch her breasts—for us to recognize what an impact she must have had on the young Francis, a child, it is to be remembered, sexually inexperienced himself and raised by a conservative and repressed mother devout in her Catholic faith.

Eventually Francis' vision of this tree of 1897 leads to a vision of Katrina herself, but one who is not only of 1897 but of all time, a Katrina outside of time, much as the moment of his parents on their honeymoon is slowly transfigured into a transcendent moment in the eternal "now." At the beginning of this vision of Katrina, Francis sees her on the steps to her house, even though by 1938 this house had been destroyed by fire for over twenty years (an event dramatized in *The Flaming Corsage*). In the vision Katrina leads Francis into a bedroom "he had never seen and where a wall of flame engulfed her without destroying even the hem of her dress" (114).[15] In the room he sees himself and Katrina as they were in various moments of time, and even as mythological figures of love in the abstract outside of any time at all:

> In the leaping windows of flame that engulfed Katrina and her bed, Francis saw naked bodies coupled in love, writhing in lascivious embrace, kissing in sweet agony. He saw himself and Katrina in a ravenous lunge that never was, and then in a blissful stroking that might have been, and then in a sublime fusion of desire that would always be.
>
> Did they love? No, they never loved. They always loved. (115)

Never and always; what never was, might have been, and would always be; then and then and now: these disparate and even nonexistent moments are conflated in this scene—and throughout the novel—without apology or qualification.

This unqualified depiction in *Ironweed* of a transfigured conception of history and time is consistent with much that we have seen in Kennedy's other Albany novels. In *Ironweed*, the narrative establishes a world that is now and forever and then and nowhere simultaneously, and thus it creates an eschatological locale—a place outside the linearity of time—in which the struggle for the redemption of Francis' soul will take place. The presence of such a universe is not insignificant when one considers the key questions of the novel: is Francis resurrectible, and is he ever resurrected? The eschatological nature of the world in which Francis lives gives legitimacy to the possibility that Francis may indeed be redeemed, for this world is, after all, the afterlife, even though it may not be heaven itself. And this sense of a transfigured and transfigurable history—indeed, of a place and time outside of history altogether—will be an important concept for interpreting the crucial and remarkable final scene of *Ironweed* in particular, a scene in which the narrative abandons the grammar of a traditional linear chronology as told in the present or past tense for a narrative in the conditional subjunctive. The conditional, what might be or might have been, is, after all, as legitimate in this eschatological universe as what was, what is, or what will be, as these several important visions of Francis' so emphatically illustrate.

Francis' Existential Journey

Although the nature of the dead who greet Francis, the ghosts he meets himself, and the visions he has all attest to the fact that Francis' "reconstituted" past is not just willful memory or self-induced hallucination, the journey that Francis himself embarks on into his own history might seem at one point to be a voluntary one, to be something he desires. After all, he did come back to Albany. And while still in the graveyard, he admits that he wants to return to the past in praying for a "repeal of time" (18). But it is important to recognize that this desire for "repeal" is not a wish to begin a quest for regeneration or forgiveness, the actual and basically involuntary quest in which Francis does engage. Instead, as Francis admits, his initial desire is to repeal time in order that he might go back in his past and kill himself before changing Gerald's diaper and thus dropping and killing the baby. In making such a wish, Francis reveals the difference between the quest he desires and the one he actually takes: what Francis wants to do is to change history, not himself. This wish also reveals at least one way in which Francis considers his errors differently from the way Gerald considers them, for the boy in his grave asked that Francis might expiate the sin of his fleeing, not the actual act of killing Gerald himself.

In wanting to destroy the moment of his "sin," and in misunderstanding that sin itself, Francis has thus not yet taken the first step toward forgiveness, embracing the sin to be forgiven, much as Martin Daugherty at first did not embrace his own sin when he made an absurd confession to a priest who barely understood English. Once Francis accepts the event, then forgiveness might occur, but in the cemetery he acknowledges what has happened only to regret that he did it and to try to wish it away or, perhaps more realistically, to try to forget it. As he says while standing over Gerald's grave: "I remember the linoleum you fell on was yellow with red squares. You suppose now that I can remember this stuff out in the open, I can finally start to forget it?" (19). Gerald, however, has other thoughts for his father:

> Gerald, through an act of silent will, imposed on his father the pressing obligation to perform his final acts of expiation for abandoning the family. You will not know, the child silently said, what these acts are until you have performed them all. And after you have performed them you will not understand that they are expiatory any more than you have understood all the other expiation that has kept you in such prolonged humiliation. Then, when these final acts are complete, you will stop trying to die because of me. (19)

Gerald's command to his father is to stop being one of the living dead he has become: the truly dead wants to help cure the figuratively so.

This journey Gerald imposes on his father begins after Francis finishes his work in the graveyard and he leaves with his friend Rudy. Francis soon after enters Albany to begin the monomythic journey that will introduce him (and Helen) to the living past and that will eventually lead Francis home to Annie, his wife. As we have already noted, the mythological and eschatological nature of this journey is made clear by the numerous mythological allusions and by the nature of the visions that Francis has, including the dead who encourage him or greet him and the past that resurfaces in his visions. The primary question that remains about this journey in this unusual world, however, is how successful it is. The myths and the magic imply that such success is possible, perhaps even probable, but is Francis' personal grail obtained? Does Francis, like Dante, reach his version of Beatrice and heaven? Or can Francis really not be raised from the dead, as Annie claimed in *Billy Phelan?*

The numerous clues provided within the narrative itself to help answer such questions begin with a rather simple and traditional metaphor used throughout *Ironweed,* the notion of cleaning or cleansing oneself. Francis' journey, as Gerald said, will be one of "expiation," a cleansing away of sin that is symbolized and paralleled throughout *Ironweed* by Francis' desire to cleanse his own physical self. While listening to the Reverend Chester at the local mission, an obligatory act if a bum wants some soup and coffee, Francis hears the preacher sing about how God's "blood can make the foulest clean" (33). Though Francis has no time for such beliefs, he immediately "smelled his own uncanceled stink again, aware that it had intensified since morning" (33). Francis then makes explicit the connection between the odor of his body and the sinful odor of his soul:

> The sweat of a workday, the sourness of dried earth on his hands and clothes, the putrid perfume of the cemetery air with its pretension to windblown purity, all this lay in foul encrustation atop the private pestilence of his being. When he threw himself onto Gerald's grave, the uprush of a polluted life all but asphyxiated him. (33)

Francis' "being," like his body, suffers from his "private pestilence," and his "life" is "polluted," metaphorical descriptions that use physical filth to signal moral decay. As Francis hints at here by identifying the origin of these various odors as the cemetery, the smells of both body and soul are also, both literally and symbolically, the "stink of the dead" (35), and thus for Francis to wash himself of that stink signals his being washed into new life as one figuratively is in baptism. Francis' desire to wash and to be baptized begins when he cleans himself in the bathroom at the mission, and he will attempt to wash himself again later at a friend's house that he and Helen visit and then in his own old home when he returns there to visit Annie.[16]

Francis' wish to cleanse himself is duplicated numerous times throughout his journey through Albany by his desire for confession and forgiveness and change, all methods of attempting to wash away the sins of the past. While observing Oscar Reo's sad state as a lounge-singer turned bartender, for example, Francis felt a "compulsion to confess his every transgression of natural, moral, or civil law; to relentlessly examine and expose every flaw of his own character, however minor" (50). And after he puts Helen in Finny's car on Halloween night, wanting for her to be warm but uneasy about the sexual favors she will have to perform, Francis "walked with an empty soul toward the north star, mag-netized by an impulse to redirect his destiny" (87). Later, when he arrives at Annie's house, he cannot explain why he has come but he still felt a "great compulsion to confess all his transgressions" (160), to "clean" his heart of all his sins.

Although Francis is not entirely certain why he has returned to Albany, other than to collect what money he can for his multiple voting, he still feels while wandering through the city this frequent desire to confess and to change his destiny. This change, silently imposed upon Francis by Gerald, begins to take shape once Francis has descended into the world of the dead in the cemetery, and accelerates once Francis hires on to help Rosskam, the junkman who lives and works in a "castoff world" of junk stored in a "cemetery of dead things" (91). While Francis rides with Rosskam, a kind of Albany Charon, the visitations of the ghosts increase in number and frequency, and Francis begins to see the visions of Kathryn and Michael Phelan and the young Francis and

Katrina Daugherty that we saw above and that so clearly establish the eschatological status of the world in which Francis is moving. The visions themselves are inspired by Francis' seeing familiar sights as Rosskam's junk wagon slowly moves toward Colonie Street, the site of Francis' boyhood home.

Although Rosskam is rude to Francis, and although Francis must threaten the junkman to get his half-day's pay, Rosskam serves not only as a kind of Charon but also as a kind of guide, a perverse Virgil leading Dante toward home. Like Virgil, Rosskam is a source of wisdom, even though he is himself a bitter and poor man. "'Some people,'" Rosskam says at one point to Francis, "'they don't know junk. It ain't garbage. And garbage, it ain't junk'" (148). It's a lesson that Francis himself will have to take to heart. Garbage is waste, something that should be thrown out because it has no value; junk, although it may seem worn and useless—worn and useless like an alcoholic who abandons his family—still has its value: it "ain't garbage." The importance of Rosskam's role on the journey is emphasized when the noise of the wheels of his junkwagon on which Francis sits is said to be "announcing the prodigal's return" (97), a biblical image that reinforces the possibly holy and thus redeemable nature of Francis.

Eventually Francis quits the gruff junkman, as Dante must quit his own guide, and he buys a turkey and returns to visit his family. When he arrives, Annie welcomes Francis home without hesitation; she is a woman, much like Penelope, waiting for and still loving her husband although he has been many years gone. Francis has trouble explaining to himself and to Annie why he has returned, although he claims that it was due in part to his son Billy's earlier invitation to come home (an event portrayed in *Billy Phelan*) as well as to his being moved at hearing that Annie had never told anyone that he had been responsible for Gerald's death. (What Francis does not mention on this return to his house is the growing presence of the ghosts, nor does he of course know of Gerald's command for him to expiate his sins.) When Francis wonders aloud to Annie why he has come back, he says, "Might as well ask the summer birds why they go all the way south and then come back north to the same old place" (160). Like the migration of birds, Francis' return is as inevitable as it is mysterious. Reilly argues that in returning home "Francis learns that running from responsibility takes him back to the starting point" (76), an explanation that avoids the issue of motivation but that nonetheless reiterates an important characteristic of the image of the migrating birds—the notion of the circular return. Like the birds on their migration, like Odysseus, who circles back to Ithaca, and like Dante, who circles slowly upward to the empyrean, Francis has completed a circle back to Annie's house. It is a shape which replicates the temporal "line" of his journey too, for the time in which Francis lives is not linear but cyclical, a history where past, present, and future blur in their circular tumble into each other.

Although his circular journey is now geographically complete in his return home, Francis has nonetheless not arrived at a specific place and moment—his home and his family of 1938—but rather at another location in his magical world in which time is again and intensely transfigured. Annie, the woman and wife to whom he returns, is after all the one who, as a young girl, gave Francis a kiss that was "out of time itself" (156). It was a kiss, a beginning of their still-enduring love, that, as Francis says, "'was just this mornin'" (163), even though decades have passed since it happened. And Francis suspects too—and his suspicions will soon be confirmed—that the backyard he looks out on from the kitchen of his home would soon "function as a site of a visitation" (163). Such descriptions reveal Annie's (and Francis') house not to be a special place free of the ahistorical universe in which Francis moves, but actually one of the more intense locations of this unusual timeless world, and this is perhaps as it should be: no specific place except the Colonie Street house of the Phelans is more important in Francis' past than Francis and Annie's home.

Francis' suspicion about the ensuing visitation, along with the sense of blessedness he feels in being back in the house and with Annie in particular, convinces him that he is in the "throes of flight, not outward this time but upward" (163), an image that explicitly recalls the figure of Dante again and that also asks us, like the metaphor of Francis cleansing himself, to see Francis' journey as one "upward" toward redemption and renewal. For years this running and flight was for Francis a "condition that was as pleasurable to his being as it was natural," a running that was ultimately a "quest for pure flight as a fulfilling mannerism of the spirit" (75). Yetman describes how integral this flight is to understanding Francis: "Literal wandering, moral errancy, deviation from any norm not self-scripted, or at least self-approved, have been functions of personality for this picaro for as long as he can remember" (101). But here in Annie's house such "errancy" is replaced by a feeling of a directed movement upward, a holy journey through "planes of escalation." As Virgil leaves Dante at the end of Purgatory, Rosskam leaves Francis so that Francis can enter the heaven of Annie's house, a place to which he ascends in order to await whatever visitation is about to come.

This notion of a symbolic ascent is reinforced by a literal ascent of Francis', this one into the Phelan attic to look for some of his old possessions. The attic, like the house in general, is another place in which history is immanent and time is intensely transformed. When Francis enters the room, he opens the lid of his old trunk and "the odor of lost time filled the attic air, a cloying reek of imprisoned flowers that unsettled the dust and fluttered the window shades" (168). In opening this trunk, in smelling the "odor of lost time," Francis first "felt drugged by the scent of the reconstituted past" and then was "stunned by his first look inside the trunk, for there, staring out from a photo, was his own face at age nineteen" (168). Once again the past is alive in the present moment, "reconstituted" now by the magic of the attic and the trunk, a transfiguration captured in the image of the youthful Francis gazing up at the old and ruined Francis of 1938: the statement that "Francis stared up at himself" (169), a description which reverses the actual and the photographed, even gives the picture of Francis an ontological value equal to the Francis of the present moment, much in the same way that the magical and the real and the past and the present are given the same value throughout the narrative.

The picture Francis sees—or that sees him—is of himself decades earlier with a group of men at a baseball park. In the picture Francis is tossing a ball from his right hand to his gloved left one. The description of this photograph repeats the conception of history apparent in the earlier visions Francis has had of a world outside of time, though now the nature of this timeless, nonlinear history is also explicitly linked to the possibility of redemption:[17]

> The flight of the ball had always made this photo mysterious to Francis, for the camera had caught the ball clutched in one hand and also in flight, arcing in a blur toward the glove. What the camera had caught was two instants in one: time separated and unified, the ball in two places at once, an eventuation as inexplicable as the Trinity itself. Francis now took the picture to be a Trinitarian talisman (a hand, a glove, a ball) for achieving the impossible: for he had always believed it impossible for him, ravaged man, failed human, to reenter history under this roof. Yet here he was in this aerie of reconstitutable time, touching untouchable artifacts of a self that did not yet know it was ruined, just as the ball, in its inanimate ignorance, did not know yet that it was going nowhere, was caught. (169)

The picture, then, is not only a symbol of Francis in his youth, back in the past, but a symbol of Francis now and, indeed, at any moment: it is a "talisman" indicating "time separated and unified," distinct moments of time put together, exactly the condition of the visions Francis has had and the condition of the city where Francis now is—where the dead walk among the living, where what was, is, will be, and might be are all present. Prior to coming to Annie's house, Francis fled from the ghosts and his own history as if they were demons haunting him, but now he has reentered history under a friendly roof and entered an "aerie of reconstitutable time" that offers compassion, comfort, and reconciliation.

One problem with this photograph as emblem, as the passage above makes clear, is that Francis seems to be doomed like the ball to be caught. As a youth in the picture he does not yet know about the tragedies that will befall the Francis of old age. The magic of the moment only seems to conceal its inevitably tragic end. "But," as Kennedy writes,

> . . . the ball is really not yet caught, except by the camera, which has frozen only its situation in space.
> And Francis is not yet ruined, except as an apparency in process.
> The ball still flies.
> Francis still lives to play another day.
> Doesn't he? (169)

Does he? And, we might add, which Francis are we talking about? The primacy of one Francis over the other in the narrative has been confused in having the picture of Francis "stare up at" the present Francis. Surely the one in the picture lives to play another day, for that Francis is even now looking into the trunk. But the current Francis' condition is still uncertain, though the hints at his redemption have been numerous—the mythological allusions, Gerald's call for expiation, the desire for cleansing, and Francis' entrance

into the "aerie of reconstitutable time," to name only a few.
And immediately after seeing the curious photograph, the
current Francis considers one specific way that he can "live
to play another day" right now, a way that he can at least be
physically restored, when he thinks that "a man can get new
teeth" to replace his decayed and missing ones (169). Thus
Francis decides, with both humor and pathos, that his
regeneration might begin with dentures.

The dentures are for some other time; for now Francis
wants to get what he has desired all day—a bath, the
cleansing he has long wanted. In the kitchen, he had
"smelled himself and knew he had to wash as soon as
possible" (168), so he collects some old clothes from the attic
in order to change what he is wearing and goes into the
bathroom.   Although he realizes how old-fashioned the
clothes are, he decides that he will wear them anyway, for the
"odor of time was infinitely superior to the stink of bumdom"
(171). Soon he gets into the tub, "baptizing" himself at last,
and in the water of his own home. While bathing he feels
"blessed" and the whole bathroom seems to him to be a holy
place:

> He stared at the bathroom sink, which now had an
> aura of sanctity about it, its faucets sacred, its
> drainpipe holy, and he wondered whether everything
> was blessed at some point in its existence, and he
> concluded yes. Sweat rolled down his forehead and
> dripped off his nose into the bath, a confluence of
> ancient and modern waters. (171–72)

Francis has at last purified himself, washing away not only
his physical smell, but the stench of death and of sin that has
been associated with this body odor throughout *Ironweed*.
Everything about the bath, from the sink to the faucets, is
"sacred" or "blessed," and Francis even comes to conclude
that "everything" in the world is at some point blessed, an
implicit acknowledgment of Francis' own worth, as was

Rosskam's comment about differentiating between garbage and junk. Significantly too, the whole cleansing occurs within the "confluence of ancient and modern waters," the merging waters of the past and present.

Once Francis gets cleaned and dressed, he descends the stairs of the house as "Francis, that 1916 dude" (172): after his ascent into the attic and his baptism, he has, in short, become the Francis of twenty-two years before. He has returned at last, it seems, to that moment prior to his great tragedy, free now perhaps to redeem the wrong of fleeing the family. The new (or the old?) Francis after his bath is stunningly handsome to his family; they are amazed at Francis' "resurrectible good looks" and at the great difference in him after his "transformation" (172). And yet despite all these clues to Francis' renewal—baptism, plans for new teeth, the younger Francis, a bath, new clothes, a resurrected and transformed man, a flight upward—this home is soon revealed to be neither a safe nor a permanent haven for Francis. His daughter Peg signals this situation when she says, in response to Francis' simple question about how she has been, that she is doing fine though "no thanks" to Francis himself (178). Although Annie and Billy protest her bitterness, Francis does not, claiming he does not expect to be forgiven. But Peg is unrelenting, wondering why her father has "come back like a ghost we buried years ago" and, if he's "nowhere," as he claims himself, why is he here in the house now (178-79)?

Francis has already admitted he does not really know why he has returned, though he is growing ever more convinced of the importance of the decision when he begins to see more clearly the "visitation" that he had earlier felt was coming, a vision that is yet another warning that his home is not the final stopping place the other clues seem to signal it is. This visitation actually began to materialize while Francis was taking his bath. While in the water, he saw "a great sunburst [that] entered the darkening skies, a radiance so sudden that it seemed like a bolt of lightning" (172). Upon looking out the bathroom window he saw that "below, in the yard, Aldo Campione, Fiddler Quain, Harold Allen, and Rowdy Dick Doolan [all ghosts from Francis' past] were erecting a wooden structure that Francis was already able to recognize as bleachers" (172). A little bit later, as Francis watches from the backyard, men begin to assemble in the bleachers, forty-three of them altogether, in addition to four boys and two dogs, a collection of ghosts reminiscent of the suitors overtaking Odysseus' palace. Francis' return home, like Odysseus', does not seem to be complete until he has fought a battle against the enemies in his own house.

Since his baptism into a new Francis has not exorcized the old ghosts, Francis yells at all of them as they sit in the bleachers in an internal monologue of explicit self-exorcism:

> I am sick of you all, was his thought. I am sick of imagining what you became, what I might have become if I'd lived among you. I am sick of your melancholy histories, your sentimental pieties, your goddamned unchanging faces. I'd rather be dyin' in the weeds than standin' here lookin' at you pinin' away, like the dyin' Jesus pinin' for an end to it when he knew every stinkin' thing that was gonna happen not only to himself but to everybody around him, and to all those that wasn't even born yet. You ain't nothin' more than a photograph, you goddamn spooks. You ain't real and I ain't gonna be at your beck and call no more.
>
> You're all dead, and if you ain't, you oughta be.
>
> I'm the one is livin'. I'm the one puts you on the map. . . . So get your ass gone! (177)

The comparisons that Francis proposes in this attempt to exorcize his ghosts signal what the narrative has indicated all along, that Francis is living in an ahistorical, timeless moment. This moment is like the ghosts themselves, who are, according to Francis, each like a Jesus, who could be said to have lived both within and outside of history, as both man and a god. Francis also compares the people he sees in his vision to a photographed image, a moment that is frozen in time but that can, if the picture is not destroyed, exist through all time.

Francis' anxious reaction to the visitation is soon seen to be proven a legitimate one, for as he watches, the ghosts start a kind of religious service in the stadium, each holding a candle and singing the "Dies Irae," the Day of Judgment, the hymn for the dead (Black, 182.) While the meaning of this scene is ambiguous, it is certainly significant in its assembling of all of the ghosts together, a culmination of the visions that have long haunted Francis. The vision might be that of a mass being held for the death of the old Francis now displaced by the new one. Or it might mean that Francis will soon join these dead too or that they all still mourn their deaths, especially those caused by Francis himself. Although this scene is the most extreme appearance of the ghosts that Francis has encountered, Kennedy goes to lengths to make sure that it is still not described as the delusions of a beleaguered and drunken man: as Kennedy writes, Francis watched the performance of the ghosts closely, for "it was transcending what he expected from dream, from reverie, even from . . . hallucinations" (180). The service in the back yard is happening, Francis realizes, "in an area of his existence over which he had less control than he first imagined when Aldo Campione boarded the bus" earlier in the story (180–81).

Whatever kind of visitation is being enacted outside of Francis' old house, and whatever kind of transformation or exorcism accompanies it in Francis' command for the ghosts to "get [their] ass gone," the encounter proves to be yet another provisional and temporary step in Francis' journey. True, the Phelan family sits down to eat the turkey that Francis himself brought with him, an episode similar to the family gathering in *Very Old Bones* that will mark the forgiveness of many Phelan sins. But Francis does not stay after the meal, opting instead for a flophouse and a night of drinking after an attempt to find Helen fails, so that it seems that the hard-bitten alcoholic was after all only temporarily "resurrected" in the attic and bath of his old home. Odysseus may have found his way to Penelope, but he has not yet conquered the suitors who are challenging him.

The provisional nature of Francis' stay at Annie's is confirmed by the continuation of the visions Francis has been having even after he leaves Annie's home. Whatever happened at his wife's house, Francis still lives in that "purgatory" he entered in his arrival in Albany. Francis' first vision after leaving his old home, which occurs in the room of the flophouse to which he goes, is of the blurring faces of several women, including Sandra, the bum who had died earlier in the story, and Katrina Daugherty. Eventually, "the faces of all the women Francis had ever known changed with kaleidoscopic swiftness from one to the other to the other on . . . three female figures" that appear in the far corner of the room where he is staying for the night (202). Kennedy's description of these three women has been labeled by Peter P. Clarke the "clearest use of myth in the novel" (171): the "trio sat on straight-backed chairs," Kennedy writes, "witnesses all to the whole fabric of Francis' life. His mother was crocheting a Home Sweet Home sampler while Katrina measured off a bolt of new cloth and Helen snipped the ragged threads. Then they all became Annie" (202). Such a description obviously equates these women with the Moirae, Fates, or Parcae who, as Edith Hamilton explains, gave

> to men at birth evil and good to have. They were three, Clotho, the Spinner, who spun the thread of life; Lachesis, the Disposer of Lots, who assigned to each man his destiny; Atropos, she who could not be

turned, who carried 'the abhorrèd shears' and cut the thread at death. (49)

As Kennedy describes them, all three of the Fates—Kathryn, Katrina, and Helen—become Annie, a resolution which Clarke believes signifies that "salvation is possible" (174). He writes of the pattern of Francis' sin and redemption and explains that he sees its culmination in this vision of the Fates:

> This redemptive pattern resembles the pattern of Aeschylus' *Oresteia* : responsibility for the death of a close family member, pursuit by Furies, trial or expiation, acquittal, and transformation of Furies to the Eumenides or Kindly Ones. Thus, in the central mythographical passage (202 [of *IW*]), the three women "all become Annie," the kindly one who welcomes Francis back. . . . (175)

Clarke thus finds in the vision of the women, and not in Francis' return to his old home, the truly convincing evidence for Francis' redemption.

Despite the optimism of Clarke's claims, however, it is probably as premature to read this vision as a sign of Francis' salvation as it is to read his return to Annie's house in the same way: Francis is, after all, still in the flophouse, and he is also about to engage in the most dangerous activity yet of his stay in Albany, an activity that will lead to more death. But there is still another reason that neither of these possibly culminating moments in Francis' journey—Annie's home or the vision of Annie in the flophouse—could actually be its culmination or climax: as Francis himself will soon understand, the ultimate objective of his journey, and indeed the path toward that journey, is limited to Francis himself. The culminating place of Francis' journey is in himself, not in someone's home or bed. Francis' journey, and the world in which it is undertaken, are, in other words, as existential as they are mythological and eschatological. Those readers who find little redeemed or worth redeeming in the Francis Phelan of *Ironweed* probably neglect to appreciate this third, essential characteristic of Francis' (and Kennedy's) world and its role in Francis' redemption.

Francis himself begins to reveal his sense of the almost inevitably existential nature of his life—indeed, of anyone's life—in a discussion he has with Rudy at the flophouse. At the house, after Francis tells Rudy to shut up, Rudy complains that he can't help it, he can't escape himself; significantly, Francis agrees: "... you can't do it," he says, "so you might as well live with it" (201). And not long after Francis talks to Rudy, he admits to himself his own, internal struggle and what he realizes is his only source for surviving that struggle: after thinking back to the strike and to his killing Harold Allen, Francis realizes "that he was at war with himself, his private factions mutually bellicose, and if he was ever to survive, it would be with the help not of any socialistic god but with a clear head and a steady eye for the truth . . ." (207). Francis realizes that he must not only survive his own divided self, but that he must rely upon that self alone to do it, not the world or God or, we might add, Virgil or Beatrice or Annie or Penelope. "The trick was to live," Francis thinks, "to beat the bastards, survive the mob and that fateful chaos, and show them all what a man can do to set things right . . ." (207). This struggle to "survive" has all along been played out on a mythological journey in an eschatological universe, in an Albany outside of time altogether. But that world has also been essentially Francis Phelan's world, not a hallucination but his own private purgatory comprised of his own personal ghosts—what Loxley Nichols calls Francis' "own underworld" (47)—a field of battle that fused the eschatological with the existential. It is a world, Francis realizes, in which he must show "what a man can do to set things right." And it is, thus, ultimately only Francis alone, in his existential struggle with himself, who can overcome his private and personal hell, who can "survive the mob and that fateful chaos."

It does not take long for Francis' conviction "to set things right" on his own to be tested. After leaving the flophouse, Francis and his friends head to the "jungle," an appropriately named hodgepodge of temporary shacks and shelters for hoboes and other homeless, an Albany version of the transient camps the Joads had to endure, a "visual manifestation of the malaise of the age and the nation" (*IW*, 208). The jungle, like so much of Francis' Albany, is a place situated outside of time, a place of "essential transiency and would-be permanency" (208) that was "maybe seven years old, three years old, a month old, days old. It was an ashpit, a graveyard, and a fugitive city" (208). It is Dante's hell (or purgatory), Aeneas's and Odysseus' Hades, Christ's tomb, a monomythic city that is both temporary and atemporal simultaneously. It is a place that is forever nowhere.

It is within this chaotic and hellish world that Francis performs what may be his final (and compromised) acts of expiation as ordered by Gerald. He gives what remains of a turkey sandwich he brought with him from his home to a homeless family—a man, woman, and "swaddled infant" (213) living in a shack and reminiscent of the transient Holy Family of the Bible. He also tells his fellow bums the story of his dropping Gerald and how Annie never told anyone about the accident, a conversation that seems to be the confession that Francis has desired all along. Yet despite his finally giving this confession, the conversation among the bums that follows Francis' story about Gerald is not a communal sign of forgiveness; rather, it is talk about the disappointing nature of women and the ways in which men become drunks. Francis thus feels his "confession" was "wasted" (215) on the apathetic ears of the hard-bitten men to whom he gave it, and what should have again been a moment of cleansing becomes yet another moment of despair; like his entrance

into Annie's house, this "confession" is another red herring
of Francis' redemption. After hearing the apathetic or callous
responses of his "confessors" to whom he told his story about
dropping Gerald, Francis felt that his confession did not
"diminish his own guilt but merely cheapened the utterance,"
and he decides that he "was as wrongheaded a man as ever
lived" and that he "would never attain the balance that
allowed so many other men to live peaceful, nonviolent,
nonfugitive lives" (215). A moment of seeming redemption is
followed only by Francis' reaffirming his spiritual despair.

As quickly as Francis' journey toward redemption is
marred by this despair, however, the despair is turned on its
head and becomes—ironically and finally—the long-awaited
means of Francis' expiation. His journey through Albany,
like the entire last twenty-two years of his life, has been an
attempt to flee his guilt and his ghosts and to seek a kind of
comforting forgiveness (or forgetfulness) from someone—if not
Gerald or Annie, then at least the fellow bums of the jungle.
But none of these events transpire, and Francis thus gives up
on ever cleansing himself of his despair and guilt. With no
options left, he thinks about who he has been during all these
years of flight and then comes to a startling conclusion about
his guilt and himself:

> Francis asserted his own private wisdom and
> purpose: he had fled the folks because he was too
> profane a being to live among them; he had humbled
> himself willfully through the years to counter a
> fearful pride in his own ability to manufacture the
> glory from which grace would flow. What he was was,
> yes, a warrior, protecting a belief that no man could
> ever articulate, especially himself; but somehow it
> involved protecting saints from sinners, protecting the
> living from the dead. And a warrior, he was certain,
> was not a victim. Never a victim.

In the deepest part of himself that could draw an

> unutterable conclusion, he told himself: my guilt is
> all that I have left. If I lose it, I have stood for
> nothing, done nothing, been nothing. (216)

The myth which Francis' expiation most resembles, then, is
not Dante—despite Kennedy's own claims—nor Odysseus nor
even Christ nor a Christian forgiven by the Church. Rather,
it is Sisyphus—or Camus's twentieth century version of him—a
Sisyphus who, unable to escape his rock and without any
options, embraces the rock for meaning. Francis' rock is his
guilt, all that he's ever had and all that he has left, and he
does not (or cannot) wash it away with the purifying waters of
the Phelan bath or surrender it through the spiritual
forgiveness he seeks from confession. His reconciliation is
thus primarily not with God or church or family—although
these might come too—but, as the above passage makes clear,
with himself. In admitting the essential nature of his guilt to
his world, Francis realizes that removing the rock of his guilt
is a hopeless task and that this removal would actually
destroy who he essentially is: his decision to embrace his
warrior-self and his acceptance of the essential nature of his
guilt is a triumph of self-assertion, as Martin Daugherty
might put it, from a man who has long struggled to escape
that very self. This understanding of Francis' role in his own
salvation is consistent with the allusion to the *Purgatorio* in
the epigraph of *Ironweed* and to Kennedy's own claim that
the book "parallels the *Purgatorio*" (Quinn, 74).[18] In
Ironweed, heaven and hell merge and interpenetrate one
another within Francis' own self-imposed and self-generated
purgatory; the sin, the guilt and the means to forgiveness and
redemption are all in one place, Francis Phelan himself: he
is both the door to (his) hell and the gate to (his) heaven.[19]

As soon as Francis confesses to the essential nature of his
own guilt—as soon as he has obtained or acknowledged his
private grail—this new Francis is faced with a kind of classic
challenge to the strength of his resolution. The test to which
the new Francis is put is instigated by a group of vigilante

legionnaires, armed and angry and intent on cleaning out the bums from the "jungle" and from Albany. They start a battle in which the self-confessed "warrior" Francis finds himself a reluctant combatant. But if he's reluctant, Francis is not timid or cowardly, for after he sees his friend Rudy struck down by one of the attackers wielding a bat, Francis leaps on the man, grabs the bat from him, and begins to fight back. The struggle which ensues—which ends in Francis killing the legionnaire—is described in terms deriving from two of the reasons that have in the past led to Francis' flights from his family—his desire to play baseball and his violent life—as if to accentuate the notion that the redemption Francis seems to have received comes not from any escape or purification of his past but from embracing that past: "[Francis] stepped forward, as into a wide pitch, and swung his own bat at the man who had struck Rudy. Francis connected with a stroke that would have sent any pitch over any centerfield fence in any ball park anywhere, and he clearly heard and truly felt bones crack in the man's back" (218). Francis repeats the swing on another man, not killing this one but collapsing his knee, and then he lifts up the injured Rudy and carries him the long way to the hospital, like Joseph of Arimathea taking the dead Christ, Sisyphus with his rock, or the Good Samaritan with the robbed traveler. Francis' efforts come to naught, for Rudy dies in the emergency room before ever receiving treatment, but the night and its consequences, yet more violence and death, confirm what Francis earlier maintained—that you can't escape yourself.[20] His trip through Albany has been an attempt to shed the guilt of violence and death, and here, as soon as he has been purified in Annie's bath, he engages in battle again and causes more death. Instead of exorcizing his ghosts, he has simply added one more, but now, and here is the key, it is to a universe that he accepts as his own and in which he promises to fight as a warrior.

The End of the Journey, Outside of Time

Only two short "scenes" follow Francis' battle in the jungle, but they are ones that have attracted numerous comments and questions. According to Daniel M. Murtaugh, these scenes "nearly defy interpretation" (302). The events themselves would be fairly straightforward—Francis looks for Helen, finds her dead, hops on a train as if to flee Albany once more, and then changes his mind and decides to return home to Annie again—were it not for the fact that Kennedy does not use a simple indicative mood, whether in the past or present tense, to write these scenes. Instead, he writes the passages with the conditional "would,"[21] so that all of Francis' actions seem to occur in some probable but uncertain moment in the unspecified future: "It would be three-fifteen" in the morning, the first of the scenes begins, as Francis works his way back to the hotel where Helen has been staying (221). Here he discovers that Helen is dead, or, as Kennedy phrases it, Francis "would . . . discover Helen on the floor in her kimono" (221). The next day—Wednesday, November 2—Francis boards a train heading out of Albany, where he is joined by the ghost of Strawberry Bill, an old hobo friend of his, who tells Francis not to worry about the police after the fight in the jungle. Francis listens and decides to return to Annie's house, the "holy Phelan eaves" (225). Here at home Francis is treated to turkey sandwiches and solicitations for Jell-O from Annie,[22] and he thinks about moving the cot in the attic down to his grandson's room to sleep, for it "was a mighty nice little room" (227).

Francis does and thinks all of this, of course, only if one wants to read the conditional tense describing the events with the assumption that the events actually occur. Daniel M. Murtaugh believes that what "really happens is that Francis hops a freight out of town. What happens in a wishful dream —and in sentences whose very grammar tries to make the dream real—is that he returns to 'the holy Phelan eaves' and the protective love of Annie" (302). Murtaugh believes that Francis' existential claim of his guilt is "the classical hero's stance . . . *in extremis*, 'the triumph of self-development' that Martin Daugherty celebrated in Billy Phelan" (302); yet Murtaugh argues that this claim, from "the vantage point provided by Annie's freely offered forgiveness," actually "fulfills rather precisely Dante's definition of damnation" (302). In other words, Francis' understanding of the essential role of his guilt and of his status as warrior is not redemption or "resurrection" at all but damnation. Murtaugh writes that it "almost seems as though this [sense of damnation] breaks Kennedy's heart," and that this heartbreak keeps him from writing the conclusion in a straightforward, indicative mode (302).

While Murtaugh's reading of Francis' damnation is plausible, other critics disagree. Edward C. Reilly argues simply and without qualification in one article (and likewise in his book) that "Phelan seeks 'sanctuary under the holy Phelan eaves' where he often watches Jake Becker's pigeons fly" in circles and then return home, as if there is no real question as to where Francis is (Reilly [1986], 8). This vision of the pigeons returning home, Reilly argues, symbolizes Francis himself as he sits in Annie's attic after his own circular flight from and return to Albany ([1986], 8). Paul F. Griffin similarly discusses in a straightforward way Francis' "homecoming," his "life in his wife Annie's attic, where he is hiding to avoid questioning in the death of a man he killed during a fight" (92–93). As with Reilly, there is really no question in Griffin's mind as to where Francis is. And for his part, Peter P. Clarke implies Francis has returned to the attic when he argues that Francis' act of throwing an empty whiskey bottle out of the train he is taking out of Albany "banishes the destructive influences in Francis's life" (174).[23] Such an act, Clarke argues, reveals that Francis is thus "reborn, reintegrated into the family and life" (175).

Although most critics seem to side with the interpretation

that Francis does return home, Kennedy, when asked if this were the case, said that he "would rather not go on record as saying what precisely [the ending] means" (Bonetti, 83). Kennedy may sound here like he's toying with his readers, but he argues too that the ending is not meant to be a "puzzle" (83), nor is it "hypothetical" (82): "What those last two or three pages say," Kennedy says, "is what Francis Phelan's condition is when we take leave of him" (83). In emphasizing Francis' "condition" rather than his place, Kennedy is actually stressing the ontological status of Francis and the universe he resides in rather than focusing on the geographical question of where the character is. Such an emphasis on condition should not be read as evasion: it is, rather, a way to emphasize that the conclusion to *Ironweed* as it is written is a natural way to depict the climax of a narrative that all along has attempted to fuse the worlds of the mythological, the eschatological, and the existential as well as the different moments of past, present, and future. Murtaugh's reading of Francis' "damnation" relies too heavily on a concern with actual place and gives precedence to the mythological and eschatological as sources of redemption: by focusing on Dante as a model of redemption and Annie as a source of forgiveness, Murtaugh ignores the consolations possible in the private and ahistorical universe in which Francis endures his existential struggles. Francis' condition at the end of the novel can be Dante's definition of damnation, as Murtaugh suggests, only if you subscribe to a picture of a world in which hell, purgatory, and heaven are all distinct places: in *Ironweed*, all of these places exist simultaneously in Francis Phelan himself. Francis is his own afterworld—which means he is inevitably damned to be himself, but he is equally blessed.

For Kennedy in *Ironweed*, the narrative of which depicts a simultaneously mythological, eschatological, and existential universe, it has never mattered whether Francis is in Albany of 1938 or 1897 or certain moments in between:

where Francis Phelan has been is a universe entirely original and unique to him and to *Ironweed*, where history and time itself are collapsed into Francis himself right now. What was, is, will be and, yes, "would be" all share an equal ontological validity because there is no distinction between them: no dependency on linearity or chronology validates one moment or condition over the other. To dramatize the conclusion of a story in such a peculiar and complicated universe, Kennedy thus places Francis not in a magical world of ghosts or heaven nor in the actual world of Albany but rather in a special world inscribed only within the conditional mode.

Ironically, it may not be in a piece of literary criticism or even a quotation from Kennedy himself but in a movie review where the nature of the mood of the novel and, by extension, the closing scenes, is best captured. In a critique of the movie production of *Ironweed*, John Clute writes of the moment in the novel in which Gerald commands that his father attempt to expiate his sins, and in the process Clute identifies an important assumption the narrative makes and that must affect our understanding of the conclusion:

It does not much matter whether Phelan imagines this task of expiation, or whether an objective miracle has occurred; through supple management of the narrative of this climactic moment, Kennedy is able to give equal weight to both mimetic and fabulistic readings, and the remainder of the book serves as a redemptive epilogue to its engendering premiss. From the very beginning, Phelan's every act is part of a pre-ordained ritual of salvation. (584)

What Clute is identifying is that the narrative of the book, in its unqualified acceptance of both the real and the magical —here the "mimetic and fabulistic"—has created a situation from the beginning of the book in which the question of which ending is the real one is, in a sense, moot: once one accepts the "premiss" based upon the "equal weight [given] to both mimetic and fabulistic readings," then the rest of the book, including and perhaps primarily the ending, is simply a "redemptive epilogue" to that premise.

Robert Gibb approaches this idea in another way when he writes that *Ironweed*, as an example of magical realism, "does not force us to make either/or choices, to view any of *Ironweed*'s events as reality or waking dream" (125). Gibb is asserting the equal validity of the mimetic and fabulistic that Clute identifies as a characteristic of the "premiss" of the novel, and it is an equality that we are asked to assume all the way until the book's end. In *Ironweed*, the dead are alive; the living Francis is "dead"; the past and present and future merge; 1897 and 1938 both are right now: in such a world, the question of whether Francis is on the train or in the attic violates the very magic of the universe of the narrative, a universe in which Francis—and Katrina and Gerald and Kathryn Phelan and Harold Allen—exist in several places at once or, rather, exist in one place outside of any moment at all. Since the distinctions between "then" and "now," alive and dead, real and magical, have long since disappeared by novel's end, why finally ask whether Francis is "here" or "there"? The "engendering premiss" of the magical world established by the narrative at its beginning does not suddenly give way at its conclusion.

What we have, then, in the conclusion of *Ironweed*, is the culmination of the existential crisis of a mythological man in an eschatological world. The novel, as Clute phrased it, is a "pre-ordained ritual of salvation," not unlike the endless and unavoidable struggle of Sisyphus to roll his rock up the hill. It is Dante spinning in place rather than spiraling upward. This "ritual of salvation" has been evident all along: the mythological parallels, Gerald's call for expiation, Francis' return to the past and its consequent possibility for redemption, the transformations at Annie's house, and Francis' own embracing of his guilt in the hobo jungle all signal the "redemption" that Kennedy himself asserts is the central focus of the novel. What must be recognized in turn is that these steps toward redemption in Francis' eschatological and mythological universe are also taken in his private existential world. In such a situation, Francis' condition once he is "saved" or "redeemed" or "resurrected" is not one in which the ghosts are finally banished or Francis finally achieves some heaven separate from his own self; his condition is not one, in other words, in which the existential is transfigured and transcended into a beatified, eschatological condition.

Instead, Francis "would be" in Annie's attic at the end, an ontological status that is self-explanatory given the timeless and placeless nature of the world in *Ironweed*. That Francis "would be" resurrected may sound uncertain and provisional but it is a condition as real and valid as any other in the novel, be it the condition of the dead, of ghosts, of the living, or of visions of mothers and lovers existing in numerous manifestations simultaneously. When the distinctions between "then" and "now" give way within the ahistorical world of the narrative of *Ironweed*, the implicit uncertainty of the conditional tense in that narrative also gives way because the opposing certainty, predicated upon a linear conception of time (and tense), does not apply: what Francis "would then be" at some uncertain time is as real and as magical, as certain and as possible, as what he is now: a mythological man who endures existential struggles in an eschatological world.

Notes

1.   For a chart of the intertwined chronologies of *Billy Phelan's Greatest Game* and *Ironweed*, see Van Dover, p. 82.

2.   The verb form used in the concluding section of *Ironweed* (in which Kennedy describes the action in phrases such as "he would see" and "he would go") is called "conditional" for the purposes of this study, although such a term perhaps oversimplifies the tense and mood of the verb form Kennedy uses and also implies a semantic interpretation on my part, although not one without foundation. (Kennedy himself calls the tense of the passage "conditional" [see Bonetti, 82]). The difficulty

in accurately labeling the tense and mood of this verb form, as this chapter should make clear, is that Kennedy is not depicting traditional notions of time and chronology in *Ironweed* and thus cannot use at the climax of the novel traditional tenses and moods, the uses of which are heavily dependent on whether the verbs describe past, present, or future action. "Conditional" seems to be the most accurate term one can use considering the "would" form of the verb phrases Kennedy uses, the ambiguousness of the ending itself, and, most importantly, the magically timeless status of the action (as this chapter will show) which the verbs describe. Francis' actions should not be considered as "conditional" in the traditional sense—that is, that they will occur *if* some other future condition is brought to bear. In some ways, the concept of the iterative "would"—implying as it does that an event does not occur in a single, identifiable moment in time—might be helpful in understanding the verb form used at the conclusion of *Ironweed*. The "continuing Tuesday and Thursday and unchanging Friday" (126-27) on which Helen has her affair with a musician is an example in *Ironweed* of using what we might call an iterative noun to describe what is in fact a moment outside of linear time.

3.   Kennedy's interest in the eschatological will be reconfirmed in *Very Old Bones*, a novel in which the narrator, Orson Purcell, calls himself an "eschatophile" (*VOB*, 184).

4.   The quotation is from an anonymous review in *The New Yorker* (7 February 1983: 121).

5.   The quotation, cited by Tierce (p. 247) is from Joseph Campbell's *The Hero with a Thousand Faces* (Princeton: Princeton UP, 1968: 30).

6.   We have already seen the similarity of Martin Daugherty in *Billy Phelan's Greatest Game* to Leopold Bloom, both newspapermen following a younger, "fatherless" man about a city. In addition to the similar use of the myth of Ulysses by Joyce and by Kennedy in *Ironweed*, one can also find specific allusions to *Finnegan's Wake* in Kennedy's *Very Old Bones* (see *VOB*, pp. 215-16) and Edward Daugherty, in his desire to write about the Irish "race" in *The Flaming Corsage*, sounds very much like the Stephen Dedalus of *A Portrait of the Artist as a Young Man*.

7.   See Tierce, pp. 248-49.

8.   Although Francis does not actually converse with his dead son, Gerald, the description of the boy in his grave shares the sense of imagination and detail that one finds in Dante's descriptions of the inhabitants of the afterlife he visits: "And because his fate had been innocence and denial, Gerald had grown a protective web which deflected all moisture, all moles, rabbits, and other burrowing creatures. His web was woven of strands of vivid silver, an enveloping hammock of intricate, near-transparent weave. His body had not only been absolved

of the need to decay, but in some respects—a full head of hair, for instance—it had grown to a completeness that was both natural and miraculous. Gerald rested in his infantile sublimity, exuding a high gloss induced by early death, his skin a radiant white-gold, his nails a silvery gray, his cluster of curls and large eyes perfectly matched in gleaming ebony" (19).

9.   In "Downtown: Where Things Happened First," in *O Albany!*, Kennedy writes of the real-life Albany trolley strike that inspired the episode in *Ironweed* in which Francis Phelan kills a strikebreaker and thus commits his first murder: "The horsecar vanished in the 1890s and the new century was only a year and a half old when the great United Traction strike (May 1901) halted trolleys in five cities. Albany was put under martial law, troops camped at Beverwyck Park, and a squad of soldiers rode on every streetcar. E. Le Roy Smith and William M. Walsh were killed when troops opened fire on a violent mob attacking a car at Columbia Street and Broadway. Smith was standing in the doorway of a store, watching the riot, when he was shot" (63). The strike itself, the date, the use of troops, the street intersection, and the death of two innocent bystanders are all part of the "fictional" story of Francis Phelan and the trolley strike in which he kills the scab Harold Allen.

10.   See Reilly (1987), p. 6.

11.   In "They Bury the Boss: Dan Ex-Machina" in *O Albany!*, Kennedy writes, "In Albany, it was rumored, even the dead voted, early and often" (293). Although not physically dead himself, Francis Phelan's actions would certainly be consistent with such a rumor.

12.   David Black, for example, describes what Kennedy is doing in presenting both the natural present moment and the supernatural world of ghosts from the past in the same way by arguing that "Kennedy literalizes [the] past in the narrative through a style of magical realism, a fusing of past and present" (177). For further material on Kennedy and magical realism, see Lori Chamberlain, "Magicking the Real: Paradoxes of Postmodern Writing," especially pp. 5–7; and Robert Gibb's dissertation, *The Life of the Soul: William Kennedy, Magical Realist.*

13.   See *Ironweed*, two pages prior to the title page where Kennedy quotes from The Audubon Society's *Field Guide to North American Wildflowers* to explain the origin of the name of the Tall Ironweed, a "member of the Sunflower Family": according to the guide, the "name refers to the toughness of the stem."

14.   See Gibb, 64, from which this notion of the spiral is taken.

15.   Such a description is reminiscent of Dante's sufferers in hell and purgatory, and as *The Flaming Corsage* will reveal, Katrina dies in a fire.

16.   See pp. 37, 71–77, and 171–73 in *Ironweed*.

17.   The timeless or "ahistorical" nature of this photograph is

curious in light of Susan Sontag's accusation (as paraphrased in Paul F. Griffin's "Susan Sontag, Franny Phelan, and the Moral Implications of Photographs") that "the falseness of a photograph derives from its unnatural ability to stop time and history" (194). Griffin, in his essay on Sontag, writes that the picture of the young Francis in Annie's attic "contradicts what Sontag sees as the fundamentally a-historical nature of the photograph. Through a fluke of exposure, this picture does convey a small slice of history; though a static image it has the power to suggest the ball's flight" (199).

18. It will be remembered that the epigraph from Dante in *Ironweed* reads as the following: "To course o'er better waters now hoists sail / the little bark of my wit, leaving behind her a / sea so cruel."

19. This solitary confrontation between a man and his own past is a field of battle different from that of Martin Daugherty, whose return to his past in the figure of Melissa Spencer is prompted in part by the familial or archetypal struggle between fathers and sons and not his own private guilt alone; different from Francis' own son Billy, who struggles in the social milieu of Albany; different from Daniel Quinn's historical and romantic challenges in *Quinn's Book*; different from Peter Phelan's attempt to redeem Phelan family history in general in *Very Old Bones*; and different from Edward Daugherty's attempt to elevate himself and his fellow Irishmen through his art in *The Flaming Corsage*. The sins inflicting Francis are his, not those of a father or some political machine; the ghosts that haunt him are from his own life and are seen by him alone; and the solution to his problems, despite the beneficent presence of characters such as Helen, Gerald, Annie, and Billy, ultimately also resides only with him.

20. Curiously, Paul F. Griffin, in "The Moral Implications of Annie Phelan's Jell-O," comes to what appears to be the exact opposite conclusion about *Ironweed*: "I turn to William Kennedy's 1983 novel *Ironweed* . . . ," Griffin writes, "to show the extent to which this work, almost despite itself, depicts a character who learns the limitations of basing his life entirely on his capacity to stand alone and so comes to revalue the relationships which bind him to the people around him" (86).

21. For a discussion of the use of the term "conditional" to describe these verb forms, see endnote 2.

22. Paul F. Griffin believes that Annie's question to Francis if he wants some Jell-O establishes a "specific and simple context," a "context of real human relationships" rather than one that is "absolute" or that exists in a "timeless celestial sphere" (93). In this context of Annie's kindness and concern, "Franny finds a new way of making sense of the world" (93). Griffin, in arguing against a "timeless . . . sphere," once again contradicts the thesis of this study (see endnote 20).

23. Robert Gibb argues that the whiskey bottle and the noise it makes when Francis throws it provide a clue that "facilitates Kennedy's change of scene" from boxcar to attic and that also "alerts us as to the nature of that change" (127). Gibb's argument about the "nature" of this change is complex and highly qualified (see pp. 127–35 of his dissertation, *The Life of the Soul: William Kennedy, Magical Realist*), but it is based on the fact that Francis hears the music of the bottle he tossed through the air while Strawberry Bill, who is dead, does not: as Gibb writes of the conversation between Francis and Bill, a "syllogism might be constructed from that exchange, for if Bill is dead and does not hear music and Francis hears music, then how can he be dead?" (128).

CHAPTER FIVE

THE ARCHES OF LOVE, THE BANNER OF BLOOD: THE MYSTERIES OF LOVE AND HISTORY IN *QUINN'S BOOK*

O f all the novels in Kennedy's Albany cycle, *Quinn's Book* is perhaps the one that, in terms of theme and narrative structure, most explicitly depends upon the concepts of history and death, the two great worlds or moments outside of the "present" that in Kennedy's fiction affect that present moment, the "now." Because *Quinn's Book* takes place exclusively in the nineteenth century and its events occur earlier than any of the other novels in the cycle, the book serves in a way as the beginning of the history of the Albany that appears in Kennedy's novels. What the concept of history itself is, and wherein lies its "truth," as Kennedy will call it, is also a question that the novel raises, both through Kennedy's transformation of actual historical events into specific scenes in *Quinn's Book* and through the adventures of Daniel Quinn, the eponymous and frequent narrator of the novel. Quinn's life is a series of quests, including one for the love of Maud Fallon, a woman he meets when he is still a young canal-boat apprentice, and one for an understanding of the historical events to which he is a witness. This public or national history shapes Daniel

159

Quinn as much as personal or family history shapes the lives of Francis Phelan in *Ironweed* or the Phelan clan as a whole in *Very Old Bones*: *Quinn's Book* is "not an odyssey in the sense *Ironweed* is, of a single man's psychology," Kennedy has said, "but of Quinn and Maud through [the] age" (Agrest, 45). Quinn's attempt to understand the "age" he witnesses —an age which includes among other phenomena race and draft riots, slavery, industrialization, and the American Civil War—is a search for what Quinn identifies as "the elusive thing that endured unchanged in spite of growth" (189). He is looking for the "coherence" (57) or the "linkage" (130) that lies behind the horror and the chaos, the "dead agonies and divine riddles" of history (288). For Quinn, this history is a nightmare of American violence which he witnesses and writes about during his career as a journalist, the career he chooses in his attempt to discover the truth behind the history he sees.

Ultimately Quinn is overwhelmed by this history and its horror in his attempt to understand it, and he ends up in despair over the death and destruction he witnesses, most especially as it appears in the Civil War. This failure to understand is paralleled with his failure through most of the book to consummate his love for Maud and to "steal" her away as his lover forever. Nonetheless, by the end of *Quinn's Book*, even though the novel is not an odyssey like *Ironweed*, Quinn does manage to complete each of his quests, though not always in the way he had thought they would be completed, a conclusion that is not surprising considering both Martin Daugherty's and Francis Phelan's unexpected sources of redemption. The answers Quinn discovers derive from a complicated series of realizations, each one influencing the other, that occur when he tries to claim Maud as his own after they have been separated for fifteen years. As we shall see, the sources of these epiphanies are various and the relationship of one to the other complex, but what they all reveal for Quinn is that he has throughout his quest been misguided in his search for truth: he realizes in the end that the truth he has been seeking lies not in the accumulation of fact—what he has been doing as a journalist—but rather in the embracing of mystery through the power of the imagination.

There are numerous sources from which Quinn in the end discovers the "truth" he has been seeking, but what is significant and similar about all of these sources is that they succeed in helping Quinn resolve his quests at a moment in the narrative in which he figuratively returns to his past, a moment in which what happened "then" is recreated in the "now." This moment occurs at the end of the novel when Quinn joins Maud, Magdalena, and John the Brawn McGee (Quinn's one-time master) in Saratoga, thus reuniting the four people who were present at the beginning of the novel during an Albany flood which initiated Quinn on his quests. Magdalena herself even decides to reenact at the end her "death" in the flood, one she miraculously overcame. Quinn finds, as Francis Phelan and Martin Daugherty do, that returning to this past, to these three people and even the specific event of Magdalena's "death," is a means for him to complete his quest, even though his past becomes available as much through the decisions of others as of Quinn himself. In a book obsessed with history—of America, of the Albany cycle, as a concept, as a source of truth, as a source for fiction—Quinn finds he can complete his quests for the truth behind public history and for the love of Maud Fallon only when he returns to his own history, only once he can do again "now" what happened back "then."

The American history that is the focus of Quinn's odyssey is that which occurred between the 1840s and 1864, the time period covered in the novel. On one level these years and their history are the background of Daniel Quinn's adventures in *Quinn's Book*, but the emphasis in the book on the concept of history and on the specific events of this time period, often at the expense of depicting the characters themselves,[1] reveals the central position of the concept of history itself in this novel. The historical events depicted in the book include the nineteenth century American cholera epidemic, the tensions between new immigrants and old, the draft riots of the Civil War, and the war itself, often but not always as these events occur in New York state or in Albany in particular. In addition to these broad, "hard" facts of history, the novel is also concerned with cultural issues during the time period covered in the book—issues such as the importance of journalism and the growth of horse racing in Saratoga. Edward C. Reilly cites many of these cultural concerns in writing that *Quinn's Book* "provides insights into boxing, betting, and horse racing. There are insights into politics and into show business; into the era's pseudosciences that include phrenology, mesmerism, and spiritualism; and insights into Albany's newspapers and their advertisements, headlines, and prose styles" (102).

This focus on military/political history as well as cultural history is also complemented in the opening sections of the novel by narrative genealogies of various families within the narrative of the book itself. Of the several genealogical passages, the longest (at least eight continuous pages) is that of the Staats family,[2] representatives of the early Dutch settlers in Albany who preceded the Irish and thus who would have preceded the Daugherty, Phelan, and Quinn families of the Albany cycle. Other narrative genealogies in the book include those of the Irish immigrant Ryan family, a slave named Joshua, the industrialist Fitzgibbon family, and several other minor and major characters.[3] In long sections of exposition, often unconnected to the actual adventures of Quinn himself, Kennedy narrates the history of these fictional or fictionalized families, tracing the lineage of immigrants as they transplant themselves in the New World (or are forcibly transplanted) and then situate themselves in American history. Taken together, these genealogies—of old Dutch money houses, impoverished immigrants, slaves, and capitalist entrepreneurs—represent the history of the diverse sociological background of 1850s Albany and offer a portrait in miniature of the historical situation of America at that time. As Reilly writes, Kennedy "fleshes out both Albany's and the nation's histories in [the] genealogies" (90). They are a lens through which to observe the broad sociological changes which affected Albany and America in general throughout their early history.

The genealogies, in combination with the political and cultural history presented alongside them, help give a wide-ranging picture, diachronically and synchronically, of the people inhabiting mid-century Albany and of the historical situation in which they lived. So noticeable is this attention to history and to various historical phenomena in *Quinn's Book* that the novel has been called by one critic "a Baedeker to its historical time frame" (Reilly, 102), as if the novel could serve as an actual resource to the history upon which it is based. While reading *Quinn's Book* in this way would be reversing the process of writing (Kennedy wrote his fiction from the history, after all, not the other way around), the notion of *Quinn's Book* as a resource is certainly accurate within the confines of the Albany cycle: the novel not only depicts the historical background against which its own protagonists act, but it also establishes the "source"—whether it be public history or personal family history—out of which protagonists for Kennedy's other novels come. Kennedy, as J. K. Van Dover writes, "saw [in *Quinn's Book*] the necessity of establishing the roots of his families and of his city" and of "setting out the historical antecedents of his people and his place" (123–24; 124).

The nature of this background as source is evident in Kennedy's depiction within the novel of numerous human "sources" to many of the families who appear later in his cycle of novels. Daniel Quinn, the narrator of the novel, for example, announces in the opening line of the book that he is "neither the first nor the last of a line of such Quinns" (5). He is, in fact, the ancestor of the George and Daniel Quinn we meet in *Ironweed* and *Very Old Bones*.[4] Quinn's friend in his youth, Emmett Daugherty, is a character in *The Flaming Corsage* and the father of its main protagonist, Edward. And Martin Daugherty, Emmett's grandson, is, of course, a major character in *Billy Phelan's Greatest Game*.

Kennedy has said while writing *Quinn's Book* that "Albany is still . . . Albany, but I'm going backward now to discover patterns that anticipate the twentieth century present. It's a preconsciousness I'm working on right now" (Quinn, 70). While many books within the cycle explore the importance of personal history to the meaning of their characters' lives, *Quinn's Book* thus explores the history of all the novels together: it is the "preconsciousness," to use Kennedy's word, of all of the Albany novels. Van Dover has argued that *Quinn's Book* "actually represents a deliberate attempt to *begin* the cycle" (Van Dover, 123–24) even though it is the fourth book in that cycle. In *Quinn's Book*, Kennedy has, like his own characters, gone back into the past, not only into the past of nineteenth century America and Albany[5] but also into the specific fictional past upon which his other Albany novels are based. Kennedy wrote in *O Albany!* that the city is a "magical place where the past becomes visible" and that his task in writing that book was "to peer into the heart of this always-shifting past" (7): this description applies equally well to *Quinn's Book*, except that instead of peering into the past of the real, historical city, Kennedy looks into the past of his own fictionalized Albany.

While the history depicted and discussed in *Quinn's Book* establishes the novel as a source for the fictional Albany and the Albany-cycle families who live there, Kennedy's incorporation of actual historical events into his fictional narrative raises important questions about the concept of history itself, especially in relation to the concept of fiction or story. Kennedy's recreation of historical events in *Quinn's Book* depends not upon a reassembling of fact into narrative but rather a reimagining and embellishment of this fact into imagined story, a process that Sven Birkerts calls "a novelistic fusion of history and fancy" (41). Such an approach not only emphasizes the notion of "story" implicit in "history," but it also echoes a discovery Daniel Quinn will make in his own way at the end of the novel, that "truth" itself resides in the imagination—the means of producing stories—and not in history itself.

One of the purposes of *Quinn's Book*, according to Peter A. Quinn, is for this "history and fancy" to fuse into a mechanism for revealing truth: as Peter Quinn argues, the purpose of the book "is to play with the mirrors of place and time, to mingle fantasy with fact, the recorded event with the mythical, the improbable with the impossible, piling one atop another until we see reflected in the resulting phantasmagoria the human truths that chronology can never give us" (308). In an interview, Kennedy explains and defends what he was attempting to do through such a fusion and why he attempted it:

> [T]here's nothing [in *Quinn's Book*] that hasn't been vividly documented in history including the cataclysms in the beginning of the book. They're taken from history. Maybe I've amalgamated them and made them happen on top of one another in ways that history had not seen fit to do, or Mother Nature had not seen fit to do, but I'm not being false to possibility.... [They] are real historical moments that I just discovered and probably embellished to a degree that makes it more dramatic. People falling into the river from the bridge, those things happened. The pier being washed away by the ice, those things happened. So I feel that that surreal or mystical or magical quality of everyday life must be addressed in

fiction if it's to be true to what it means. (Reilly [1989], 16)

Kennedy's conception of truth in history (and one Quinn himself discovers) resides thus not in the possibility of regaining the sense of presence or truth of the past through a retrieval and rehearsal of fact; instead, truth derives in part from accepting the magical and from using the imagination to see the extratemporal world of myth and story within the historical. Only through these worlds outside of time can the "truth" of what everyday life means be perceived.

The crucial role of the imagination in understanding history or the past is made explicit in the opening sections of the novel through Kennedy's adaptation of historical events into fictionalized ones. In these sections, Kennedy takes real and separate events from history, a great fire and flood, and conflates them into one moment, including in his narrative along the way some of the actual legends and myths about the events that have been handed down through history. In *O Albany!* Kennedy wrote of the "legend" of the "Great Fire of August 17, 1848," which "started from a washerwoman's bonnet . . . inside a shed next to the Albion Hotel at Broadway and Herkimer Street" in Albany (*OA*, 67), and this story and others are included in Quinn's description of the flood near the beginning of the novel:

> The cold had descended upon the city so suddenly after the flooding of the riverbanks that men were forced to bring their livestock to high ground. Canaday [a friend of Quinn's] mentioned one man who brought his horse into his front room, and wisely so, for horses tethered untended in water found their legs frozen in the instantaneous ice that rose 'round their bones. Before the night was out, one man in Greenbush would grow furious at his inability to extricate his horse from deep ice and, in watching the horse dying standing up, the man himself would die

of a congested brain. Carriages would become ice-locked, birds would freeze to the limbs of trees, and not only ice but fire would ravage the city wildly and indiscriminately. The bonnet of Bridie Conroy, an Irish washerwoman, would catch fire from sparks on the burning quay and Bridie would run crazed into the night, tumbling headlong into a shed full of hay, and igniting what history would call The Great Fire—six hundred buildings, many of them shops, all burned to cinders: five thousand people without lodging from the blaze that would yield its fury only to the heavy fall of snow that was just now beginning. (36-37)

History thus reappears in *Quinn's Book* imbued with legend and story; it is fact reimagined, maybe even into myth, much as happened in *Legs*. Quinn's history is closer to myth or to story than to what we would call historical truth: he even writes of the apocalyptic-sounding "fire rising out of flood" (11), an event that is itself evidence of "the gods gone mad" (11) and of a "cosmic, mythic rage" (9).

Kennedy, and Kennedy's narrator, thus both turn history into legend, story, and myth. Kennedy has claimed, as will *Quinn's Book* itself, that this process, in its dependence upon the imagination, gets us closer to the "truth," though at times it seems an inevitable or natural process anyway. Quinn reveals the naturalness of this process, in fact, in telling about what happens to the history of one of the Staats ancestors, Jacobus, a man who fathered a child with an Indian woman. Within a month after Jacobus's death, Quinn says, "Jacobus's name was only on the tongues of cads and vulgarians, and within a year in the most proper social groupings, Jacobus had faded into a shadow of figure of doubtful legend, one who, like the silver-tailed shoat and seven-titted cow, may or may never have existed" (27). Fact, as Kennedy lets us know here, and in a novel itself which uses historical fact, can easily become fantasy once it becomes part of the past. Imagination and prejudice step in to fill the gaps in knowledge that time opens up: at least in embracing imagination one is being true to the processes of human understanding and not presenting a false sense of the truth of history.

This question of where "truth" resides in history is one that is important in understanding how Kennedy uses history in *Quinn's Book*, but it is also important to the character of Daniel Quinn himself as he attempts to come to terms with the horrors of history to which he is a witness.[6] His search for the meaning of the world he observes, his search for the truth, the "linkages" behind the reality he sees, begins at the same time that he also begins his confrontation with the other great mystery in his life, his love for Maud Fallon. His immersion into these mysteries—his "fall," as Reilly calls it (97)—occurs when Quinn is caught up in the great Albany flood in December 1849, the flood about which we read above.[7] The disaster is the cause of Quinn and Maud meeting and thus initiates Quinn into the mysteries of love, but the flood, along with the fire that follows it, also serves to introduce Quinn into the horrors of history: the flood and fire are nature's version of the military and civil atrocities that will soon haunt Quinn's days as a journalist.

The specific events surrounding the flood which initiate Quinn into these mysteries begin when Magdalena Colón, a well-known courtesan and music hall dancer also known as La Ultima, stages a publicity stunt in which she promises to pay a hundred dollars to any skiff operator willing to carry her, Maud (her niece), and their maid from Albany to Greenbush across the frozen and dangerous waters of the Hudson. A man named Carrick is the only one to volunteer, but his boat is quickly knocked out of control by the ice floes in the river. John the Brawn McGee, the brutish operator of a river skiff, and Quinn, John's apprentice and a boy recently orphaned by a cholera outbreak, set out after Carrick's boat, but before they can reach it a floe of ice smashes it in and sends everyone into the water. Carrick, his assistant, and Magdalena's maid all die; Quinn rescues the young Maud, cold but alive, before she goes under water; and John, using his boat hook, lifts out of the icy water the lifeless body of Magdalena as well as her trunk, the true object, as it turns out, of John's rescue mission. John's reaction to the tragedy, as Quinn describes it, is less than sorrow-filled: "'One dead slut,'" he says after the rescue (8).

But Magdalena and her death will not be as simple to dismiss as John thinks. To begin with, the flood that kills Magdalena also kills hundreds of Albany citizens, and many of them superstitiously blame Magdalena for the tragedy as well as for the great fire that follows it (in Kennedy's fictional version of events at least) and that kills yet more people and destroys the homes and businesses of thousands. Once John the Brawn and Quinn get Magdalena's body, her trunk, and Maud ashore, an Albany woman, newly mourning the death of a relative in the flood, turns on Magdalena's corpse in anger, blaming the dead dancer for all the misfortune. Quinn says that the woman

> rose up from beside her inert man, let seethe through her teeth a single word—"Herrrr"—and, following upon this with the maddened and throaty growl of a jungle feline, flew across the space that separated us, pounced upon the courtesan's lifeless body, sank her teeth into that pallid cheek, and came away with a blooded wad of flesh in her mouth, which she savored with a bulging smile and then spat onto the dead actress's chest. Stiffened with loyalty to our corpse, I leaped into the tableau and yanked the toothy bitch by the arm, flinging her aside so that John the Brawn might lift our dead lady out of more harm's way. (13)

This cannibalism is only the first of several vividly gory

scenes in the novel. In *Quinn's Book*, Kennedy pulls no punches, risking the shock of his readers in immersing us into an explicitness that perhaps mirrors Daniel Quinn's own experiences later in the book. But even though this violence against Magdalena seems a desecration of her body, it actually begins the transformation of Magdalena from "one dead slut" into something much more interesting, a perverted Christ-figure. The mourning woman's attack on Magdalena literalizes the traditional Christian notion of the Eucharist—in which Christ's "body" is eaten—although the woman's attack also corrupts the notion of the Eucharist at the same time: Magdalena's body is eaten not out of spiritual desire for eternal life but out of vengeance for the end of a life, and that body is ultimately spat back as a curse upon itself.

Despite this perversion of the Christian symbolism, other events following the disfigurement of Magdalena's body signal her transfiguration into a kind of perverse Christ figure. One of these signs will be Magdalena's power, even in death, to reveal the future, much as Christ, as an omniscient god, would theoretically be able to do.[8] While hurrying Magdalena's body to the home of Hillegond Staats, an acquaintance of Magdalena's who Maud believes will care for them, Maud tells Quinn to close the eyes of Magdalena's corpse: "'If you look in their eyes you see your fate,'" Maud says (17). Despite her warnings, Quinn looks into the dead woman's eye when it flits open a few moments later, and eventually he sees "a procession of solemn pilgrims moving through a coppice" (17). This procession includes Maud, an unidentified old woman, John the Brawn, a "figure wrapped in furs," Quinn himself, and a black dog (18). As Quinn watches, this vision changes to "a ragtag troop of men swarming down a city street and smashing the windows of a newspaper office with stones and clubs" and then to a young man "talking soundlessly" who is thrown by two thugs into a carriage that whisks him away (18). As we will learn, each of these visions is indeed a part of Quinn's future, a verification of both Maud's superstition and Magdalena's magical powers. The first vision Quinn sees in Magdalena's eyes, in fact, will come true not long after Quinn arrives at the Staats mansion, when he is part of a group which processes to a mausoleum to discover and then help rescue a runaway slave.

Even considering the cannibalism-as-Eucharist and Magdalena's ability in death to reveal the future, equating Magdalena with Christ seems farfetched in many respects, since she accomplishes no immediate kind of redemption for her followers and since her message before her death, in her role as a courtesan, was one primarily of erotic love. Nonetheless, Magdalena also possesses one of the most significant characteristics of the Christian god—and of Legs Diamond, for that matter—a miraculous power over death. When Magdalena is first brought into the Staats mansion, Hillegond has her body placed in the *"Dood Kamer*, or dead chamber, the room set aside in substantial homes of the old Dutch to accommodate death" (21). This special room, however, does not accommodate death for long, as we witness in what is perhaps the most outrageous scene in all of Kennedy's work. As Quinn tells us, soon after Magdalena is brought in, John the Brawn "raised and carefully folded her skirt above her waist" and, with Hillegond, Maud, and Quinn all watching, climbed "aboard Magdalena Colón and began doing to her gelid blossom what I had heard him boast of doing to many dozens of other more warm-blooded specimens" (29–30). This scene may be shocking in its own right, but Kennedy does not stop there. Unbelievably, Hillegond is herself so aroused by the sight of the necrophilia that she encourages John to make love to her, and then, in the middle of their lovemaking, with Quinn and Maud still watching, Magdalena herself miraculously rises up, "now resurrected from wilt by the sunny friction of joy" (30) and demanding that John continue making love to her. Quinn notes what he

sees as the lesson of this outrageous, grotesque scene, namely
that love has the power to overcome death, and in doing so
he explicitly reveals (while simultaneously denying) the
similarity between Magdalena and Christ:

> I had never seen anyone return from the dead before
> Magdalena Colón was resuscitated by love, the same
> commodity used by the Christ to effect a similar end.
> I draw no blasphemous parallels between John the
> Brawn, the amatory instrument, and Jesus; or
> between Jesus and Magdalena, especially in light of
> what she reported to us about her deathly interlude.
> But the power of love is more various and peculiar
> than we know. (33)

Quinn may not draw any blasphemous parallels, but
Kennedy doesn't seem afraid to do so. And we should
remember, as shocking or possibly distasteful as this resus-
citation is, Francis Phelan and other characters such as Legs
Diamond have shown us that Kennedy is not afraid to have
his characters transgress the laws that usually separate the
living from the dead.

Quinn himself, despite the unforgettable circumstances
to which he is a witness, will at times forget the power of love
he observes here in the years which follow, for he will long be
separated from Maud, a woman with whom he falls in love.
In the end, though, he will return to her and Magdalena in
an attempt to be "resuscitated by love" himself out of the
despair he acquires from witnessing all the death of the Civil
War. In helping Quinn at the end, Magdalena will, it turns
out, be a source of salvation like the Christ to which she is
comparable, even if in a perverse way, although this salvation is reserved for Quinn and Maud, takes place only at the
end of the novel, and occurs with little active participation
from Magdalena herself. For the most part, Magdalena serves
as a Christ figure in *Quinn's Book* less as a source of salvation
and more as an emblem of the interpenetration of the

traditionally distinct conditions of life and death: as the eternal god of Christianity was said to enter history, and then die to overcome death itself, so too Magdalena possesses the power to cross over between these distinct worlds, from life to death and back again, a power, as we noted above, that is not unusual for characters in the Albany cycle.

This attention in *Quinn's Book* to the now familiar theme in Kennedy's work of the shared reality of life and death surfaces in several other scenes surrounding Magdalena's own resurrection. One of these scenes is the discovery of the runaway slave Joshua, whose presence is revealed by Will Canaday, a wise journalist and friend of Hillegond's who arrives at the Staats mansion amidst all the excitement of the resurrection. Canaday leads a group of people from the main house to a Staats mausoleum in the very procession that Quinn saw in Magdalena's eye, and here the group discovers two escaped prisoners chained together, Joshua and a white man who has just committed suicide. Joshua is not only literally chained to one of the dead, creating a symbolic tableau of the inescapable connection between life and death, but he is himself described as a "man in such debilitated condition that he looked more dead than the corpse above him" (38), a reversal of the two conditions of living and dead that mirrors the more profound reversal enacted by John the Brawn upon Magdalena.

After the group frees Joshua, still alive though he resembles the dead, they help him into the house in order to aid in his escape, and in the process the novel reveals even more its attention to the way life and death interpenetrate one another. As the rescuers lead Joshua back to the mansion, they also carry with them the coffin of Amos Staats, one of Hillegond's ancestors—a task that Quinn calls the "second resurrection of the evening" (42)—because the coffin was disturbed in all of the excitement of freeing the slave. Once inside, Maud, eager to see what the body looks like, opens the coffin and stares at a corpse perfectly preserved even though it is over seventy years old, a condition that once again distorts the ordinary relationship between life and death.

The arrival of Amos Staats's body in the house not only calls attention to the merger and mixing of death and life in the novel, but it is also the moment in which Quinn first acts upon his love for Maud, the other great mystery in addition to history to which he is introduced in these opening scenes. This love between the two young people emerges almost magically—a love at first sight—out of the flood and fire and cannibalism and necrophilia, out of the horrible history and death the two witness. When they first arrived at the Staats mansion after the flood, with John carrying the still-dead Magdalena, Maud made Quinn promise that he would "steal" her, "no matter what the cost, no matter how long it takes" (19), even though the two have just met and even though Quinn has no idea from what he must steal her.   Maud simply tells him that he has "first right to [her] life" since he has rescued her from death (19), signalling the unusual connection of their love with the notion of death—a connection that will be sustained throughout the novel and that is made emphatic once Amos Staats' coffin is brought inside. As Quinn tell us, his and Maud's love is "consummated" as they admire Amos's corpse:

> "He's so beautiful," Maud said. We stared together at
> his beauty until she turned her gaze to my own face.
> "And you are beautiful as well," she said, and she
> kissed me with her mouth upon my mouth. She kept
> her mouth there and my arms went 'round her. We
> kissed under the spell of death's beauty, then stopped
> kissing to gaze again at Amos. (43)

"Death" has been the origin of the love between Maud and Quinn in the fatal flood where they met; it is also the source of their mutual promise to sustain their love forever because of Quinn's rescuing Maud from death itself: and now, standing above Amos's corpse, the first physical sign of Maud and Quinn's love for each other comes under "death's beauty."

Unlike Magdalena's resurrection, in which love—in the guise of eros, at least, or whatever it is that one wants to label the necrophilia—allowed for the renewal of life, the resurrection of the beautiful Amos ends in Amos's own destruction. His lifelike body, inspiring as it is to Maud and Quinn, is nonetheless destroyed upon being exposed, as Quinn says, to "the air of our pernicious age" (43). In the scene in which the body disintegrates, Kennedy intertwines all of his major concerns in the novel and the several great mysteries that will befuddle Quinn himself, as the symbolic dust of death and history from Amos's corpse is cast upon the two young lovers. As Quinn narrates it, Amos's body

> exploded upward and outward, his hands and face disappearing beneath a great graying puff of dust tinged with pale blue, a puff that ascended fully six feet above the coffin and spread over us all in a melancholy haze. The dust demarcated the end of something, the final burst of heroism, perhaps, whose like was no longer accessible to our commonplace lives. The sadness of lost glory was implicit, most especially to Maud, who cried as if a demon held her in its jaws. She clutched me, threw her arms about my neck and kissed me again with passion and energy, ground her pelvic center against my own and kissed all of my face with a ferocious gluttony.
>
> She kissed me, she kissed me, and I kissed in return. . . . The dust was falling onto our head and shoulders, the air slowly clearing; and though we did not interrupt our kissing, I could see from my eye's corner that the face of Amos was gone, as were his hands. . . . Having seen this and understood none of it, I returned my eyes to Maud and kissed on until we were pulled apart. . . . (43–44)

It is hard to know what to make of all this erotic appeal of death in Kennedy's book, though Freud would certainly understand the connection between these two great desires. But it is an appeal that Quinn is only too glad to follow through with. Despite being pulled away from Maud by the others in the room, Quinn forces himself upon her lips once more until they are again separated. Hillegond, in observing their passion, says simply, "'They know love'" (44). They may—Kennedy, at least, seems to want us to think they do—but they also know death and history, literally immersed as they are in dust, a symbol of the inevitable death and decay brought on by the passing of time.

The unusual source and resolve of Maud and Quinn's love predicts an unusual life for them as a couple. And as the novel reveals, their love will indeed be unusual, though it is ironically not at all full of the intense, death-influenced passion described at its outset. Once the excitement of the flood, the resurrection, the runaway slave, and the exploding corpse all dies down, John the Brawn takes Maud and Magdalena on a canal boat to seek his fortune with them and abandons his young apprentice, leaving Quinn sleeping on the shore as the boat leaves town. And despite their intense initiation into their mutual love, Maud and Quinn will then be separated, except for rare and chance meetings, for the next fifteen years.[9] It should come as no surprise, considering how immersed in death Maud and Quinn are when they first meet, that their separation is overcome in the end only at another "death," a wake that Magdalena holds for herself at the conclusion of the novel in preparation for the death she once had and wants to have again.

Quinn recognizes that his simultaneous discovery of the important mysteries of his life—history and love—as well as the discovery of the thin border between death and life itself, will shape his life for years to come: "I was bewildered," he says in reaction to all of the events surrounding the flood:

Nothing seemed to conclude. I was in the midst of a whirlwind panorama of violence and mystery, of tragedy and divine frenzy that mocked every effort at coherence. I now felt a physical sadness overtaking me, my body and brain losing their security and being thrust into hostile weather. I knew that apart from my family's being swept away by the cholera, what had happened to me in recent weeks was the most significant phase of my life thus far, the core of that significance being, and preeminently so, Maud. (57)

Once Quinn is abandoned by John the Brawn, he will turn his attention to this "whirlwind panorama of violence and mystery" in order to try to find the "coherence" (58) behind it, the consoling truth behind historical events (such as the cholera epidemic) that might give some meaning to their horror. This interest in the "meaning" behind the "panorama" is, in fact, implicit from the outset of the novel, even before Quinn's abandonment by John sends him on his quests. While observing the flood, for example, he says that all of the events he and the others witness defy any possibly logical explanation and, because of this condition, deprive one of a meaningful position in the world:

[The flood] generated in us such fear of the Lord, of nature gone wild, of cosmic, mythic rage against our vulnerable puniness that we were negated as individuals and became as grains of sand, as desiccated leaves. We survived only because we survived. There is no other ascribable reason or logic behind who was saved and who wasn't, any more than there was logic in the way I alone of my family had come through the cholera unscathed. (9–10)

Quinn's search will be an attempt to come to some position by which he can endure or even make cohere the mysteries and horrors of history, the "cosmic, mythic rage" that is "without reason or logic."

Quinn's adventures in his pursuit to understand history —or, more accurately, the book's descriptions of this history itself—occupy much of the narrative after the four primary protagonists are separated. The comings and goings of Quinn, Maud, Magdalena, and John are all subsumed into stories of the historical situation in which they live, stories which include wars and riots, the Underground Railroad, the growth of horse racing and journalism, stage productions, and boxing matches. Daniel Quinn wanders through all these events, observing and wondering and oddly separated from Maud throughout, pondering all along what the answers are to the mysteries of his life, the horror he witnesses, and the love he does not yet possess.

The preeminence of this historical over the personal in many of the sections of the book seems confirmed by Quinn himself, who describes himself as a living embodiment of his personal family history and even, to some extent, the greater public American one. As he says at one point, "My parents were gone themselves, along with their unknowns, all now remaining of what they deemed valuable embodied in me, this urchin particle floating in time, waiting for the next blow to fall" (71). He is the living embodiment of all that remains of his family's history, and he is also a sort of Everyman victim of history, suffering through his "vulnerable puniness" and "waiting for the next blow to fall." Specifically, Quinn sees himself as the suffering Irishman, the representative ancestor of all those Irishmen to follow in the other stories of the Albany cycle. As Quinn writes once to Maud after witnessing the poor conditions of one Irish family, the Ryans: "Maud, I speak to you now of the Irish . . . to tell you of the Ryans and their misery and how it distracts me, for it is part of me: Joey Ryan—with broken nose, dead father, sickly mother—is surely myself in another guise, just as Molly Ryan, that tiny waif, could be you" (111). Quinn is thus both someone who attempts to find some coherence in the "mythic rage" that is history, as well as a representative individual—and an emblematic Irishman—standing in his "vulnerable puniness" before that mythic rage itself.

Throughout Quinn's search for meaning, his attempt to come to terms with this rage, he carries with him a "potato platter," a disk that is an explicit symbol of the mysteries he is pursuing. This platter or "Celtic disk" is the sole inheritance Quinn receives from his parents and thus is also his only connection with his own past, his own history as an Irish immigrant in America. The platter is hidden (unknown to Quinn) in the bottom of a birdcage that Quinn's mother made him bury as she lay dying. When he asks her why he must bury the cage, she answers, "'Because I brought it from Ireland'" and then goes on to explain that "'a birdcage isn't all that it is. . . . Study it well and mind you that there's value in it that you can use someday'" (64).

Quinn buries the cage, and after his mother and the rest of his family have died from cholera and after Maud has abandoned him, he returns to unearth it. He discovers that the cage has a false bottom and in it he finds the platter, "a circular metal disk bearing an odd trompe l'oeil design":[10]

> Now it was a screaming mouth with vicious eyes, now a comic puppy with bulbous nose and tiny mouth. Depending on where the light hit the eyes they were glassy, or sad, or hypnotic. . . . I believed the disk was valuable in some way yet to be understood. It was like nothing I'd ever seen. It might be a platter. It might be gold, or silver, for it had not rusted. But even if it wasn't precious metal it had value as a thing to look at. I stuffed it into my sack and left the house, brimming with a brand-new faith in the unknown that I had found at the bottom of a birdcage. (73)

Throughout his adventures, Quinn from time to time pulls

out this disk and ruminates upon its odd design and its meaning. As he is waiting for one of his periodic reunions with Maud, he dreams of the disk, which spoke to him "in a pair of cryptic phrases: 'Under the arches of love,' it said, and then 'Under the banner of blood,' neither phrase holding intimate meaning" for him at that time (129). Cryptic though they may be, the messages obviously allude to the two great mysteries in Quinn's life, his love for Maud and his inability to understand the violence of the history he observes. Quinn as yet is unable to see the exact connection of the disk with these other mysteries although he still believes it has some connection to his life: he says at one point that "only an intuition persisted that one day I might find the grand significance of this oracular object, as well as how it related" (129-30) to all that he had already witnessed, including the Irish immigrant riots, his love for Maud, the slave Joshua's escape, and the explosion of Amos Staats's corpse.

Although Quinn may not know exactly what role the disk has in his quest, he does acknowledge that it is the disk, what is called at one point "The Great Platter of the Unknown" (228), that encourages him to think of the need for coherence in life. As he says after he dreams of this disk:

> The message emerging from my febrile imagination during these tumultuous days [when he is helping to discover a secret Society] was a single word: "linkage": and from the moment I was able to read that word I became a man compelled to fuse disparate elements of this life, however improbable the joining, this done in a quest to impose meaning on things whose very existence I could not always verify. . . . (130)

Although the confusing design of this mysterious platter symbolizes Quinn's own confusion, Quinn also connects it with his chance to overcome that confusion. As he says, the disk is one source of his "faith" (73) in the secret that might resolve the confusion he feels from his witnessing history: the disk somehow inspires him to believe in the mysterious "linkage" that might "fuse disparate elements of [his] life" and thus allow him to "impose meaning on things."

Quinn's attempt to impose the meaning in which the disk inspires him to believe is made primarily through writing—specifically, journalism—a vocation he first encounters after he is abandoned by John the Brawn. Once Maud disappears, Quinn joins up with the newspaperman Will Canaday, looking toward the older man as a mentor, and through him Quinn discovers the power and allure of journalism. With Canaday, Quinn helps unravel an intrigue involving Dirck Staats, Hillegond's son (an adventure which includes one of the scenes Quinn witnessed in the eyeball of Magdalena's corpse). Quinn discovers that Dirck once uncovered a nefarious secret society and that he transcribed everything he knew about this society into a secret code so that no one would realize what he had uncovered.

After Dirck is kidnapped and eventually mutilated (his tongue is cut out, making writing his only means of communicating), Will Canaday publishes provocative articles that unravel the secret power of the society and that help bring it down. As a witness to and participant in these events, Quinn discovers "the power of the word to transform this simple abduction of a man into an event that alters the trajectory of history's arrow" (77). This "power" Quinn discovers is one to which he seems almost naturally attracted. As Dirck himself says to him, "Our society seems ever to be confessing its flaws to you, just as you seem to have been born to witness tragedy and to elevate people from trouble" (133), a belief Dirck holds so strongly that he leaves Quinn a bequest that will free him of his financial insecurity as an orphan.

The realization of the "power of the word" and Quinn's own natural attraction to it ultimately convinces him to pursue a career in journalism, the medium which will be his means of carrying on his quest for understanding for years to come. Kennedy emphasizes the importance of Quinn's accepting his role as a writer by focusing intently on the moment in Quinn's life in which he discovers this vocation. This moment arrives in 1850 after Quinn has met up with John, Magdalena, and Maud again. Not long after attending a ball with Maud and others, Quinn returns to his room as confused as ever, especially about his relationship with Maud:

> Poor Quinn. Consider him. He saves a life, discovers love, finds it reciprocated, is obsessed and rightfully so, . . . finds the object of his obsession to be madcap, takes her home, kisses her, all but swoons with confounded desire, goes to his rooming house, fails to sleep, rises, lights his writing lamp, plucks from his writing case his pointless pen, finds a point, imposes it upon the pen, unrolls his paper, uncaps his inkwell, poises his pen above the well with the intention of wetting the point and writing, refrains from dipping because his condition allows no clarity of thought, puts down the pen, paces up and down in his bedchamber, takes up his collection of Montaigne's essays, opens it, and finds two passages underlined. . . . (169)

The passages he reads are philosophical ruminations on "'How the Soul Relieves Its Feelings on the Wrong Objects, When the Real Are Wanting" (170), the very kind of scolding Quinn realizes he needs to have considering his obsession with the frequently absent Maud. The essays irritate him, for after reading them he realizes even more strongly how "madcap" is his own obsession with Maud. In his ruminations, Quinn soon remembers a fight he once witnessed in which John the Brawn knocked down a famous fighter, and at last he comes to the magic discovery of his vocation as writer:

> . . . at that memory [of John's knock-down] Quinn picks up his pen, dips it in his ink, and writes one sentence: "They call him John the Brawn and he doesn't know enough to pull his head in when he shuts the window, but he knocked down the best fighter in the world," and having written that, puts down his pen, smiles, walks up and down the bedchamber, and understands that he has just changed his life. (170)

Quinn's discovery of writing and of journalism in particular does change his life, for it becomes his method of witnessing the mysteries and enigma of history, what he calls the "worlds beyond worlds that he cannot understand" (169).

Quinn's quest to "understand" these worlds may take place through his role as a journalist, but his writing only pushes Quinn through the questions he has; it does not provide the answers to those questions or the consolation he seeks for a world he cannot understand. Indeed, his entry into journalism introduces him into the worst horror he will yet face, the Civil War. As Quinn himself says later in retrospect, "The decision I made so long ago, to live my life according to the word, reached its apogee in the war and then descended into the bathetic dumps of faceless slaughter" (280). For years he will live through this slaughter, recording it for others while sinking into despair, slipping far away from Maud and his promise to steal her, far from the magical powers of Magdalena Colón, and as far as he has ever been from understanding the world.

The extent of Quinn's distance from what (and who) is meaningful to him is emphasized by the fact that Maud actually becomes engaged to another man, the industrialist Gordon Fitzgibbon, while Quinn is engaged on his career as a journalist. Although Maud may be significant in Quinn's life—the "core" of his being, as he says (57)—she pursues her own life away from him, a life which reveals her slowly being transformed into a modified version of her aunt. Magdalena has taken to including in her shows announcements of the spiritual beliefs she has adopted since her "death," as when she tells an audience before a performance in Syracuse that she would like to give "her thanks to God for resurrecting her from the dead" (143). Her message is that one should not fear dying, that it is merely a return to the "birthplace of dreams" (143). She adds that "'there is always the chance of turning around and coming right back'" from the dead, a fact she knows well, and that she "'can't imagine a more pleasant experience than dying'" (143).

It should come as no surprise that, after such proclamations, Magdalena finds that her famous Spider Dance—"in which she shook off an attack of imaginary arachnids that were climbing her skirt and bodice, and in so doing revealed more flesh than was generally provided to American audiences outside of brothels" (143)—is ridiculed by the audience who has just listened to her speak of being resurrected. Maud comes to Magdalena's rescue, however, by successfully infusing both of Magdalena's powers, spirituality and sexuality. Maud's own spiritual talent is an ability to communicate with the dead or at least with mysterious spirits who speak to her through knocking, a phenomenon that dispels the doubts and silences the insults of audiences when she reveals her powers on stage.[11] As impressed as these audiences are with Maud's magical abilities, they are even more impressed with her own version of the Spider Dance, one she first performs when Magdalena is laughed off the stage in Rochester. Maud's dance is one in which "in learned emulation of her aunt she whirled about in recklessly flying skirts, her wild abandon silencing all hooters, and at length provoking them into cheers and long applause as the curtain fell" (144).

Magdalena's failure as a dancer/spiritualist is repeated

in the failure of her other great art, that of lover, a failure
that can be attributed, like her failure at dancing, to her
intense interest in the "other" world. John the Brawn,
Magdalena's lover since they left the Staats mansion, says to
her after some unsatisfactory lovemaking, "'You had more
life when you were dead'" (145), an accusation that is more
of an accurate observation than an insult and that raises
once again the curious reversal of life and death found
throughout *Quinn's Book*. As Peter A. Quinn writes, "*Quinn's
Book* warns us: The dead are not dead" (308); and the
living—as John realizes after making love to Magdalena—are
not necessarily alive. Indeed, after John's comment,
Magdalena realizes that she wants water, the very cause of
her dying, for she believes water will be "capable of assuaging
. . . the agony of death" (145) so that she might therefore be
reborn into the vitality she had before her "first" death. "'I
must lie in a lake and recover my passion,'" she says to John
(145), and he obliges her by taking her to Saratoga Springs.

   That Magdalena had more life when she was dead is a
paradox not unlike one Maud herself cannot accept, namely
"enantiodromia, the ancient Greek concept of running in
contrary ways" (152-53), a notion that Maud's classics
teacher in Madrid once taught her. Maud is unable to
practice or accept what those who believe in enantiodromia
accept, such as "believing in the unbelievable" (153). What
Maud does believe in is herself; as she says cryptically at one
point, "I am never what I was. I am always new, always two.
I am, and I am, and so I am" (164). In making such a
proclamation, Maud, like Magdalena before her, announces
herself as a quasi-mythical goddess: Magdalena as the
resurrected Christ-figure, proclaiming the superiority of the
afterlife and knowledge of the mysteries of the world, has not
only shaped Maud into a dancer and mysterious commu-
nicator with the world of the dead, but also into a Yahweh
figure, she who can say, "I am who I am."

It is to these two "goddesses," as well as to John the Brawn McGee, that Quinn returns once he leaves the horrors of the Civil War in 1864. Fifteen years after their initial adventures together, Quinn and the three individuals who introduced him to his quests for the meaning of history and for the satisfaction of love are reunited. Quinn returns to Maud in particular because he believes that somehow she will be not only the answer to his quest for love but also the source of his recovery from the despair into which he has fallen during the war. As Edward C. Reilly argues, "Quinn has realized that his rebirth, after the *death* of the Civil War, resides in Maud" (97). Quinn acknowledges this faith he has in Maud to be a possible source of rebirth or illumination for him when he equates her with his Celtic disk:

> Quinn equated Maud with his Celtic potato platter: both of them agents of change and illusion, both of uncertain origin and significance—the platter waiting underground for another generation to unearth it, quantifying its own value and mystery in the shallow grave; and Maud propounding mysteries of the cosmos with every Maudbreath. Buried, they eluded. Resurrected, they grew lustrous. (178)

Although Quinn does not yet understand what the roles of Maud and the disk may be in his quests, he hopes that both of them, similar as they are as "agents of change and illusion," may grow "lustrous" once they have been resurrected, the disk from where he buried it, and Maud from the years that she has been separated from Quinn.

In his attempt to use Maud's "lustrous" nature to heal himself, Quinn rejoins his former lover in 1864 for a less innocent version of the embrace they shared fifteen years earlier while Amos Staats's body exploded over them. The embrace is Quinn's attempt not only to consummate his love and thus complete one of his quests, but also a symbol of his attempt to "fuse" what previously had been separated, to form his own "linkage." Although Maud is engaged to another, she undresses before Quinn at one point, wanting him to see all of her, and then she assumes the very position the dead Magdalena once had in the Staats *Dood Kamer*: Maud "lowered herself into a supine position on the table, freeing up her robe and chemisette. Quinn . . . could only watch with awe her reenactment of Magdalena's posture, the array of her apparel before resurrection" (209). Eventually Maud "closed her eyes and let her arms fall into the same position as Magdalena's of yore" (209). Quinn and Maud's encounter together is thus a return to their history, another moment in the Albany cycle, like Martin Daugherty's with Melissa Spencer, of repeating "now" what happened back "then" in the past. In *Quinn's Book*, Maud not only returns to her own past in order to try to use it as a means toward redemption (particularly for Quinn), but she also returns specifically to a resurrection she and Quinn both witnessed. In other words, Maud attempts to resurrect the past by reenacting a resurrection, a phenomenon that Quinn desperately needs, drowning as he has been in his own obsession with death and the horrors of history and war.

Maud has been preparing for her role in saving Quinn throughout her separation from him as she has been slowly transformed into the person of her aunt: since witnessing Magdalena's death and resurrection, Maud has come to know, like her aunt, "a place where the miracle of love rises gloriously out of death" (207). Yet despite this knowledge and despite Maud's attempt to reenact the resurrection, the reunion of the two lovers fails. Maud says, just as Quinn is about to consummate their love, that her "blood" tells her that they are not yet ready (209). Some unknown is still missing, the mystery of their love not yet ready to be solved, the disparate elements not yet fusible. Quinn, though disappointed, does not despair, for he still feels after the failed embrace that Maud is "the instrument by which he would rid himself of death and war, put life once again on horseback" (218).

With this belief in Maud's power, Quinn follows her to a bazaar honoring the Civil War, where she convinces Quinn to give a speech. Before he speaks, Maud sees the "trouble" behind Quinn's "pacific smile," what perhaps her blood sensed in telling her not to consummate her love with him: it's the "war" that's still troubling him, she realizes, and so she decides to begin her own speech with "Keats, telling Quinn that he was perhaps half in love with easeful death" (220). The poem Maud reads, presumably "Ode to a Nightingale," seems to have no effect on Quinn, however, for his speech verifies her intuition of his obsession with death. What he says is brutally realistic, an insult to the crowd who expects to hear tales of military adventure and glory. Quinn gives them instead a speech about "the war's reality" (222): as he says, "A pile of dead people, that's the reality I'm talking about. The bigger the pile, the bigger the reality . . ." (222). His speech goes on to discuss Union soldiers killed by their own cannon fire, a rebel soldier killed by his own men while attempting to surrender, "dead boys . . . spread shoulder-to-shoulder over about five acres," a measles epidemic, his own injury in the war, and the execution of a deserter (Peaches Plum, a childhood nemesis of Quinn's) (222–27). "Death's all that matters," Quinn says toward his conclusion, "and I know you all want the reality of that . . . " (226).

Quinn seems to be at his nadir at the bazaar. He tells his audience that all that is left of him is "a kind of fatal quizzicality" (227), a resigned curiosity that has replaced the energetic quest of his youth when he was "solitary, furious, eccentric, growing bold" (61). With his quest incomplete, death an obsession, and Maud engaged to another, Quinn has returned to a woman he hopes will be the "instrument by which he would rid himself of death and war" only to be rejected by her. He is as confused and lost as he has ever been. As he says of himself, "Quinn is a psychic idiot. Quinn experiences everything and concludes nothing. *Tabula rasa ad infinitum*" (239). After years of observing and witnessing and searching, his mind is as blank as when he started, when he was "bewildered" and when "nothing seemed to conclude" (57).

Despite this bewilderment, however, by mentioning his "quizzicality" Quinn is also revealing that he still possesses the desire, if not the energy, to uncover the answers to the mysteries that he has long been seeking. And as it happens, Quinn does not really need this energy, for the answers soon arrive in a series of events and discoveries that tie together all of the important concerns in Quinn's life—the Celtic disk, death, the role of writing in understanding reality, and love—while requiring nothing more on Quinn's part than his own ability to think.

This process by which Quinn resolves his various quests begins with his better understanding of the meaning behind the Celtic platter. He takes this disk out not long after his and Maud's failed lovemaking and says, "I concentrated on my disk and it changed: convexity into concavity—a fat tongue into a hollow mouth; and in this willful ambiguity by the Celtic artist I read the wisdom of multiple meanings" (239). These multiple meanings make Quinn remember one of Will Canaday's pieces of advice from many years earlier, before Quinn set out on his own: "avoid gratuitous absolutes" (135, 239). It is a lesson Quinn has forgotten, for his entire quest has been for an absolute, for the truth behind the reality he sees. Now, however, the multiple meanings of the disk remind him of another option, the wisdom of multiplicity.

This newfound appreciation of multiplicity over the absolute helps Quinn realize yet another flaw in his approach toward his quests: his vocation as a journalist, he comes to conclude, his means of looking at the world, has been misdirected, for its basis in logic and reason and fact keeps it from grasping the mysteriousness that is the essence of the multifaceted and paradoxical world. Journalism, or at least the practice of recording history, is not, in short, the path to wisdom. This important discovery comes from a most unlikely and quotidian source, the new job Maud's fiancé is thinking of starting. When Quinn engages in small talk with this fiancé, Gordon Fitzgibbon, Quinn discovers that Gordon is considering leaving his work in industry in order to run for Congress. "The idea of a man entering into a new career at midlife was strange to me, and appealing," Quinn says (265). "I had thought only of continuity since I began educating myself, and so the idea of a mind change . . . seemed like a mutation of the species" (265). Quinn acknowledges this talk with Fitzgibbon as his "change of mind on the word" (265),[12] and after this moment he reflects on the limitations that his journalistic mode of writing has imposed on his quest:

> All that I had written for Will [Canaday] and for the *Tribune* seemed true enough, but a shallow sort of truth, insufficiently reflective of what lay below. Joshua's life, or John's, or my own could only be hinted at by the use of the word as I had been practicing it. The magnificent, which is to say the tragic or comic crosscurrents and complexities of such lives, lay somewhere beyond the limits of my calling. . . . How was I ever to convey to another soul, even in speech, what I felt for and about Maud, what grand churnings she set off in my inner regions? How could I know those workings, even for myself alone, without a proper language to convey them? I was in need of freedom from inhibition, from dead language, from the repetitions of convention. (265)

The journalistic method he has been using on his quest cannot, he understands now, arrive at the truth he seeks, that which "lay below"; he needs instead a "freedom" from the conventions required by this method, and he discovers the means to this freedom when he again contemplates the "mystery" of his Celtic disk:

> And with that thought [of the disk's mystery] I knew that what was wrong with my life and work was that I was so busy accumulating and organizing facts and experience that I had failed to perceive that only in the contemplation of mystery was revelation possible; only in confronting the incomprehensible and arcane could there be any synthesis. My wretched inadequacy in achieving integrity of either mind or spirit after having witnessed so much death, deviltry, and treachery was attributable to this. I had become a creature of rote and method at a time when only intuitions culled from an anarchic faith in unlikely gods could offer me an answer. (265–66)

Quinn has thus, at last, discovered a means to resolving his quests, to achieving a "revelation" or "synthesis." His journalistic investigations into history had tried too hard to discover a reason and a logic, an absolute, behind all he saw. What he needs instead, he comes to understand, is to contemplate mystery, to confront the "incomprehensible and the arcane," the only way in which a "synthesis" is truly attainable. In this contemplation is the wisdom of appreciating the mysterious and the multiple and the arcane, a far different procedure from the "accumulating and organizing [of] facts and experience" that had been his attempt to discover truth.

That Quinn discovers that the "contemplation of mystery" is superior to the accumulation of fact sounds impressive, but what does it mean for Quinn as a man acting in the world? The answer for Quinn comes not from Maud, as we might expect, but from Magdalena and her reenactment of her first death. Her role in helping Quinn is admittedly more accidental than anything, although it is her own wisdom about the mysteries of death that at least enables her to provide for her coincidental help. Magdalena's obsession with death, unlike Quinn's, is not a narrow sense of despair but rather a celebration of the beauty of death and the complex interrelationship between "both sides of existence" (278). When Magdalena thinks she is "about to die for the second time," she says that she wants a "wake to acknowledge her passing over into lovely death, but held while she [is] still alive and able to enjoy both sides of existence at the same time" (278). She, unlike Maud and Quinn, accepts and even enacts the enantiodromia, the paradoxical and "incomprehensible" and "arcane," in embracing simultaneously the usually contrary and distinct worlds of life and death.

When hearing of Magdalena's planned wake, Quinn offers to write the handbill advertising it, and he realizes in preparing to write this ad that he wants "to do justice to the woman" by moving "beyond the barricade of empty facts into some grander sphere" (280). He wants, in short, to act upon the discoveries he has made thanks to the Celtic disk and to his talk with Gordon Fitzgibbon. To do Magdalena justice, Quinn says that he must devise "a set of images that did not rot on [him] overnight" (280). In this way, he says, he "might confront what was worth confronting, with no expectation of solving the mysteries, but content merely to stare at them until they became as beautiful and valuable as Magdalena had always been, and as Maud now was" (280). His writing of the handbill reflects his newfound desire to contemplate the mysterious rather than to solve the mystery; it's a faith that even leads him to believe that he might discover the "harmony"—the coherence or linkages—he has long sought: "I was persuading myself," Quinn says, "that if I used the words well, the harmony that lurked beneath all contraries and cacophonies must be revealed. This was an act of faith, not reason" (280). In such statements Quinn reveals that he has not abandoned the power of the word to resolve his quests but that he simply must use words in a new way. As Quinn says, "rather than writing Magdalena's obituary, I began to write her story, taking the facts . . . from my imagination, where, like a jungle flower, she had long since taken root" (280). He has, in the end, replaced fact with imagination as the source from which he writes: he replaces history with story, the pursuit of truth with the wisdom of contemplation.

This emphasis on imagination over the accumulation of fact reflects an endeavor Kennedy himself practiced earlier in *Quinn's Book*, when he wrote history not as an obituary, not as facts about the past, but rather as an imaginative recreation that he felt might actually better arrive at the truth of that history.[13] As Kennedy has said himself, "What sets a good fiction writer apart from the journalistic guppies is that he, or she, understands that the truth comes up from below, that it develops from the perception of the significance of experience, and not from the experience itself" (McCaffery, 165). In opting to use imagination rather than merely repeating the historical or factual, Quinn is following the same credo, one through which he can find the "harmony" he has long sought. Quinn abandons the journalism that has led to "a shallow sort of truth, insufficiently reflective of what lay below" (265) for the realm of the imagination which can discover "the harmony that lurked beneath all contraries and cacophonies" (280).[14]

The discovery of the Celtic disk's essential mysteriousness, Quinn's acceptance of the "wisdom of multiple meanings," Magdalena's inspiration as a living example of the beautiful intertwining of the worlds of the dead and the living, and Quinn's rejection of the accumulation of fact for the greater truth of story and imagination—all of these resolutions and discoveries coincide at Magdalena's "wake," a reenactment of the source of the quest itself, Magdalena's drowning in the flood on the Hudson. In an unexpected way these resolutions offer an answer to Quinn's quest for the truth behind history, teaching him at least of the folly of his pursuit and offering him an alternative means toward achieving wisdom. What is yet to be resolved, however, is Quinn's desire for Maud, the object of his remaining quest, but he achieves this during the wake too, almost as if it were a gift for having overcome the other quests on which he has been engaged. After the wake, Quinn kidnaps Maud as he had long ago promised he would, taking her from her fiancé to a room in the house in which Magdalena's wake is being held. As Quinn's search has brought him full circle to the reenactment of the drowning at which his search began, so too does it bring him to the same Maud and the same love he once knew fifteen years earlier: as Reilly writes, "Maud realizes that their love has not only endured but has come full circle, the latter symbolized by her pink frock which she says is 'the same color as the one I was wearing when we met' [253]" (97). This time Quinn's and Maud's reenactment succeeds: as they both undress in an anonymous room in the mansion, "Maud and Quinn [are] at last ready for love" (289) and Quinn can thus at last complete his quest.

The success of Quinn's quest for Maud, although consistent with Quinn's other successes, is oddly imposed on the protagonist, a gift almost from Kennedy himself. This sense encourages the feeling one has had all along that *Quinn's Book*, despite its title, does not belong to Quinn but to his time and his place. As Kennedy admitted above, the book is not an individual odyssey but an exploration of the age in which Quinn and Maud live. Quinn's struggles have shared space with, and sometimes have given way to, the consideration of this age: the "history" in *Billy Phelan's Greatest Game* or *Ironweed* is the individual protagonist's; the history in *Quinn's Book* is both Quinn's and America's. The resolution of Quinn's questions about this history—and about his love for Maud—takes place once Quinn returns to his past, once he goes from what is happening "now" to what happened back "then," when he joins Magdalena for her second death. Quinn resolves his questions about history, in other words, by going back into history. But this return shares center stage with a larger history too, with the past of mid-nineteenth century America and of the fictionalized Albany of Kennedy's cycle of books.

NOTES

1. As Van Dover writes, "Daniel Quinn's choices and views may lack a firm basis in character, but the action of the novel is located unambiguously in space and time" (107).

2. The Staats family, Van Dover reports, were an actual Albany family "which figured prominently in early Albany history" (113).

3. See Reilly, pp. 90–92.

4. Curiously enough, if a short story of Kennedy's is to be included as a contribution to the Albany cycle as a whole, the grandson of the Daniel Quinn of *Quinn's Book* is also called Daniel Quinn and marries a woman named Maud. In "The Secrets of Creative Love," published in *Harper's*, we read of this twentieth century version of Daniel and Maud and in the process learn, as Van Dover reminds us, that the Daniel Quinn of *Quinn's Book* was killed in a duel (125). Van Dover also mentions another curious parallel, that the "penultimate sentence of the story . . . is identical to the antepenultimate sentence of the novel" (126–27). According to Van Dover, the original conception of *Quinn's Book* called for alternating chapters occurring in the nineteenth and twentieth centuries respectively, although the short story is not "the result of a discarded stage in the composition of the novel" (127). What it is, of course, is yet another example in Kennedy's work of the inter-penetration of then and now, one Daniel and Maud in the present reflecting another in the past.

5. Peter A. Quinn rightfully says that *Quinn's Book* is "a historical novel about Albany . . . in the same way Joyce's *Ulysses* is a historical novel about Dublin" (308).

6. Kennedy also enacts the theme his own narrative pursues in *Legs* when he contributes through that novel to the very mythicization of Jack Diamond that *Legs* itself attempts to dramatize.

7. The function of this historical tragedy as a source of love is emphasized in Kennedy's publishing the initial chapter of *Quinn's Book* in *Esquire* under the title "A Cataclysm of Love" (*Esquire* 106 [November, 1986]: 241–53).

8. Christ's knowledge of the future is mentioned by Francis Phelan himself in *Ironweed* when he tells the assemblage of ghosts at his house to leave him alone: "I'd rather be dyin' in the weeds than standin' here lookin' at you pinin' away, like the dyin' Jesus pinin' for an end to it

when he knew every stinkin' thing that was gonna happen not only to himself but to everybody around him, and to all those that wasn't even born yet" (*IW*, 177).

9. The narrative never really dramatizes sufficiently what causes the two lovers to remain separated, especially once they attain adulthood and could thus be free of John and Magdalena. Their separation does have a thematic or metaphorical justification, namely that Quinn must first undergo his quest for historical understanding before he can complete his quest for love. Maud, in effect, becomes Quinn's grail, available to him only once he has endured the challenges of his own quest to understand history or, at least, himself. But the practical, believable reason for why the two lovers are separated to such an extreme is never completely dramatized in the story, perhaps contributing to the cool critical reception *Quinn's Book* received.

10. See the Appendix for a drawing of this Celtic disk as provided in the front of *Quinn's Book*.

11. See pp. 115, 149, and 152 in *Quinn's Book* for various episodes in which Maud communes with the dead or with spirits.

12. Fitzgibbon is also representative of greater national change in *Quinn's Book* in his purchasing of the old Staats mansion once Hillegond dies. According to J. K. Van Dover, the death of Hillegond, an "emblem of aristocratic elegance, hauteur, and noblesse oblige" (113), and the purchase of her house by the industrialist Fitzgibbon, "signifies the extinction of [the] old order in America" (113) and the rise of the democratic, capitalistic order which replaces it.

13. The use of "imagination" to alter historical fact is, of course, also a focus in *Legs*.

14. One is tempted to read such a belief biographically once one knows that Kennedy became a successful novelist after decades of making a living as a journalist.

CHAPTER SIX

UNEARTHING THE FUTURE OF THE PHELANS

V̶ery Old Bones, the fifth book of Kennedy's Albany cycle, is structurally the most complex of all the Albany novels. Like Joyce's *Ulysses*, it begins and ends on the same day. In Kennedy's case, this day is Saturday, July 26, 1958, the day on which Peter Phelan, one of Francis Phelan's younger brothers,[1] has his will read to his family although he is still alive himself. Between the opening of the novel at dawn on July 26 and the closing of the novel after lunch on the same day are revealed numerous events in Phelan history from 1887 up to the present moment of the narrative. These events are ostensibly narrated from the point of view of Orson Purcell, the unacknowledged, illegitimate son of Peter Phelan, although Orson could not possibly be a witness to all of the events he narrates, many of which occur in places he is not and some of which even occur before he is born. The story Orson tells goes back and forth and back again in time, moving with no consistent pattern between numerous dates, a cyclical design not unlike the structure of the Albany cycle as a whole. In its cyclical form, the novel enacts the important theme evident throughout Kennedy's work of the interpenetration of the past and the present: the reader is constantly moving between various moments of time, 1958 and 1887, 1954 and 1934, October

197

and September and March, now and then. This complex structure reveals the understanding evident throughout Kennedy's work that we cannot appreciate what is happening now unless we also—and simultaneously—understand what was happening before.

By the date of the narrative which frames *Very Old Bones*, Orson Purcell has had a not very successful career in the military and in writing. He has also suffered at least two psychotic breakdowns, the second of which he is recovering from when the novel opens. Part of his career as a writer, Orson tells us, is the book we are reading. It is a memoir that five years earlier "began as a work of memory, passed through stages of fantasy, and emerged . . . as an act of the imagination" (8), an appraisal that mirrors the process Kennedy has explored in novels such as *Legs* and *Quinn's Book* in which historical fact is transformed through art into such products of the imagination as myth, legend and fiction.[2] The particular "act of the imagination" that is *Very Old Bones* is written by Orson, as Thomas R. Edwards says, "in the hope of reconstructing and making endurable the sources of his being" (54), for Orson's impetus in writing this memoir is his obsession with his lack of a family who will claim him as a son, his sense of the painful emptiness of being a source-less person.

Orson's concern for "reconstructing . . . the sources of his being," which he assumes, at least biologically, are the Phelans, is carried out in a narrative act of archaeology investigating the history of generations of the Phelan family. *Very Old Bones*, as Bill Ott says, "takes the reader on an archaeological dig through the Phelan closet," a dig which unearths a shameful and often secret family record not only of violence, jealousy, and insanity but also of denial and repression, of a refusal by the Phelans to accept what they have been and, consequently, who they are now. The result of such shame and secrecy is a family that in 1958, the present time of the narrative, is all but "dead"—a familial version of Francis' private condition in *Ironweed*. Those alive are embittered and suffering, from old age as much as from their own personal anguishes, and no Phelan heir is likely to be born from any of them. As the novel of the title implies, there are some very old skeletons in the Phelan closet, ones that have been denied for decades and have led to a moribund and pathetic family, soon, it seems, to be gone for good.

These bones in the Phelan closet are what is unearthed in part thanks to Orson's search for his own "sources," but, as so often happens in Kennedy's fiction, Orson's expedition into the Phelan past is also an opportunity to sanctify that past, to learn and grow from it. Orson's revelations about Phelan history in *Very Old Bones*, supported by equally important revelations by other characters, do not engender expressions of disgust or pity, but rather provide an opportunity for the Phelan family not only to discover long-denied ghosts but to exorcize them too. Through Orson's memoir; through the memories of Molly, Peter's sister; and, perhaps most importantly, through Peter Phelan and the paintings he does of Phelan ancestors, the Phelan past is brought into the present moment, "then" is made part of "now." And as with Francis Phelan in *Ironweed*, Daniel Quinn in *Quinn's Book* and Martin Daugherty in *Billy Phelan's Greatest Game*, these protagonists in *Very Old Bones* magically transform their shared present moment by going back to their shared past and its hidden bones, a process which leads them to resurrect the dead in their history—including themselves—into a living family to embrace.

For the Phelan family to be resurrected, it of course must first be dead, and the narrative of *Very Old Bones* dramatizes what its title implies, that by 1958 the Phelans, after decades of decay, are all but moribund—as one review humorously puts it, the Phelan family "makes the House of Atreus seem a model of health."[3] The last and seventh child to be born of the matriarch Kathryn Phelan and her husband Michael

—the original sources of the house of Phelan—is Tommy, a simple-minded "moron" whose birth in 1891 was for Kathryn a curse on the Phelan family. As Molly Phelan explains it, Sarah, the eldest Phelan daughter, "always said after Tommy was born simple that there shouldn't be any more Phelan children. That was Mama's idea, of course. Mama stopped sleeping with Papa after Tommy. No more, no more, it's a sign, I know it. We all heard them fighting about it" (220–21). The sign seems to have been an accurate one: the generation after Tommy's includes a stillborn (and illegitimate) baby; the insane and bastard Orson, significantly named Purcell, not Phelan, since Peter has never claimed him as his son; Gerald, accidentally killed by Francis in 1916 (an event significant in *Ironweed*); Billy, the one true Phelan remaining but childless at fifty-one and alienated from his aunts and uncles because of what he perceives to be their cruel treatment of his father; and Peg, Francis and Annie's eldest daughter, whose steadfast nature could offer hope to the family except that she is married to George Quinn and thus is—in this patriarchal Phelan world—technically a Quinn. This Phelan family is closer to its end, to its "death," than to any future as a recognizable family, a condition that is not lost on the Phelans themselves. As Molly, one of the Phelan children, says of the family, "We always had too many empty graves in our family. We always prepared for death, never for life" (211). Or, as Orson wonders, "Was ever a family so sonless, so cold, dark, and bereft of a future as these fallow Phelan *fils?* (215).

Such decay in the Phelan family is a state mirrored in the city of Albany itself, always a crucial—if not integral—part within all the books of the Albany cycle. As Orson and his cousin Billy wander around Albany on the central day of the narrative, when Peter Phelan is to read his will, Orson reflects on the condition of the city now that its nightlife has been destroyed by the passing of time and the passing of new laws to curb the gambling and gaming and drinking:

The Monte Carlo gaming rooms were gone, another victim of the crackdown: end of the wheel-and-birdcage era on Broadway; Louie's pool room was empty, only Louie's name left on the grimy windows; Red the barber had moved uptown and so you couldn't even get shaved on the street any more; couldn't buy a deck of cards either, Bill's Magic Shop having given way to a ladies' hat store. A ladies' hat store. Can you believe it, Billy? (36–37)

Billy cannot. He wanders "around the old turf as if it wasn't really old, as if a brand-new crap table might descend from the sky at any minute" (37). But Orson knows otherwise: on Broadway now there is "no lightning. No thunder. No dice. Just the memory of time gone, and the vision of the vanishing space where the winners and losers, the grifters and suckers, had so vividly filled the air with yesterday's action" (37).[4] While wandering around this moribund section of town, Orson and Billy also discover what serves as a sign of the decay in the world of Albany (and an emblem of the focus of the novel itself) when they hear that a set of bones has been accidentally unearthed in town by a construction crew. The bones, it seems, include both mastodon and human remains, victims of the ice age and (probably) of gangsters, symbols of something once vital but then left buried and forgotten. Now, of course, they have been unearthed.

As *Very Old Bones* unfolds and the Phelan's own skeletons are gradually unearthed, what becomes evident is that the Phelan history is not only scarred by shame and tragedy, most of it brought on by insanity in the family, but that the decline that results from these tragic events is itself accelerated by the Phelan trademark of denial. In fact, in many ways the insanity and the denial are products of each other, or at least twin symptoms of the same curse. The epitome of this denial is Kathryn herself, the Phelan matriarch whose shade we saw in *Ironweed* eating weeds in her grave out of her insatiable desire for revulsion. As Peter explains in *Very*

Old Bones, "the thing she knew best was denial" (272). He claims it is the "antithesis" to the "indulgent madness" of Malachi, Kathryn's brother whose murder of his wife is an important subject of Peter's paintings (272). This denial is so emphatic that after the murder of Lizzie McIlhenney, Malachi's wife, Kathryn "even denied herself the pleasure that had probably been hers with the conception of Peter (the subsequent children were conceived under duress)" (272). This sexual repression finds its most virulent manifestation in Kathryn's belief that Tommy was a curse on the family rather than a product of sexual love. But Kathryn also struck Francis, her eldest son, hard enough to send him into the family china closet when she heard of his sexual dalliances with Katrina Daugherty. Her overbearing and restrictive nature eventually chased Francis from the house, as it also did Peter in 1913 after a fight about the Daughertys and the staging of *The Flaming Corsage*.[5] So strong is Kathryn's practice of denial that all her life she wore a

> maternal uniform—black cotton in the summer, black wool in winter—that asserted that unbelievable resistance to anything that smacked of vanity, though not even that: of lightness, of elevation. Her children and relatives had tried to sway her with gifts of floral-patterned dresses, colored skirts and blouses, but the gifts remained in boxes for years until finally Kathryn gave them to the Little Sisters of the Poor. (114)

These gifts, like Kathryn's desire for pleasure, remain boxed and hidden away. All her life Kathryn denies herself any chance of joy or happiness, whether sexual or sartorial.

Kathryn's acts of denial led to the exile of two of her own children, and these acts also began a legacy of bitterness and decline that haunts the Phelan children for decades after her death. This legacy is carried forward primarily by Sarah, the oldest Phelan daughter. As Orson says of her early on in the novel, Sarah's "horizon of pleasure in anything but the pragmatic was extremely limited" (6), an ironic understatement considering how ferociously Sarah repressed any attempt at pleasure in her life—including her threatening a boyfriend with scissors to keep him from coming near her, going to confession in order to tell about her brother's sin for fear that it might be her damnation too, refusing to take a short vacation with her sister and brother, spanking her simple-minded brother Tommy when he was in his sixties for his own pathetic acts of sexual pleasure, and protesting the installation of electricity into the Phelan Colonie Street house in 1934.

Sarah's status as prude, spinster, and judge, the epitome of emotional and sexual repression, was a curse cast upon her in the form of her father's dying wish. As Michael Phelan lay dying from a train accident in 1895, Kathryn convinced him to request that Sarah stay home to care for her. "'I don't care who gets married," Michael obligingly says on his deathbed, "as long as Sarah stays home with her mother" (105). Sarah is only twelve when she receives her father's wishes, and, as Orson reflects on the day of Kathryn's wake, ". . . hadn't [Sarah] done admirably well what her father asked in the thirty-nine years since his death? Oh hadn't she?" (105). Sarah had, becoming a "mad virgin, . . . the dying words of Michael Phelan her dungeon, the courage of her saintly, sinless mother the second-generational iron maiden of her fate" (273). This fate "imposed on the young girl the scullery-nunnery existence that made Sarah deny and eventually destroy her own life rather than admit that lives of sensual pleasure were not only possible, but sometimes eagerly pursued. . . ." (272-73). As Kathryn's bitterness exiles Francis and Peter, her desires send Sarah into an inner exile in the very house on Colonie Street from which her brothers flee.

So similar to her mother is Sarah that she gradually becomes a new version of Kathryn herself, even attaining the title of "Little Mother," a condition that reaches its apex on the day of Kathryn's wake in 1934. When Sarah descends into the parlor to confront the long-absent Francis,[6] for whose departure from the family she has been greatly responsible, she arrives dressed "in total mourning, even to the black combs that held her hair, her dress a high-necked, ankle-length replica of the recurring dress that Kathryn Phelan had worn most of her life" (114). Sarah has become one of the living dead, not only in the extent of her mourning and her long history of life-denying repression, but in donning the "maternal uniform" of her mother so that Sarah herself symbolically becomes the very woman whose corpse lies in the front parlor of the house. As Francis watches his sister enter the room in her mourning clothes, he remembers Sarah's effort over the years to become her mother, an attempt which at last seems to have succeeded:

> Francis looked at Sarah and retreated in time. Here was the mother incarnate in Sarah, now fifty-one, a willful duplicate; and Francis remembered that Sarah had even wanted to call herself Sate when they were young, because people called their mother Kate; but Mama would have none of that. Sarah would be Sarah, which was no hindrance at all to emulation, as this presence now proved; uncanny resemblance, even to the combing and parting of the hair and the black-and-white cameo brooch that Kathryn always wore at her throat. (114)

A few moments later, while looking at Sarah, Francis says to her and the rest of the family, "'I seen [my mother] wakin'. I seen her dead, and now I see her again, not dead at all" (115). Even the simple-minded Tommy is astounded by the similarity between the two women: "'Sarah looks like Mama,'" he says (114).

Like Martin Daugherty in *Billy Phelan's Greatest Game*, who confuses himself with his own father in his illicit relationship with the actress Melissa Spencer, Sarah is unable to distinguish herself from her own mother. In the process, Sarah continues the dangerously repressive and (self)-destructive behavior of Kathryn, even up until her own death. Sarah's decline when she becomes ill in 1954 is surprisingly fast and shocks Orson until he decides that it was a death the timing of which was controlled by Sarah herself: she

> calculated her own weakness until it was the equiv-
> alent of a newborn: helpless, pulled into a realm not
> of its own choosing, the newborn and the imminently
> moribund bound for an encounter at the symbiotic
> boundary of life and death. And she died two hours
> into November 17, 1954, her mother's ninety-fourth
> birthday. (224–25)

Sarah willfully closes the circle of hers and her mother's existence, their shared life of repression and bitterness that begins and ends on the same day. And she will even follow her mother into the afterlife exactly as her mother had done before her: "Sarah left explicit instructions for her wake. She was to be laid out in the same style dress that Kathryn Phelan wore to her grave, and in the same style coffin, which was to be placed in the same position in the front parlor. A solemn high funeral mass should be said for her, as with Kathryn Phelan" (225).

Sarah's denial of herself, of joy and of history even, is not singular in her generation of the Phelan family. None of her siblings, except the simple-minded Tommy (and the dead Julia), is free of the great temptation to deny and to repress, not only their own desires and urges, but also what has happened in their past or what is happening to them now. Even Francis Phelan, the hero of *Ironweed* and a minor character in *Very Old Bones*, shares this characteristic, a fact we learn when he returns briefly to Albany and the old

Phelan home in 1934 when Kathryn dies.[7] As Francis sits in
the family dining room during Kathryn Phelan's wake, he

> saw only one thing in the room that surprised him:
> the picture of the family taken at Papa's forty-fifth
> birthday party at Saratoga Lake, where they had a
> camp that summer, the summer of the year Papa
> died. There was Francis at fifteen and Tommy as a
> baby. Francis would not approach it, not look closely
> at what was then; better off without any vision of a
> past that had led to these days of isolation from both
> past and future. Gone. Stay gone. Die. Go live in the
> cemetery. (118)

Francis tries to banish this vision, to deny its presence and
importance, just as his mother and sister denied for years any
pleasure in their lives. The history which has exiled Francis
is one he would just as soon forget.

Francis sees the picture of his father because his siblings
all invited him into the house for a meal, asking him what he
plans to do for the funeral, if he might even be a pall
bearer—all his siblings, that is, except Sarah, who announces
that Francis will not be staying. The two have long despised
each other, Francis seeing in Sarah not only the duplicate of
his hated mother but also the girl who told Kathryn about his
sexual escapades with Katrina Daugherty. When Francis is
left alone with Orson (then only ten years old), he takes the
opportunity to sneak away, running out the back door of his
old family house. Orson and Peter, however, surreptitiously
follow him, and they both see Francis jump onto nearby
train tracks as if to kill himself and then jump back again.
Peter's meandering reflections about Francis as he watches
his brother's near-suicide reveal his ambivalent feelings
toward his older brother, feelings characterized in great part
by his jealousy of the bohemian life Francis leads and that
Peter himself would like to. But Peter's thoughts also reveal
how this eldest brother, the supposed heir to the Phelan

family, is also the end of the Phelans: "I see you, Francis," Peter thinks to himself, "in your termination, the end of family tie, the beginning of nothing. . . . I salute you as my brother in the death of our history. You more than I knew how to murder it" (124–25). Francis' denial, his rejection of the family, is thus more than a personal "sin," for it also implies the denial of the future of the Phelans themselves.

As Francis stands waiting for the train, secretly watched by Peter and Orson, he himself reveals how the history he tries to deny still haunts him as he thinks of Katrina Daugherty, the woman whose sexual advances many years earlier were responsible for his alienation from his now-dead mother and the rest of the family: "Jesus, lady," Francis says to an imaginary Katrina, "you don't go away easy, do you? Like a life you lived afore you was alive" (125). Though a part of the past, Katrina continues to haunt Francis (as she also does in *Ironweed*); she is indicative of his inability to deny, despite his efforts, the history which has created him. As he stands on the train tracks, his thoughts run from Katrina to all the other women in his life, including his wife and Helen Archer (from *Ironweed*), all people who are part of his history, the life that he tried to ignore by not looking at the family picture and the past he is trying to run away from again by either killing himself or jumping a train out of Albany. The picture and the women are part of a history which Francis wishes to deny, and it is a denial that is indicative of the unhealthy condition not only of Francis himself but of the whole Phelan family in his and their refusal to acknowledge who they are.

Like Sarah and Francis, Molly Phelan, the youngest daughter, also has something she hides, although it is not joy or physical desire. Molly, unlike her sister Sarah, has tried to live a happy life, and has even had sex before getting married (she's a widow when the novel opens). Molly also has long realized the unhealthy condition of the children of Kathryn and Michael Phelan, a realization evident in her reaction when she listens to Sarah beat Tommy, even though he is sixty-three years old, after Tommy lifted up a woman's skirt with his cane: "The situation was old, Molly's guilt was old, the themes that provided the skeleton of events taking place this minute were older than Molly herself, and she was sick of them all, sick of her helplessness in the face of them" (197). Molly knows that Sarah's beating of the simple-minded Tommy is not an isolated event but another moment in the "old" history of the Phelans, an event resulting from Sarah's sexual repression and her isolated life in the Colonie Street house as well as Molly's own inability to intervene in Sarah's excesses.

Molly has spent over twenty years in this sickness and helplessness after her husband, Walter Mangan, died in 1937, only two years into their marriage. Like so many events in Kennedy's Albany cycle, Molly's relationship with Walter is defined by death. She remembers the timing of their first meeting, for example, by recalling that their relationship began six months after the death of her mother, when she met Walter at a resort in Saratoga. And their meeting itself occurred when Walter took pity on Molly after an injured waxwing she was nursing died. The death of the bird upset Molly, but as she says to Orson's wife Giselle in 1954, "'I've been grateful to it ever since, because that's how I met Walter. The cedar waxwing introduced us'" (206). Walter took the dead bird and had it stuffed and preserved for Molly, and she still carries the dead bird with her at the present time of the narrative, over twenty years after its death. Walter's marriage proposal to Molly was appropriate considering how the death of the bird and death in general defined their relationship: "'How'd you like to buried with my people?'" he asks her one day (209).

Like Daniel Quinn of *Quinn's Book*, whose relationship with Maud is framed by the twin deaths of Magdalena Colón, Molly's only years of love and true happiness are defined by death—introduced by the death of the waxwing, confirmed by a decision to share grave plots, and ended by the tragic death of Walter two years later in an auto accident on his way to Virginia. Despite Walter's morose marriage proposal, Molly has him buried in the Phelan graveyard, not the Mangan's, and he is laid to rest there not knowing the most significant secret of Molly's life, a literal collection of bones that haunts her. Although she never told Walter, she became pregnant with his child before they were married, and the shame of her situation forced her to attempt through drugs to abort the baby. For a while it does not seem to work, but four months into the pregnancy the baby is stillborn, probably as a consequence of the drugs. Molly endured the delivery on her own, and no one, including Walter and Sarah, ever discovered or knew about the pregnancy. After the child's birth, in 1936, Molly wrapped up the body and buried it in the cellar of the Colonie Street house where she and Sarah lived. It is a secret she keeps to herself until 1953 when she confides to Orson about what happened. "I called the baby Walter Phelan," she tells him, "and baptized him with water from the sink in a teacup and he's down there still, in a far corner of the cellar, with boxes of horseshoes and jam jars on top of him all these years, God forgive me" (221).

As Sarah has denied pleasure and joy in the Phelan family, Molly has in turned denied an integral part of her life, a baby that is the result of her few brief moments of love and happiness. The bones are indeed, as Orson calls them, the "mortal remains of love" (229), but remains that are never discussed out of fear of the judgment of others. The skeleton is also the mortal remains of the Phelan future: Molly named the baby Walter Phelan, and he could have thus carried on the Phelan name had he survived. At the present time of the narrative of *Very Old Bones*, the only other possibility for the continuation of the name is the fifty-one-year old bachelor, Billy.

Like Molly and the other Phelan siblings, and like Kathryn too, Peter also practices what seems to be the standard Phelan procedure of denial. Peter's denial is, in fact, alive and not-so-well in the figure of Orson Purcell, the son he has had with Claire Purcell but whom he denies is his own. It is Orson, in fact, who describes Peter's denial in a possibly imagined interview he has with his father: "I suggest that you cannot even take that deepest part of yourself seriously," Orson says to his father,

> that you have trouble acknowledging your status as a human being, as well as the status of your son, whom you treat as one of your works of art, disclaiming responsibility for him, allowing him to float free in the universe, devoid even of the right to the intentional fallacy. (136)

In part Peter's denial stems from his jealousy, for he feels that Claire could have been made pregnant by a magician she worked for at the time of Orson's conception. While Peter's suspicions have merit, the evidence for Orson's paternity, including his physical resemblance to both Francis and Peter, indicates that Peter's denial is more a manifestation of will than of sincere doubt. Peter's tendency in discussing Orson's parentage is to deflect any attempt at inquiry about the topic, such as when he responds to Orson's challenge to acknowledge the similarity between Peter's own art and Orson himself by retreating into abstract and meaningless aphorisms about aesthetics. When Orson wonders if he is right in assuming that Peter treats him like one of his pieces of art, Peter responds evasively by saying, "Art is the ideation of an emotion" (137). And later in the conversation, when Orson again draws a similarity between himself and Peter's paintings by saying that "mystery is the secret of art and paternity," Peter simply says, "As you like it. As you like it," never willing to admit how he likes it himself (137). Each oblique attempt by Orson to get Peter to claim him as his son is met by an equally oblique comment from Peter veering the conversation away from the topic. Like the other Phelans, Peter denies, to Orson and the world if not to himself, a key part of his own past.

Even though Peter denies that Orson is his son, Orson himself practices no such denial—he is convinced that Peter is his father. Ironically, it is the moment in which so much of the Phelan practice of denial is brought to light—Kathryn's wake—that also marks the moment in which Orson begins his gradual assimilation into the Phelan family, despite Peter's refusal to include him officially. Peter takes the ten-year-old Orson with him to the family wake, not to introduce him as the latest member of the family but because Claire Purcell, Orson's mother, is on the road performing. Many years after the funeral, Orson considers what he realized at the wake, specifically as he watched Francis get up and sneak out:

> Now, reconstituting that moment twenty-four years later [in 1958], I remember that my sadness at the loss of [Francis'] presence was the first time I was certain that my father really was Peter, and that I really did belong in this family. I had seen some-thing in the man's face that resembled what I saw in my own face in the mirror: a kindred intangible, something lurking in the eyes, and in that smile, and in the tilt of the head—nothing you could say was genetic, but something you knew you wanted to acknowledge because it was valuable when you saw it, even though you couldn't say what it was. And you didn't want to lose it. (119)

Like Quinn, who finds his love Maud in the "death" of Magdalena, Orson finds the certainty of his family—his history—during the celebration of the death of Kathryn. Both episodes are part of the pervasive cyclical nature of Kennedy's stories—death always leading to new life, the end of one family member in *Very Old Bones* in particular serving as the beginning for another.

Kathryn's wake will actually be more than just an important moment for Orson and his particular problem as a "bastard," for Orson's introduction into the family coincides with the novel's introduction of Peter as a source of healing for that family. Peter acknowledges at one point that there's a "darkness" (18) in his family, and he symbolically overcomes this darkness when he returns to Albany for the funeral and decides even before going home to buy chandeliers for the house and to have electricity installed there for the first time. It is a gesture of defiance against Sarah, who refuses the gift, but more importantly against the just-departed Kathryn, who had been "dark-willed" and who had always considered electricity "diabolical" (90). The Phelan children had for years "rarely brought visitors home, so shamed were they that their house . . . had slowly become a museum of everybody else's rejected past" (90–91). Wanting to put an end to such shame, Peter brings the chandeliers to the house in order "to be done with gloom" (92), both the actual gloom of darkness and the emotional gloom of the home of Kathryn Phelan. Once he gets the boxes holding the lamps inside, Peter lifts up one of the chandeliers from its box with the words, "'Fiat lux'" (92), an appropriate announcement since he is godlike in his casting light on a house that has previously hidden itself in a dark and stagnant past.

As Peter's role as a source of illumination for the family is revealed in these events, so too is the family, and Francis in particular, revealed to be a source of inspiration for Peter. (It is an inspiration that will be repeated in Peter's painting of Malachi and other Phelan ancestors at the end of the novel.) This inspiration derives primarily from what Francis and Peter do during the wake. When Francis runs from the house and Peter follows him to the train tracks, Peter witnesses his brother contemplating suicide but does nothing to try to stop him, a decision that will greatly affect Peter's artistic production. Orson tells us that Francis' stepping back off the tracks and the guilt Peter feels for not trying to stop him lead Peter into a year in which he produces no paintings but in which he nurtures an artistic madness that eventually becomes the energy for paintings about Francis himself, works that Peter calls *The Itinerant* series.[8] These paintings become the first source of real fame and wealth for Peter, but they also confirm the mutual need of Peter for his family and the family for him. As Peter brings light to the Phelans through electricity (and eventually through his Malachi paintings), the family presents itself as a subject that will lead Peter to his long-desired artistic success. Orson says that Peter went to the wake rather than to the simultaneous opening of an exhibition of his own work because "kinship maintained the major share of control over Peter's life" and that Peter's "art, in the end, could only bear witness to this" (86). If Peter feels obligated to kinship, to helping his family, this obligation is returned in his family's unknowingly helping him with his artistic success.

For Peter, then, Kathryn's wake becomes a moment in which his role in the family, and the family's role in his life and work, are first made evident. It is also, as we have seen, the moment in which Orson first truly feels he has found his family. Yet oddly enough none of these discoveries or discovered roles leads to any significant resolution for Peter, Orson, or the Phelan family. Although Peter is proud of "having brought the light to Colonie Street" (105), it is a light that Sarah's own gloomy nature will counter for decades. Sarah will, in fact, literally destroy Peter's light when she unscrews the bulbs and unplugs the lamps in the house during a fit of depression in the 1950s. And Peter's paintings of Francis will also be a brief touch with success, one that fades as Peter loses touch with his own artistic strengths: in the years that follow the reception of *The Itinerant* series, Peter

> foundered badly, dabbling in cityscapes, portraits, and in the new non-figurative, non-representational

abstract mode, whose exercises in symbolic color and form, devoid of the human being, he could admire when done by others, but only loathe as pretentious failures when he created them himself. (233)

Peter forgets that he needs those "human beings" for his own (and worthy) expression, especially the human beings from his own family.

Like Peter, Orson also fails; in his case it's a failure to gain a family officially, to be acknowledged by Peter as a son. After Francis' near-suicide, Orson even says that Peter grew "remote" from him (133), a phenomenon Orson himself does not understand and one that seems peculiar in light of Peter's symbolic step of introducing Orson to his "putative" family in taking him to the wake (3). Kathryn's death seems to be the moment of cure for Orson and for the Phelans—the repressive Kathryn is dead, the house is lighted, Peter discovers a source of artistic success, Orson finds a family—but none of these discoveries endures, and, as *Very Old Bones* eventually reveals, the Phelans fall again into their decline, one that includes as it always has insanity, death, violence, depression, and denial.

The difficulty Orson has in officially finding his place in the world, in dealing with his "bastard" state, and the failure of the wake to affect a conclusive change in his status as an unclaimed son, eventually take their toll on him as he grows into adulthood. Orson reveals that he discovered very early that his past would be an obsession for him when he acknowledges that "bastardy might be an enduring theme" in his life (17), and eventually this obsession takes on serious ramifications for his mental health. While serving in the army in Europe after World War II, Orson falls in love with and marries Giselle Marais and, in order to finance their romance, enters into an illegal international currency scam, an endeavor that results in his arrest. The pressure of the romance with Giselle, whom Orson idolizes, the humiliation of his arrest, and his own mental imbalance ultimately lead to the first of two nervous breakdowns Orson will have in the novel. This first one after his arrest ends with Orson standing up in a German bar taking bites out of himself in order to create the stigmata of Jesus Christ on his body. When he is finally subdued and hospitalized, an army psychiatrist gives a long explanation to Giselle of Orson's problems, which stem in great part, the physician says, from Orson's concern with his uncertain parentage. Orson listens to the psychiatrist's explanations, all of which he admits he readily agrees with. As the psychiatrist says,

> [Orson] believes he is a bastard, an unwanted child. He was seriously neglected by mother and father, though he exudes love for them both. . . . He has found no career direction, and has completed nothing of significance to himself. He left the publishing world, rejects teaching and journalism, loathes the army, and rues the inertia that allowed him to be called back to active duty. He sees nothing worth doing, including completing the last contorted sentence of his unfinished book, which now ends on a high note of suspense with a comma. . . . (72)[9]

The psychiatrist also believes that this obsession Orson has with his bastard status directly affected the way Orson reacted to his recent arrest. According to the psychiatrist, after Orson was abandoned by the man who led him into the currency scam, Orson became "once again the bereft bastard, without parent, without salvation. He is the unredeemable, loathsome, fear-ridden orphan of the storm, living in the shadow of an achieved father, crippled, he thinks, by the genes of unknown ancestors, and now with a future that holds only degradation, possibly of a lifelong order" (73). On top of these problems, Orson has complicated his life even more by falling in love with and marrying the eminently desirable Giselle. She is, as the psychiatrist says, the "goddess of the unattainable moon" for Orson (72), a status which encourages his constant insecurity over how a man such as he can please and keep such a wife.

Orson's problem stems from the fact that he is not certain where he comes from or who his family is, whether that family is the one he might establish with Peter or with Giselle. Orson is, as he describes himself, a "happenstance of history" (136): while Francis and Sarah and Peter and even Molly are prisoners of their fates as Phelans, of the "sin" and denial the family has exercised for decades, Orson is utterly free, "bereft" as an orphan "without parent" and "without salvation." Ghosts from the past haunt Francis on his 1938 walk through Albany, but what haunts Orson is that he does not know his past—he is not certain what ghosts, if any, await him. Orson wants to embrace his past, while Francis tries to escape his.

As it turns out, Orson's insanity, brought on by his bastard state and by his idealized wife, becomes, like the wake itself, a step in his movement into the broader Phelan family (a movement that will also contribute to the healing of the Phelans as a whole). Since Giselle is about to start her career as a magazine photographer at the time of Orson's breakdown, she decides to send him back to New York to live with Peter, thus reuniting father and son, at least to the extent that they live in the same place. After Peter and Orson are together for a few months, Orson tells his "father" that he wants to bring Giselle to live with them. Peter encourages the idea, claiming, half in jest, that he wants to see anybody who would actually marry Orson. Orson describes the friendly banter between the two men, and in doing so provides his interpretation of both his and Peter's growing awareness of their close relationship:

> Peter smiled. I examined the smile to evaluate its meaning. Was it a real smile? It looked like a real

smile. I decided to return it with a smile of my own.
Son?
Dad? (146)

Orson's questions are unspoken and unanswered, but the
asking of them, at least in Orson's mind, signals that he at
least believes that Peter is beginning to see him as the son he
has never claimed Orson to be.

This exchange, in good part a result of Giselle's decision
to move Orson to New York, also signals the beginning of
Giselle's clear yet complex role in Orson's eventual integration into his "adopted" family. Orson later will even claim
that Giselle is "obliquely responsible" (283) for the climactic
healing moment of the reading of Peter's will. As a beautiful
and talented woman (so much so that Peter himself falls in
love with her), Giselle seems to infuse a needed vitality into
the "old" and dying Phelan line. And as the latest member of
the Phelan clan, she sees a family where the family cannot
see one themselves, a role she carries out as a photographer
as much as a wife: not long after she arrives in the United
States from Europe, she takes a picture of Orson and Peter,
"the first photograph ever taken of Peter Phelan and Orson
Purcell together" (149–50). In the picture, Orson says, "it was
later said by some who saw it [that] the two men bear a
family resemblance, though Peter's mustache destroys any
possibility of establishing a definitive visual link" (150). As
the dialogue of "Son?" and "Dad?" is undermined by the
interrogative and the interior monologue, so too is the
possible certainty of the picture undermined by the attri-
bution of the opinion of others ("some who saw it" noted a
resemblance between the two men) and by qualification ("the
mustache destroys any . . . definitive visual link"): nonetheless, both the conversation and the photograph reveal
Orson's obsession with his ancestry and introduce Giselle in
her role in helping to resolve that obsession.

Despite Giselle's good intentions of reuniting Orson with
his father (and coincidentally with his psychiatrist, who

returned to the United States from Europe at the same time
as Orson), Orson's life in New York is little better than what
it had been before. Directionless, Orson remains obsessed
with his status as a bastard, obsessed now too with the often
absent and seemingly unattainable "goddess" who is his wife.
Orson describes these days in New York as one repetitive and
meaningless cycle of drudgery as he works at his editing job
and attempts to write a book of his own:

> For months . . . my life had been repetitive ritual:
> rise from narrow bed, dress in sordid clothing, eat
> meagerly and without relish, go out into the world to
> edit a book you loathe, confront what you now knew
> to be an unpublishable novel of your own making,
> come home in darkness to reinhabit your father's
> bohemian gloom, and write your daily letter to
> Giselle. (165)

Under these depressing conditions, Orson decides not to live
any longer under any "delusions" but simply to wait for the
end of his life and whatever that life might bring along the
way, a step which includes for him the "elimination of the
past" (184). This turning away from the past, he believes,
makes him an "eschatophile," a lover of the end times, of the
future (184). He grows "thrilled" by the "lovely, lovely
darkness" of the end of life (185) and decides to throw out all
of his past and "unmemorize" his own life:

> I would throw out all that I had written, all my letters
> (including those from Giselle; especially those from
> Giselle.) I would throw out all books that did not
> enhance solitude. I would throw out memory. I would
> throw out the memory of Miss Nelson, in whose home
> I roomed when I first went to Albany to live. . . . I
> would also throw out the memories of Quinn [Orson's
> cousin]. . . . And I felt lightened already. It would be
> a pleasant thing to unmemorize my life. It would

prove I was no longer afraid of time. I would sit in my window and watch the garabageman take away the evidence that Orson Purcell had ever existed. (184-85)

The pain of Orson's impossible search for the past leads him to dump his own private past altogether. Thanks to his continuing rejection as a Phelan, he ironically seems to be becoming just like them, practicing their habitual trait of denial.

A few months after Orson moves in with Peter, Giselle finishes her job in Europe and joins her husband in the United States. Orson thus finds himself living with the woman who has been his "goddess of the unattainable moon," a woman whose standards he feels he cannot attain. When the book he is writing is rejected by the publishing house for which he works, Orson, losing control of himself, steals some money and spends an extravagant weekend wining and dining his wife. He then goes off to the old apartment of the bohemian writer (now dead) whose memoirs he is editing, and in solitude he attempts to "unmemorize" his life for good by trying to drink himself to death. His efforts fail, however, as Peter, Giselle, and eventually Molly too rescue him and help him to recuperate. He is taken to the hospital, and then is eventually moved by family members into a cabin near a lake resort in Saratoga owned by longtime friends of the Phelan family. There Orson earns his room and board by working at odd jobs around the property for the older couple who own the house and who can no longer take care of it on their own. This move to Saratoga under the guidance of Molly and Giselle and Peter turns out to be much more than another step in Orson's battle against his insanity, however, for once installed in the cabin Orson begins what will be his healing from both his insanity and his bastardy, and from there he also observes the simultaneous healing of the Phelan family—three crises which will find a final shared means of resolution through Peter and his paintings of Malachi.

As if to emphasize this interconnected healing of Orson and the Phelan family in general, the healing process for both parties begins when Molly and Orson, aunt and nephew, find that they are in love with each other during Orson's stay in Saratoga. This "love" is very much the ro-mantic and erotic kind—after the necrophilia in *Quinn's Book*, one should not be surprised at what happens in a Kennedy novel—though beneath its incestuous overtones lies a purer love also, a sincerely innocent concern for and admiration of the other, and from this sincerity derives the beginning of Orson's recuperation. Orson feels, in fact, that Molly's concern for him while he is sick helps him to "perceive a future" (216), a notably different attitude from Orson's earlier desire to eliminate his past and simply wait for his end to come.

The concomitant changes in Orson and the family, and their mutual and interconnected effect upon each other, are captured in a passage from *Finnegan's Wake* that Orson cites while talking about his recuperative time at the resort: "*But you're changing, acoolsha, you're changing from me, I can feel . . . yes, you're changing, sonhusband, and you're turning, I can feel you, for a daugherterwife from the hills again. . . . I pity your oldself I was used to. Now a younger's there. Try not to part!*" (219, "italics Kennedy"). Orson likewise is changing, moving from the oldself: he is an insecure son and husband now being helped by a lover-aunt. Neither Orson nor Molly ever acts on their love for each other beyond one or two moments of impassioned kissing, but the love itself helps to draw Orson out of his insanity and deeper into the family. "In the year after Molly and I fell in love with each other's failed love," Orson says, referring to their respective troubles with love, "I could at last say without equivocation that I had acquired a family, although a failing one" (223).

That the family is "failing" has been evident for decades,

but Orson is speaking of yet another moment of extreme crisis in the Phelan family, this one centered around the year 1954. It is in June of this year, around the time Orson is healing in Saratoga, that the simple-minded Tommy is brought home by a policeman for his having lifted up the skirt of a woman with his cane. As we mentioned above, Sarah is so incensed by Tommy's actions that she beats him severely, even to the extent of injuring his spine. The results are disastrous. Chick Phelan, infuriated at his sister and fed up with the house, proposes to his longtime girlfriend and moves to Florida. Molly falls into a "melancholy" brought on by her years of loneliness and the decades of the Phelan decadence against which she seems impotent. And Sarah, terrified when she stays behind by herself when Molly and Tommy go to Saratoga, falls into a depression and closets herself in the house. Molly returns later to find the family house "in total darkness at late afternoon, every window barricaded against the light by black drapes Sarah had nailed to the walls. Sarah had also unplugged all lamps, and removed all bulbs from the ceiling fixtures . . . " (223). The depression soon turns into a physical decline, one in which Sarah's "strength and will centered on the downward rush to death" (224) until she dies, as Orson noted above, on the anniversary of her mother's birth. Her death, however, does not end the tragedies of the "failing" family. Peter, aware that someone must help Tommy now, moves back to Albany, but, in the midst of another surge of artistic excess (brought on by his discovery of the Malachi story), he suffers a heart attack. And two years after Sarah dies, Tommy has a fit of pain from his spinal injury while he is at work at the Albany filtration plant, and he falls into the water and drowns.

Could the Phelan decline be worse? Francis has been dead at this point for over a decade. Sarah and Tommy have recently died, the latter from an injury given to him by his own vengeful sister. Chick has fled the house. Molly is depressed. Peter is seriously ill. The man watching them all,

Orson, is an insane bastard—literally. Orson also doubts the fidelity of his wife, Giselle, who must spend most of the time traveling in order to practice her photography, and the primary suspects for the adultery in Orson's mind are even relatives, Orson's cousin Quinn and his own father Peter. And yet even as the long decline of the Phelans seems at last to have reached its last gasp, these Phelans miraculously (the religious metaphor is apt) find a way to recover and renew themselves: as is usual in Kennedy's work, what seems to be the end is really a new beginning. How this new life is achieved in *Very Old Bones* is also a familiar process in Kennedy's works, for it depends on revelations about the Phelan past, revelations that allow some very old bones in the Phelan closet at last to be unearthed. The Phelans, like so many other Albany cycle characters, go back into the past to help heal their present.

The first of these revelations occurs during Sarah's wake when Molly, inspired by the love Orson and she have professed for each other, reveals to him the secret of her stillborn baby and its burial in the Phelan basement. Her love for Orson has already been the means of his further insinuation into the family, and now it is also the means by which one of the Phelan secrets can at last be unearthed. Molly convinces Orson to help her dig up the remains of the baby, and they wrap up the tiny body, almost all dust now, and secretly place it underneath the pillow in Sarah's coffin in order that the baby can be buried in holy ground. The act is a first step in ceasing the denial of family secrets and of reality itself, a denial which has for so long exacerbated the Phelan psychosis. It is also a symbolic step toward reuniting the Phelan family in bringing the disparate ancestors, including father and son, together in the cemetery neighborhoods Francis walked through at the beginning of *Ironweed.* In burying the baby in the holy ground of the cemetery, Molly and Orson are also, in effect, sanctifying the family's past, even the least bit of it, an "unborn" and possibly aborted bastard.

The second of the revelations about Phelan history (after Molly's baby) goes back even farther into the past than the birth and death of Molly's child, and it also affects the Phelan family as a whole, including Orson. This discovery involves the unearthing of information about the events surrounding Malachi McIlhenney, a man whose story might have been forgotten except that Sarah, one of those who knew about it, inadvertently revealed the whereabouts of the story herself. When Molly returned from Saratoga to discover the darkened Colonie Street house and Sarah ill inside, she also found Sarah reading an old newspaper, although no one realizes what the story is that she is reading until Sarah dies and the family finds the newspaper hidden in a crawlspace in her closet. In this and similarly concealed papers, the family discovers what happened in 1887 concerning Malachi, Kathryn Phelan's brother and a forerunner of all the Phelans. Malachi, depressed by his inability to make his way as an Irish immigrant in America, slowly goes crazy, and inspired by a foolhardy neighbor burns his wife to death in thinking that she is a witch and that the devil must be purged from her. His insanity and his act of murder are witnessed by Kathryn while she is pregnant with Peter. (Francis, Sarah, and Charles [Chick] have already been born; Francis, seven years old in 1887, vaguely remembers some of the incidents and commotion.) But after Kathryn only Sarah knows of the incidents in any detail, and for decades she, like her mother, hides the newspapers recounting the story.

Malachi's actions are the beginning of the Phelan decline, both in the genetic insanity Malachi will pass on (even unto Orson) and in the way that this insanity and the ensuing violence is denied—primarily by Kathryn and Sarah —for decades. Orson claims that he has "generalized about cause and effect in this family, but one proximate cause of what made Kathryn, Sarah, Peter, and the rest of us behave in such diverse but consistent ways was chronicled in that newspaper story Molly saw Sarah reading" (231). The discovery of the newspapers, however, begins to change the harmful effects of the very story these papers tell about Malachi. Their removal from the crawlspace parallels the unearthing of the bones of Walter Phelan, Molly's baby, and ends a long period of denial for the Phelan family as a whole.

Peter in particular explicitly counters this denial when he produces the story of Malachi in a series of paintings that he calls the *Malachi Suite*. According to Orson, Peter "saw, in the story of Malachi and Lizzie, and then in the way that Kathryn and Sarah had nursed that story and secretly kept it alive, a pattern that need not have been . . ." (231). To reverse this pattern and cure the shame of insanity and its long denial, Peter returns to those events and brings them forward into the present—in fact, into the eternal present in his art. Orson claims that Peter would never have been able to complete his series of paintings if he had not "projected himself into the lives of the people who had lived and died so absurdly, so tragically, in the days before and after his own birth" (20). In returning to the past—like Francis in *Ironweed*, like Martin Daugherty, like Molly, like Daniel Quinn in 1860's Albany—Peter alters the decades of the denial of that past by revealing it through his art. His themes, as Orson claims, always said, "this is evidence that yesterday did exist; this is what yesterday looked like" (84), assertions far different from the years of denial.

Peter's process of accepting and revealing history is not only different from the denial that the Phelans, including Peter himself, have practiced for decades, but it is also far different from Orson's despairing desire to "unmemorize" his life. Peter Phelan not only uses his own personal memory, but much more, including family memory, history, and artistic imagination. It is through this last procedure, in fact, that Peter metaphorically "sanctifies" the past by converting it from historical possibility into artistic truth, much as Kennedy did in *Legs*, as Kennedy and Quinn himself did in *Quinn's Book*, and as Orson is doing in his memoir which is *Very Old Bones*. Peter's imagination does not distort historical reality but actually makes it "more true," removing it from the contingencies of history and time into something timeless, a picture on a Grecian urn, art in the eternal now. As Orson says of Peter, "he felt that whatever he imagined would somehow reflect what was elusive in the historic reality, elusive because its familiarity and its ubiquity in real space and time would make it invisible to all but the imagining eye" (272). Peter uses his imagination to make visible what has before been ubiquitous but denied, to let people see what has been hidden in the dark of Phelan history. Peter's "imagination," Orson says, is that "which makes the long-dead world, with a fine suddenness, as Keats put it, fly back to us with its joys and its terrors and its wisdom" (20); it is here, in the profundity of joy and terror and wisdom, where lies the truth revealed and then blessed by Peter's art:

> Peter Phelan, obsessive artist of Colonie Street, subsumed in the history of his family, all but smothered under his ancestors' blanket of time, had willfully engaged it all, transformed history into art, being impelled to create, and purely, what Picasso had called "convincing lies"; for Peter believed that these lies would stand as a fierce array of at least partial Phelan truths—not moral truths, but truths of significant motion: the arresting of the natural world at an instant of kinetic and fantastic revelation. (264)

As Walter Phelan was transformed from a nameless corpse in a basement into an accepted Phelan laid to rest in sacred family ground, so is the story of Malachi transformed from a hidden and shameful event in the past into an object defined by its figuratively sacred status as art. *Very Old Bones*, as one review quotes Kennedy as saying, is about "'the power of art to transform life,'"[10] and what the Phelans have after their transformation is truth—not the received truth of religion nor even the absolute truth of historical fact (as Quinn knows is inadequate) but artistic truths, truths of beauty, as Keats might say, and of "fantastic revelation."

The process Peter follows in producing his paintings—the retrieval and sanctification of the past through art—is significant, but so too is the motivation that inspired him to do the paintings in the first place, his growing concern for the Phelan family. The tragedies of 1951-1956 lead Peter "to perceive," as Orson tells us,

> that individuals, families, or societies that willfully suppress their history will face a season of reckoning, one certain to arrive obliquely, in a dark place, and at a hostile hour, with consequences for the innocent as well as for the conspirators. Peter saw this first in my collapse, and then in the rolling boil of divine vengeance visited upon his brothers and sisters in these years. (189)

Peter's realization of the dangers of denial is encouraged by what Orson calls Peter's "unflagging love for his brothers and sisters" as well as his feelings for Orson, "about whom [Peter] had begun to fret in unreasonably paternal ways" (189-90).

In addition to the metaphorical sanctification enacted by Peter's painting of the Malachi story, the paintings also have a real, practical effect—they make Peter wealthy. And in light of the money he is earning from the paintings as well as his failing health, Peter proposes to give this wealth away by fulfilling the terms of his will while he is still alive.[11] His reasoning for such an action indicates his awareness of the suffering the Phelans have endured as a result of the history he has just painted: he is giving his money away, as he writes himself in his will,

because I further believe that out of the collective evil
to which so many members of this family have been
heir, heiress, and victim (the scope of which I have
only in very late years begun to understand), there
can come some collective good, and because one
known form of good is the easing of the financial
woe that periodically besets us all . . . .(262)

To read the terms of this will and formally to reveal his
Malachi paintings, Peter plans a family lunch. It is an unusual event, the performance of an act that usually accompanies death while the "deceased" is not only alive but
present at the reading—a description that conjures up images
of Magdalena's second and staged death in *Quinn's Book*.
The lunch, as Orson says, is about "all the Phelans, and their
ancestors" (252)—and, one should add, their descendants, for
Giselle, now two months pregnant, is also in attendance. The
lunch also includes the embittered Billy Phelan, who "never
wanted anything to do with the house, or its people, after his
father's experience" (251). Orson managed to convince Billy
to attend by showing him Peter's paintings, by thus revealing
to him the Phelan past, the origin of both Billy and,
"putatively," Orson himself. The significance of the effect of
the paintings to change Billy's mind are not lost on Orson:
"That Malachi was still influencing our lives . . . supported
my idea that we are never without the overcoats, however lice-
ridden, of our ancestors" (253).

For years Kathryn and Sarah, and in their own ways
Molly and Francis and Peter too, ignored such overcoats out
of shame of their lice, but now these coats, thanks to Peter's
artwork, are being used to reunite the Phelans. The paintings
(and the will) bring the new (Giselle and her baby), the old
(Molly and Peter), the self-exiled (Billy) and the rejected
(Orson) all together for a celebration of family. Despite
Peter's rejection of "any pragmatic or moralistic element to
art," his paintings, Orson tells us,

already had an effect on the moral history of the
family, and would continue to do so through the
inevitable retellings of the story associated with the
paintings; and these retellings would surely provide
an enduring antidote to the poison Malachi had
injected into the world. (272)

As Gerald T. Cobb writes, Malachi has "bequeathed to his
descendants a host of dysfunctions, including alcohol abuse,
rigid religiosity tending toward superstition and violent
jealousy" (412); Peter, by contrast, has bequeathed through
his paintings a legacy of understanding and generosity, a
means to countering Malachi's own malicious legacy. And
the obvious sign of Peter's success is the lunch itself, what
Orson calls "the provisional healing of a very old split in this
family" (276), a gathering of the Phelan clan. The food served
at the meal itself significantly is lamb, not only a traditional
Irish feast for this Irish family, but also a symbol of the
resurrection.[12]

While the paintings help heal the Phelan family in
general, they also help Orson out in particular. In the stories
about which Peter paints, Orson is able to understand his
own behavior in the mirror of Malachi's insanity, and he at
last can be consoled about his illness. When he thinks about
whether Malachi was "predisposed to disaster," Orson admits
the following: "all I could do was project myself backward
into my own disturbed history, into [my] isolation . . . where
there is no need to engage the actual world because the
private world is always sufficient to the day. Reality conquered by the ego: Malachi's story precisely" (253–54). Thus,
despite Peter's refusal to accept art as didactic, it has served
just such a purpose not only for the Phelans but also for
Orson in particular in his realization of the similar
egomaniacal conditions of himself and Malachi. Orson
admits that the consolation of seeing himself within a
comprehensible history of illness has helped him heal: "I now
like to think that I am coming out of this benighted

condition," Orson says, "and in my own peculiar way am again an engaged citizen of the bright day, working within the race" (254).

Orson has come out of the dark, a "benighted condition," into a world figuratively illuminated by Peter as the Colonie Street house once literally was by Peter himself, and he has come into a "race," a history of a family that Peter has captured on canvas. And Orson can claim himself a member of this race with some confidence now also, for perhaps the most significant result of the paintings and Peter's subsequent will is the adoption of Orson as an official member of the Phelan family. In moving to Albany to help the sickened Peter, Orson had already become not only "the magister of the Phelan house" (223) but also the "putative son" and even, in helping Peter, "father to the putative father" (3): Orson became, in effect, the magister and father of the very family who has not yet adopted him as their latest son. But Peter's act of painting is identified by Orson as "a form of atonement" (275) for Peter's many years of denying his paternity. This atonement, Orson writes, is for the behavior of the men in the Phelan family throughout their history, including Malachi and Peter himself, especially Peter's "own behavior as son, husband, father" (275). As proof of this atonement, Peter includes in his will, in addition to the distribution of his monies, the following bequest: ". . . concerning Orson Michael Purcell, my unacknowledged son by Claire Theresa Purcell, I do now fully and publicly acknowledge him as my true and only son" (263). Thus Peter's lunch allows not only for the healing of the Phelan family in general and for the consolation Orson finds in an insane ancestor, but also the overcoming of Orson's own personal "bastardy," the obsession of his life. Orson finds his place in the family history just as that family comes to accept that history itself; as Orson says at the reading of the will, "If, through the years, I had been slowly imagining myself acquiring this family, then this was its moment of realization, and perhaps the redirection of us all" (275).

As part of his adoption into the family, Orson is also to be the executor of Peter's estate, including all of his artwork. But there's one provision:

> that he legally change his name to Orson Michael Phelan, and that he thereafter remarry, forthwith, his present wife, Giselle Marais Purcell, to insure that her unborn child of this moment . . . will legally bear the Phelan name; and that if this issue be not a male child, that Orson pursue yet again the conception of a male heir with his wife of the instant . . . in order to insure at least the possibility of the Phelan name continuing beyond Orson's own demise. . . . (263)

Orson has, then, not only at last found a father and a name, a history and a place for himself in that history, but he has become the conduit through which the Phelans will reach into the future. By going back in time, back into history before he was even born, Peter was able to resurrect through his imagination the Phelan bones long buried in secrecy; history was thus acknowledged and purified through art, and thanks to that acknowledgment not only could the current state of the Phelan family be celebrated at a lunch but the future of the Phelans, and of Orson himself, could also be, if not guaranteed, at least promised. The Phelans, moribund and doomed since Malachi and through Kathryn and Sarah and on to Billy—their last, worst hope—now can celebrate who they are and have hope for whom they might be in the future.

To signal this new condition of the Phelan family, Giselle once again takes a significant photograph, this time of those assembled to hear the reading of the will. As Orson describes it, ". . . another formal photograph in modern Phelan family history came into existence; my second with my father, Peter's first with Billy and Peg, and so on. The new combinations were quantifiable" (282). There are new and quantifiable combinations because there is a new family. Billy, long estranged from his aunts and uncles, is now a part of the picture, despite his continuing protests, as is the newest Phelan, Orson, and the other people who might assume his name, Giselle and the unborn child. Orson acknowledges the power his wife has had in this important day, a power signaled by herself as the potential source of the new Phelans, when he says that she was "obliquely responsible . . . for this day of reunification, this time of our dawning into unity" (283). As a photographer she will also be responsible for capturing that day in art, much as Orson has captured the whole process leading up to her photograph in the memoir that is *Very Old Bones.*

Although it is not mentioned in these closing scenes in the novel, one would be hard pressed not to think of Kathryn Phelan's wake and its effect on the family, for there too the family was liberated, united, and even enlightened, but to no lasting effect. And indeed, Orson includes a hint of such foreboding when, as soon as he praises Giselle for her role in reuniting the family, he qualifies his praise by adding, "if indeed it was unity, if indeed it was dawning" (283). Later he wonders if Giselle will regret giving up her career as a photographer in order to be a mother and if she might come to "think of her own name . . . as her fate: for [Giselle] means 'hostage'" (285). Orson knows and admits that such "simple conversions" as Giselle Purcell to Giselle Phelan, as professional photographer to mother, "are for minds more simple than hers" (250). And even Orson's final comment illustrates the equivocal nature of the lunchtime celebration: after kissing Molly and Peg and Giselle out of his pleasure at the family lunch, Orson deflects the curious and concerned looks of those he kisses with a smile that lets them know he has not fallen again into insanity. It is a smile, he tells us, that said he was "as sane as any of them" (292); but that is a phrase of consolation which hardly can console, for being as sane as a Phelan is not always being sane at all.

But if Orson's skeptical questions about the likelihood or ease of Giselle changing destroys the euphoria of the family gathering, it also eliminates the possibility that Orson and the others are continuing the long Phelan tradition of denial. Although the pleasure of the family gathering is tinged with realism by Orson's skepticism, his questions and comments reveal a clear understanding of the current situation of the Phelans. Orson reveals his own willingness to embrace this conception of the family when he describes the kind of bones he would construct for his own closet now that he has been accepted as a Phelan, bones that are pulled from the numerous ailing members of his own family as well as the odd assortment of people from his past, such as the criminal he worked with, Meister Geld, and a whore he once slept with: "If I really was a magician," Orson says,

> and could command the spirits the way Malachi thought he could, I'd build a skeleton that would have Lizzie's ribs and fingers, Tommy's chipped backbone, Francis' all-but-gangrenous leg with the bone showing, Billy's broken ankle, Sarah's near-fleshless arms with bones pushing through skin and with tubes dangling, Peter's arthritic hips, Walter Phelan's partial skull, Meister Geld's toe and thumb, the handless armbone that my sugar whore loved to suck, and I'd have the creature dance to the 1911 tune Giselle brought [to the gathering] to lighten things up with music from the past. (291)

Orson has learned well from his new father: the skeletons of the past are to be unearthed and embraced, not hidden in shame. And the skeletons Orson himself wants to have, the ones he imagines, are comprised of the most shameful parts of those from his own history. Orson's lesson seems to be that any family, even one whose members are deformed, is better than no family at all, as he well knows. As Thomas R. Edwards writes, the image of Orson's Frankenstein Phelan "suggests" that "our possible mutuality in sorrow, guilt, and loss, may be what measures the human worth of kinship" (55); and as Orson believes, any kinship, no matter how scarred and mutilated, is better than no kinship at all.

In the end, the reading of the will and Orson's attitude toward it are characterized neither by vain hope nor unnecessary skepticism, for the reunification, reconciliation, and resurrection evident during the gathering should not be read as a significant moment of permanent and blessed change in the linear progression of Phelan history. For Kennedy, the reconciliation of the Phelans on July 26, 1958, is a turn in the wheel of history and their history in particular, part of the cycle of passing events that have been dramatized in the five Albany novels thus far. In Kennedy's work, as Loxley Nichols writes of *O Albany!*, "nothing is ever past, nothing ever ends" (48), a thought Orson echoes in discussing his possible "remarriage" to Giselle: "It seemed facile," Orson says, "to think of the remarriage as a beginning when it was merely a supercharging of an old steam engine that might or might not make it over the next rise" (287). The remarriage is a supercharging, another turn in the wheel, another hill to climb before life goes down and (maybe) back up again, as the lunch itself is a recharging in a Phelan history in which decline is followed by rebirth, illumination by darkness, death by resurrection, then by now, and now even by then. In *Very Old Bones*, the descent of the entire Phelan line was at last stopped through the familiar Kennedy image of an artist embracing and purifying history, but that history is not going to stop happening, and what is a moment of brightness now will. soon be a moment of darkness in the future that will require another hero to look back to illuminate it. In *Very Old Bones*, now falls back into then, Peter into Malachi, Orson into the Phelans, the young Phelans out of the basement and into the graveyard,

the old Phelans out of the crawlspace and into a future that
will one day be their past.

NOTES

1. A helpful genealogy of the Phelans accompanies the text of *Very
Old Bones*.

2. *Legs*, it will be recalled, both dramatized and enacted the
mythicization of the real criminal Jack "Legs" Diamond. In *Quinn's
Book*, Kennedy himself incorporated actual historical events into his
narrative, although he manipulated the nature of those events to suit his
own fictional purposes. This manipulation could be described as
Kennedy's own version of the mythologizing of events from history.
Daniel Quinn within the same novel likewise discovers that the pursuit
of historical truth is futile; what needs to be done instead, he decides, is
the contemplation of the mysterious through the imagination.

3. From an anonymous review in *The New Yorker* (27 April 1992:
106).

4. To appreciate the changes Orson is referring to, it might be
helpful to consider the concluding paragraph of *Billy Phelan's Greatest
Game*, a novel which takes place when Broadway is still alive: "And with
Footers beside him, and Martin trailing with an amused smile, Billy went
out into the early freeze that was just settling on Broadway and made a
right turn into the warmth of the stairs to Louie's pool room, a place
where even serious men sometimes go to seek the meaning of magical
webs, mystical coin, golden birds, and other artifacts of the only cosmos
in town" (282). By the time of *Very Old Bones*, there is no cosmos at all,
and all the magic is gone.

5. *The Flaming Corsage*, it will be remembered, is Edward
Daugherty's play about his affair with Melissa Spencer. It is the play
Martin Daugherty goes to see in *Billy Phelan's Greatest Game* and, of
course, the focus of the last novel of this study.

6. Francis has been gone from Albany since 1916, the year in
which he accidentally killed his son Gerald. His other return, that was
covered in *Ironweed*, occurs four years later in 1938. While returning for
his mother's wake, Francis does not visit his and Annie's home.

7. Francis comes back, but he is not there to mourn: as he says, he
returned never counting "on anything more than seein' she was really
dead. I figure, she's dead, I'm free" (115). His comments confirm what
Peter himself saw in Francis' face when Francis looked at Kathryn's
coffin: "Peter read the look on his face: The bitch is dead . . . lower away"
(100).

8. It is interesting to consider that Francis is also the subject of the

character Edward Daugherty's play, *The Car Barns* (as well as Kennedy's *Ironweed* of course).

9. Such a description sounds quite similar to Martin Daugherty, himself unable to finish his own book and also obsessed with his father; and to Daniel Quinn, specifically when he is in despair after the failure of his own quests.

10. The quote is from an anonymous review, "Very Old Bones," in *Bookman's Weekly* (August 10, 1992), p. 445.

11. It is for this moment that Peter's true power of healing seems preserved, and for which the final healing of the Phelans and of Orson in particular seems to have waited ever since Peter's limited and literal attempt at illumination at Kathryn Phelan's wake in 1934. One is tempted, in fact, to find significance in the puns of the two crucial moments of the narrative: in 1934, the Phelans could only "wake" to their problems and to the possible solutions to those problems, but in 1958, at the assertion of Peter's "will," these solutions could actually and successfully be applied.

12. In addition to celebrating the family in drawing all the members together (except Chick, who decides to stay in Florida), the lunch scene in *Very Old Bones* also seems almost consciously to draw the preceding Albany cycle novels into itself. The conversation at the lunch mentions Legs Diamond (of *Legs*) and Morrie Berman (of *Billy Phelan*); Billy Phelan is of course there at the house, talking about his father (from *Ironweed*); and mention is made too of Daniel Quinn, the son of Peg Phelan (Francis' daughter) and the namesake of the earlier Daniel Quinn (of *Quinn's Book*).

CHAPTER SEVEN

BACK WHERE HE STARTED

*K*ennedy's sixth Albany novel, *The Flaming Corsage*, fills in details about a key moment in the history of the city of Albany (Kennedy's fictional one and the real one) and about the Daugherty family, one of the three main Irish-Catholic families of the Albany cycle. In dramatizing the passionate but doomed marriage of Edward Daugherty and Katrina Taylor, Kennedy helps flesh out characters, such as Edward, who so far have been in the background of other works. Edward, a playwright noted by his son Martin as being "inescapably absent" as a father in *Billy Phelan's Greatest Game*,[1] is here granted center stage. And we see from the eyes of Katrina the seduction of the eighteen-year old Francis Phelan that was such a significant moment to the Phelan family and, in consequence, to the plot of both *Ironweed* and *Very Old Bones*. Through its particular focus, *The Flaming Corsage* expands on the history of the Albany cycle, but it also simultaneously ties that history together more tightly. The intricate web of relationships among the Albany citizens grows more precise as Kennedy turns his attention to these Daughertys and uses their experiences and points of view to clarify what we know about his Albany and its citizens.

While *The Flaming Corsage* may indeed enlarge our

237

understanding of the cast of the Albany cycle, it is, of course, a novel in its own right. Yet it is perhaps the one work in the cycle the appreciation of which is most closely tied to an acquaintance with the other Albany novels. While the two main characters, Edward and Katrina, are finely drawn, they do not present themselves with the same depth and complexity as, say, Francis Phelan or Orson Purcell. And while readers acquainted with the earlier novels will be able to recognize Melissa Spencer and appreciate her significance to the cycle, those unfamiliar with the earlier work may only see a sensual and manipulative but otherwise unimpressive woman. On the one hand this might be a criticism of the novel; but on the other hand it reveals just how intricate and intertwined the Albany cycle has become. Maybe only William Faulkner, in his Yoknapatawpha novels, has had a corpus of work in American fiction which compares with the breadth of the literary project Kennedy is undertaking in the Albany cycle, and even Faulkner's is not as intricately woven and its parts as mutually dependent as Kennedy's.

As one might imagine, this attention to familiar Albany characters in *The Flaming Corsage* is not the only way that the book fits into Kennedy's cycle. The novel, like several of its predecessors, uses in its narrative the interweaving of various moments in time, enacting that common phenomenon in Kennedy's fiction of the interplay of then and now. The opening scene, which takes place on October 17, 1908, dramatizes one of two key moments in the story—the attack of a jealous husband on his wife and Edward Daugherty—but then it quickly switches back in the next chapter to September 1885 where we see Edward as a young man spending time with his friend and ultimate nemesis Thomas Maginn. The novel proceeds through the events of 1885 for several chapters, jumps for a few pages to October 16, 1908, and then jumps back to 1894 to when Edward and Katrina are married. From there it goes from 1895 to 1903 to 1910, back to 1906, then on to 1907, 1910 and, eventually, to 1912.

Most of the chapters are provided with the dates of the action described in those sections, but many of the closing chapters are not, and this gives them an air of being outside of time altogether, a status similar to many other scenes throughout the cycle, most notably in *Ironweed*. And, in fact, many of these final chapters *are* "outside" of time, for they include transcriptions of police reports and passages from some of Edward's plays. Kennedy has before in *Very Old Bones* alluded to the Keatsian notion of the eternal nature of the work of art, the truth of beauty in the Grecian urn, and certain works in *The Flaming Corsage* are at times explicitly removed from the chronology of the other chapters of the book by Kennedy's not labeling those works with dates (though of course not all of the works, such as the police report, can be categorized as art).

In addition to providing an example of Kennedy's appreciation of the eternal or at least atemporal nature of art, the plays detailed in the novel, those dramas written by Edward, embody and also depict a prime concern of Edward Daugherty's artistic passion, the use of art to make sense of history, whether that history be personal or public. This challenge to understand history is one we have seen before in various forms—Daniel Quinn attempting to shake off the death of the Civil War, for example, or Orson Purcell writing a memoir to help him understand his "bastard" state. In *The Flaming Corsage*, the challenge which Edward Daugherty takes on is not as abstract or as extensive as Quinn's (whose challenge concerned understanding history itself) nor is it focused so exclusively on the personal as Orson Purcell's. Daugherty is instead hoping to use his art in order to understand and elevate the Irish and the Irish heritage from which he comes and, eventually, to understand his own role as a member of that heritage. Kennedy's Albany cycle has primarily been about Irish-Catholic characters of that town, and it has almost always been about these characters struggling with and through their past; but in *The Flaming Corsage*,

Kennedy is explicitly concerned with the "Irishness" of these Irish as he depicts Edward Daugherty working to understand and honor his own "Irish" past as well as the past of the Albany Irish in general.

Daugherty's concerns with understanding his city and his culture are an artistic mission, a desire to wed his aesthetic passion to his tribal concerns. But he also hopes with his art to raise not only the Irish but himself as an Albany Irishman "out of the ghetto." The son of an activist laborer, Daugherty is well aware of the suffering of the Irish worker in Albany and highly conscious of the class distinctions between the aristocratic (and Protestant) barons who founded Albany and the mostly Irish laborers who worked for these barons and in the construction of the adjacent canal. Daugherty is especially conscious of these distinctions because of his romantic interest in Katrina Taylor, the daughter of Jacob Taylor, a man who is not only a leader among the Protestant business aristocracy but who also is the industrialist whose "goons" beat up Edward's labor-activist uncle, thus rendering the man competent only to "shovel sawdust" (26). Jacob disapproves of his daughter's marriage to this "mick," as Edward's friend refers to him, and Edward hopes to fashion for himself a life as a writer which will not only prove the value of his art but which will also lead to the elevation of his own socio-economic status. "[Katrina and I will] move onto the grand stage," he says at one point to Katrina's parents, and "I'll prosper formidably and achieve heights no lawyer or doctor who might court Katrina could ever know . . ." (37). Thus in raising up the historical image of the Irish, Daugherty hopes to raise himself up too. He wants not only to go back "then" and honor the history of his people, but he simultaneously hopes to escape the dishonor which they have received for centuries.

Like other Albany heroes—Francis, Molly, and Peter Phelan; Orson Purcell and Martin Daugherty—Edward will attempt to embrace history in order to effect some change in the present. But despite Edward's being as conscious of the power and significance of that history as any other character in the Albany cycle, we will see that such knowledge does not, ironically, ensure the redemption or resurrection which characterizes so many of the Albany novels. Edward acknowledges the role of history but underestimates its power, one that even art, a vehicle for so much transformation in Kennedy's work, cannot master in *The Flaming Corsage*.

Edward's initial attempt at using and himself overcoming the history of his people—namely the working-class Albany Irish—appears in the form of his first novel, *The Mosquito Lovers*. The title refers to the Irish convicts, the "expendable martyrs" (5), who worked on the construction of the Erie Canal and who had to endure such hardships as the infestation of mosquitos and the threat of malaria these insects represented. Despite the publication of this novel in 1885, when Edward is 26 years old, Edward himself does not yet feel that an artistic voice has been given to his people. As he waits one day in the study of Katrina's parents, planning to confront them about his plans for marriage, he looks at all the English history books and their "confirmation of ancestry" (31), the ancestry which represents oppression over the Irish. The books "weigh" on Edward, and he muses to himself: "But where are the books of *my* lineage, *my* ancient history? My history has not yet been written" (31).[2]

While waiting in the Taylors' library, Edward goes to the shelves and identifies books on Albany's Dutch history, works by the Founding Fathers of the United States, and classics by such British writers as Shakespeare, Dickens, and Thackeray. But he finds mention of the Irish, despite their significant role in the history of Albany, only as deserving subjects of English oppression. Edward reads in one book, for example, of how Cromwell understood that the Irish "'respect a master hand, though it be a hard and cruel one'" (31), and how the Irish are "abominable, false, cunning and perfidious people"

(32). The attitude of Cromwell is exemplary of the attitude of the book Edward is browsing through—and, by extension, of the Taylors—toward the Irish.

Edward is "weighted" with the vicious racism of such history, and also by the silence of his own people's history, his own novel notwithstanding. Edward's hope is to confront and correct that history, but it is more than an abstract aesthetic challenge to which he must rise. He is in the Taylor's study to persuade them of his worthiness not as an artist so much as a son-in-law, and so while the attitudes of the British history he is reading are a scandal and shame, it is also, he realizes, the kind of history into which he is marrying. "Here you are, Edward," he says to himself, "seeking the hand of a woman bred of Cromwellian dust, you, whose father, by memory passed on, traces your lineage back to Connacht then and now" (32). Kennedy's earlier novels all operated on the notion that the past may be past but it is not over; it continues to haunt and to shape the present moment. Here too in *The Flaming Corsage* Edward Daugherty sees the past taking shape in the present: he recognizes that his lineage is "Connacht then and now." And if that past is alive now, then so too are the vestiges of its shame and anger and hate, its racism and its violence and its desire for revenge. And yet he stands amid these vestiges and artifacts to begin his search for love and for redemption for himself and the Irish of Albany.

While waiting for the Taylors, Edward considers in particular his own past and how his family was kicked off their Donegal land and sent to suffer in the rocky terrain of Connacht. He then reviews in his mind all the hardships—the homelessness and starvation, the dying and suffering—of the Irish people, calling the generations that follow from this suffering the "rock's foetus" (33) because they survived off of the rocky soil that was their only hope for sustenance. Edward describes this foetus, these Irish, as a "doomed creature mutilated in the womb" with "neither tongue, nor brain, nor soul," and then follows their struggles in his mind through famine and into "modern exile on Connacht Block in Albany" (33) and finally into the North End where his family now lives.

At this point Edward's imagination certainly seems capable of picturing the horrors of history, one of the challenges of his artistic mission, but it is not yet clear how capable he will be at raising up that history through his art or of raising himself up into a family which symbolizes the worst of that history. Edward himself considers that his own history has now led him to "heights where you can court the modern get of an ancient devil"—namely, Katrina—but then he scolds himself, claiming that he is "demonizing" Katrina in order "to make her the equal of what her parents think" he is (34). In using such thinking, Edward is not, in other words, raising himself up, but lowering Katrina.

If such demonization is a sign of the difficulties Edward will face in his marriage and career, he is at the moment of his talk with the Taylors still confident enough to pursue his dreams—artistic, social, and romantic. As he says to the Taylors, "I have talent and I have energy and both will last me a lifetime" (37). Some of Edward's confidence, misplaced as it will prove to be, derives from his sense of already having overcome his ghetto Irish background and made his initial forays into the other side. He is about to publish his novel, an affirmation of his artistic talent, and he has advanced in his romance enough so that the obstacle to his love is not Katrina but her parents and the lineage from which she comes. But Edward's confidence in his ability to transcend his place and time and the condition of his race[3] derives ironically from help he received from an annuity payed to him by the industrialist Lyman Fitzgibbon, Geraldine Taylor's father and thus Katrina's grandfather. This annuity, a gift Lyman gave to the Daughertys after Emmett saved Lyman from a lynch mob in 1840, is funding Edward's life and career until he turns thirty; in other words, Edward has effectively been given the life of the "other side of the tracks" without ever having to work his way through that transcendence. "It was Lyman's duty as an unmurdered man," Kennedy explains, "to see that Edward escaped what fate had ordained at birth for his kind" (34). And it works: "Edward *was* transformed," Kennedy writes, and the greatest evidence of this was that Edward not only published his novel but also became confident enough to walk into the study of an enemy of his race and ask for the hand of this man's daughter's in marriage. But it remains to be seen whether that transformation was complete enough, and legitimate enough, to withstand the challenges that Edward is setting for himself—artistically, socially, and romantically.

Edward's confidence in his power is revealed in the ploy he uses to try to convince the Taylors of his worthiness. Instead of ignoring or forgiving the history which separates him from them, he raises it up and challenges them to see both him and themselves for who they are. When Katrina's parents arrive in the drawing room in which Edward waits, he spends most of his speech to them explaining how history does not matter, but he does so ironically, namely by outlining the horrors of their shared history, the great burden it represents, and the great shame it must be to the Taylors themselves. Edward refers to the "Dublin slums" and the "stony field of Connacht" and to the Taylors' ancestors, the "avaricious land barons" and those who "grew rich off the slave trade" (36). He goes on then to praise with tongue in cheek how the Taylors have managed to overcome their own sad past. He points to the books Geraldine and Jacob keep in the study, those texts Edward has just skimmed through, and claims that the presence of these books on the shelves is "clear proof the past is behind us, that we're in a new world with a new light on our own days" (37). He admires the Taylors for having the "strength and courage to keep . . . the record of those unspeakable crimes" (37). And yet, despite this ironic acknowledgment of the causes of the division between himself and his potential in-laws—an irony certainly lost on the Taylors—Edward argues that he and Katrina will "transcend whatever society tried to do to us" (37). Edward is well aware of how history has separated him and his people from his future in-laws, but he is also confident enough—and enough of a true Kennedy protagonist—to embrace that history and attempt to use it to shape himself anew in the present.

Edward calls his speech to the Taylors his "Manifesto of Love and History" (37), a title evoking Daniel Quinn's quests as he pursued his interest in history through the Civil War and his desire for love in the person of Maud Fallon. The tragedies that will affect Edward's life in the future prove how naive he is in issuing his manifesto, but the obstacles which Edward faces, and which betray his naiveté, are not offered by the Taylors and their heritage alone, for Edward also faces disapproval from his own people, most notably from his father, Emmett Daugherty. It was Emmett's brother who was beaten by Jake Taylor's "goons," thus revealing that the historical conflicts of which Edward speaks are not history only. Eventually Emmett will come to appreciate his son's choice of a wife, but prior to the marriage he refuses to speak with her. He does not want to accept his daughter-in-law as the Taylors themselves do not want to accept Edward.

In arguing with his father about his marriage, Edward puts forth again both his consciousness of the history from which he comes and his understanding of how he sees his art affecting that history. "Do the wars of the father have to be the wars of the son?" he asks (52), and then he defends his own solidarity with the Irish by pointing to his writing of *The Mosquito Lovers* as a condemnation of how his people have been treated. Edward claims that, unlike his activist father, he is not a "soldier in the class war," though he amends that by saying he wants to advance—and have his fellow Irish advance—by their brains rather than their backs (or fists):

"Where are the minds of *our* people?" he asks Emmett. "Why aren't we running the foundries and lumber mills . . . ?" (52).

Edward sees his father's labor radicalism as an unnecessary extension of age-old rivalries. "I want to get beyond [radicalism]," Edward says. "I want to leap over the past and live in a world where people aren't always at each other's throats" (52), a wish which might actually reveal the source of Edward's naiveté. As Kennedy has shown repeatedly in his books, no one "leaps" over the past: it is a terrain which one must cross on foot. Edward, however, claims that he's not losing or abandoning his past in his leap. He sees himself as a "new being" (52) and asks in his defense, "Do I lose my past by shaping a future? Do I disinherit myself?" (52).

These are significant questions—especially in the Albany cycle—and not only because Edward is trying to gain his father's blessing on his marriage. *Does* Edward disinherit himself? Obviously he cannot, as no one can, especially in Kennedy's universe. But what Edward fails to address here is how much his inheritance—and Katrina's too—will affect him. He may not lose his past by shaping a future, but how much does that past shape the future for him? How much does he underestimate the power of history, the very phenomenon he claims to address and use in his art? Edward himself acknowledges that his own identity—the self he is inheriting—is a mystery to him. In mentioning how his father raised him but Lyman Fitzgibbon educated him, Edward admits that he is "some kind of new being with no known habitat" (51). It is a lack of understanding, of place, and of history which will prove fatal, not to him but to his dreams, both artistic and personal, and to his wife. While Edward defiantly believes that he can embrace and yet overcome his and Katrina's troubled past, he is unprepared for the troubled future that past will bring.

* * *

Edward's dream of becoming a representative upper-class Irishman—and in the process of honoring and helping his fellow tribesmen—is made manifest in his own personal dream of marrying Katrina. he marriage represents (and also offers) for Edward his own personal ascent into social, economic, and professional respectability. And as we saw above, it is also living proof of Edward's own artistic vision, one which believes the Irish can indeed raise themselves up from their own painful history. But the marriage is more than a pragmatic or aesthetic affair, for the union of Katrina and Edward is also a passionate one, though this passion is itself of an uncertain nature. Both Edward and Katrina seem hesitant or unwilling to try to understand the nearly inexplicable passion which draws them together. Edward considers Katrina "perfection" (12), and when he acknowledges that this is foolhardy, he says in response that he doesn't want to attempt to find flaws in her: "To what end?" he asks. "Is it so wrong to embrace perfection? Am I a dunce to believe in it?" Katrina herself, in talking to her chambermaid, scoffs when the maid wonders if Katrina is "sick in love" with Edward. "'I'm sick because my body seems to want this marvelous man,'" she says. "'I would never call it love'" (40).

The odd and unexamined passion of these two mismatched lovers leads them to a secretive meeting in a cemetery, a place which might itself be considered odd were we not so familiar with the role of the dead in the life of Kennedy's Albany heroes and heroines. Katrina considers the cemetery "the most beautiful place" she knows (42), and it is here that she surprises Edward by seducing him into sexual intercourse. The whole seduction, however, has an air about it of a test, not only of Edward but of Katrina's own feelings. Katrina told her maid that she knew the difference between soul and body (40), a distinction which can only make one question the nature of Katrina's love for Edward, a love that seems primarily predicated on the yearnings of the flesh and not on the love of the entire person. When she and Edward are finally together in secret, Edward wonders aloud if he might at last hear a long-awaited answer to his proposal for marriage. Instead of saying yes or no, Katrina instructs him to come close to her: "'I want to know how I'll react,'" she says (45). Edward and Katrina study each other's faces for a moment, and then she kisses him and concludes that she likes it. After they kiss some more, she says, "'It's clear that we now have to do the rest,'" (46) as if "the rest" is the next step now that the first one has met with her approval. Edward is perplexed by Katrina's desire for sex and tells her that he loves her even more, but Katrina's response reveals her own sense of uncertainty: "'I sense the ecstasy I've heard about,'" she says to him. "'I want to be certain it exists'" (46). And when Edward calls her a "wonder," she responds, "'You're all the world to me now, Edward. But I must confirm that you are truly real'" (46). Katrina seems to be using her body to discover what she cannot find in her own mind or soul—the ecstasy of love, the reality of her lover. It is a passion to match Edward's own artistic one, but, like Edward's own desires, it is fraught with dangers from the beginning: her own uncertainty matches Edward's naiveté.

Katrina and Edward eventually do marry, though neither of the couple's parents bestows their blessing on the event. Katrina herself is not without reservations over her decision. Not only does she need sex to help her discern what she wants, but she is also well aware of what she is giving up in marrying Edward. Even before she decides to join him at the cemetery, she wanders around her house and notes family heirlooms—a Bonaparte candelabra, an Ismari vase, a Peale portrait—as well as pictures of her ancestors. She is recognizing her own history, that past from which Edward is taking her, both her personal family history and the greater public one of her wealthy, aristocratic ancestors. "I see a proud elevation of spirit and mind in the splendid people of my life," she says. "I will lose my birthright to these things if I marry Edward" (39). These are the same "people," it will be remembered, whom Edward identified as the avaricious land barons and slave-trading capitalists who made his own people suffer.

Several years into their marriage, Edward comes to realize the regret Katrina has in abandoning her own familiar history. In an attempt to compensate her for her loss, Edward builds a house for Katrina that was a "scaled-down replica of the Taylors' Gothic Revival town house" (68). To "assuage" Katrina's "loss of the resplendencies she had left behind" in marrying him, Edward refurnishes their house, according to Kennedy, in the "halcyon Elk Street image—crystal, engravings, chairs, fabrics, lamps—all in the Taylor mode, so that [Katrina] might simulate her past whenever her fits of neurasthenic nostalgia descended" (68). Such rebuilding and remodeling is hardly the leaping over the past Edward claimed to be able to do, though it is a practice reminiscent of other Kennedy characters—such as Sarah Phelan—who also strove to reject the present and live in their past.

The need Edward feels to pretend with Katrina that she is still living in her past signals the challenges that he and his wife face as they attempt to fulfill Edward's pronouncements as articulated in his Manifesto of Love and History. But the "History" here is ironically one of the challenges to that "Love," as are, again ironically, Edward's and Katrina's respective aesthetic and erotic passions. Although Edward offered his artistic talent and energy to the Taylors as the means by which he would raise himself up and bridge the differences between his background and theirs, that passion soon begins to threaten the marriage itself. Edward identifies one source of the difficulty he and Katrina begin to have in their relationship as Katrina's anger at the fact that his talents lured her away from her own past. By the eighth year of her marriage, Kennedy writes, Katrina lapsed into "prolonged silences," "vacant stares," and "listless, infrequent sex" (68), and the culprit for this, Edward believes, is Katrina's bitterness toward him for "luring her away from her maidenly joys with his eloquent tongue, his hot love" (68). Seduced by Edward's talent and energy, Katrina now finds herself removed from her personal history of luxury and from her own family, and she holds the loss against her husband.

While Katrina's bitterness is what Edward eventually identifies as the problem in his marriage, he also admits to another, more obvious problem, and that has to do with the ill will engendered by his writing of a play, *The Baron of Ten Broek Street*, a work described as a "satiric social comedy about a wealthy lumber baron (very like Jacob Taylor)" (66). It has to be said that the play was not written only as an act of vengeance against his father-in-law or as a statement of Edward's own socio-political biases as the child of working-class Irish. The play was, Edward admits, an attempt to "balance his bias" (66), for Edward's earlier play, *The Stolen Cushion*, had, in fact, satirized the Irish bourgeoisie. Both plays reveal Edward's attention to the history out of which he comes and his hope that his art can use that history to overcome the injustices of the past and offer reconciliation and improvement to those in the present. He says of *The Stolen Cushion*, for example, that he hoped "to raise the Irish to the intellectual level of nativist Americans, prove the educability of greenhorn multitudes, as he had proven his own, and show those same multitudes how to transcend the peasant caste into which they'd been born" (66-67).

While these lofty—and admittedly arrogant—goals may have been Edward's motivation, they were not the result of his work. *Cushion* angered the Irish of the city, including Edward's own father, and *The Baron of Ten Broeck Street* angered Katrina and the entire Taylor family. In light of the reception of *Cushion* and *Baron*, and in light of the troubled marriage he lives in after almost a decade, Edward decides to try to rectify the troubles he has caused, and he begins by focusing specifically on his marriage to Katrina. The most important step in this process comes when he announces to the Taylors that he is withdrawing *Baron* from production. Such a decision is, he admits, a "capitulation," but one he feels he must do or else his "marriage would bleed to death from Katrina's imagined wounds" (68). It was those very wounds which led him to build the fake-Taylor house for her, and now he has pulled back on his own artistic mission, "all for the venal streak at the bottom of [Jacob Taylor's] elegant heart" (68).

While withdrawing *The Baron of Ten Broek Street* is a conscious stroke designed to help heal the divisions with his in-laws and in his marriage, Edward also admits that he has tired of the political nature of his plays and is turning to more personal concerns. "Changing the world is elevating work," Kennedy writes of Edward's own thinking, "but better if he could dramatize the mind of Katrina" (67). As Edward will find out, such dramatization is a challenge as difficult as the one he faced in writing his social commentaries. And ironically, these difficulties are exacerbated by unfortunate events which occur at the very moment that Edward is attempting to reconcile with the Taylors and to stave off the dissolution of his marriage.

These events center around a hotel fire, one that is based on an actual historical event, the fire at the Delavan Hotel in Albany in 1894 in which fifteen people died, mostly hotel employees stuck in their rooms because of blocked emergency exits.[4] Kennedy has taken this significant historic event and placed it as a crucial moment not only in the plot of *The Flaming Corsage*—it provides the novel with its name—but, in turn, in the lives of many of his fictional Albany citizens from other novels. The fire and its aftermath, in affecting the lives of Katrina and Edward so profoundly, also affect characters we have seen before in other works. Francis Phelan's seduction by Katrina and Martin Daugherty's alienation from his father—integral parts each of several of the Albany novels—can be traced in part to the tragedy at the Delavan Hotel.

That the fire affects the Daughertys and Taylors at all results from Edward's decision to assemble his in-laws at the Delavan Hotel for Christmas dinner in 1894 in order to announce that he is withdrawing *The Baron of Ten Broeck Street* from production. Edward announces to Katrina that the whole evening is intended to get the Taylors, and Jacob in particular, to "reverse" his "loathing" of Edward (63). In his attempt to achieve this goal, in addition to announcing he is withdrawing his play, Edward also presents Geraldine Taylor, Katrina's mother, with a fur coat and Jacob with a racing horse, ostentatious Christmas gifts which are an attempt, in effect, to bribe his in-laws away from their disdain for him.

In the middle of what becomes an awkward, hesitant attempt at familial reconciliation, the maitre'd of the hotel announces that there is a fire in the building. The diners, all eating in an upstairs restaurant, rush for the elevator and staircases. Katrina's sister Adelaide first leaves with Edward and the others and then returns to get the fur coat her mother had left behind; Adelaide's husband, Archie, runs back to get her. In the chaos and panic, Edward pushes Geraldine into the elevator, effectively helping her escape with her life, and he carries the wheezing Jacob to safety along with a stricken woman. As they are all about to exit the building, an explosion in the elevator shaft sends a flaming stick through Katrina's corsage and into her chest. Edward puts out the "flaming corsage" and pulls out the burning stick.[5] Once outside, Edward realizes that the eruption from the elevator shaft has pinned Adelaide and her husband on the roof of the hotel. In a dramatic rescue witnessed by Edward and the Taylors from outside, both Adelaide and Archie are able to escape from the burning roof, though

Archie is helped down by firemen while Adelaide panics and jumps onto the ground.

Although it would seem from these events that Edward should be considered a hero and that the Taylors and Daughertys are blessed to have escaped, the weeks following the fire reveal its true significance and its tragic implications for Edward. Geraldine catches pneumonia from her standing in the cold after the fire, though she will survive the attack. Cora McNally, Katrina's old housemaid and confidante, dies in the fire, as does Cora's sister. And while Adelaide walked away from her leap from the building, an undiagnosed ruptured spleen leads to her death a week later. Two months after that, in the "unbanishable melancholia that followed the death of his daughter," Jacob Taylor himself dies of a heart attack (81).

The fire and its aftermath have two specific consequences for Edward and his marriage. The first is the blame Katrina places on Edward for what happened to her family. Although the fire was a freakish event unconnected to anything Edward did, and although he rescued or tried to rescue many members of the family, Katrina's thinking about how events might have been different ends up with her blaming Edward. After Adelaide's death, Katrina reflects on what she might have done to "divert the course" of her life: "by not letting Adelaide run away from them at the fire, by not siding with her parents against Edward, by not yielding to Edward's plan to win back their goodwill with his dinner and gifts. By not marrying him" (79). Eventually Katrina will go even further than wondering if she should even have married him. After Jacob dies, Katrina "came to believe what her mother had said first: Edward killed Adelaide and Jacob" (81).

In addition to Edward's being blamed for the death of Katrina's sister and father, the second ramification of the fire is Katrina's slipping into a quiet but sustained melancholia bordering on insanity. This instability manifests itself in a lifelong obsession with death itself. Immediately after the tragedy, Katrina begins a vigil at the sight of the fire, watching as workers sift through the debris for the bodies of the dead. She is there, she says, to "'bury the dead,'" as if those who had died, including Cora McNally, were her responsibility as their guardian (77). After the bodies of Cora and her sister are uncovered, Katrina offers to pay for their burial. When people are curious about why this stranger is being so generous, Katrina says enigmatically, "'We can't help whom it is we love,'" before adding, "'We must learn to avoid love. Love is a mask of death, you know'" (80). The people around her do not know, for they do not understand her. Still she goes on: "'Death is venerable. You can always count on death'" (80).

Edward soon appears to take the distraught, irrational Katrina away, though he is perhaps the one person not surprised by what is happening to her. As he says to her, "I know how you love death, how you need it" (80). It was in a cemetery, after all, the most beautiful place Katrina knew, where she decided to discover and simultaneously consummate her feelings for Edward. As she strolled through the cemetery with Edward on the day they met and had sex there, she was, in fact, comforted by the sight of all the graves of famous Albany ancestors. It was, as Kennedy writes, the "gilded world of the familiar dead, a world into which [Katrina] had been born and raised" (45). Death is described as a consolation, a comfort to Katrina, but it has also been an inspiration for her. At Edward's curiosity about why she chose to consummate her relationship with him in a cemetery, she considers a beautiful sculpture of the Angel of the Sepulcher and recalls the New Testament story concerning the discovery of the empty tomb of Jesus. When the tomb is discovered, the Angel asks of the women there, "'Why seek ye the living among the dead?'" (46). It is a question to parallel Edward's own: Why, Katrina, do you seek answers to your life among these graves of the dead? Kennedy explains Katrina's imagined answer to the Angel:

[Katrina's] answer came that, in her, there had taken
root the truths of her poet [i.e., Baudelaire]: that
death is the divine elixir that gives us the heart to
follow the endless night, that is the mystical attic, the
poor man's purse, the mocker of kings, the accursed's
balm, the certain loss that vitalizes possession. She
feared [death] not at all, and chose to behave as if
each moment were the ultimate one; and this
consistency, to the end of her days, would astonish all
who knew her. (46–47)

And it would be the fire at the Delavan Hotel above all else
that would allow Katrina and her obsession with death to be
so astonishing.

The extent of Katrina's instability will become evident in
a concrete way in her very house, the one Edward had constructed so that Katrina could live in a miniaturized version
of her familial past. Even twelve years after the fire, the main
sitting room of the Daugherty house reflects "Katrina's
devotion to the revered dead" (115). Portraits of Geraldine
(now deceased), Jacob, and Adelaide hang on the wall, as
does one of Baudelaire, Katrina's favorite poet. On a table is
a bust of Persephone, the goddess of the underworld. A
pendulum clock is hung on the wall and permanently kept at
8:53, the moment when the flaming stick pierced Katrina's
chest and ignited her corsage. The room, Kennedy writes, is
a "chamber of venerated memory," a "sumptuous crypt of
exhausted life" (115). It not only honors the dead but, in fact,
includes them, for the room is a "tomb" for the "Katrina-that-
was" (115). Like Francis Phelan before her, Katrina has
become one of the living dead. So obsessed has she been with
the past and with the notion of death that she has now
ceased to live effectively in the present. History (or at least
her personal history), the very artistic obsession of her
husband, has itself become her tomb. Even her choice of
maids reflects this imprisonment: Loretta McNally, the
younger sister of the maid who died in the Delavan fire,

eventually serves the Daughertys as Cora McNally had once served the Taylors.

Katrina's instability of course has ramifications for the stability of her marriage to Edward. As the decoration of her house makes clear, Katrina sees the fire as the transformative moment in her life. A passage in her diary reveals the results of this transformation for her and Edward:

> We were united through the fire in freakish fusion, like Siamese twins with a common heart that damned us both to an intimacy that not only knew the other's every breath, but knew the difference between that every-breath and the signal breath that precedes decision, or unbearable memory, or sudden death. We now live out an everlastingly mutual curse: "May the breath of your enemy be your own." (81)

What was supposed to have been the evening of Edward's transforming his marriage into the blissful pairing he had once imagined it would be has turned into the exact opposite: Edward and Katrina have gained a new intimacy, but one energized by a disdain so great that they have become each other's own worst and inescapable enemy. It is an ironic rejoinder to a conversation of theirs in the cemetery. After they had sex and professed their passion for each other—they seem loath to use the word "love"—Edward exclaimed, "'Only death will undo us'" (47). It does indeed, though in ways they had not expected: not their deaths, but the deaths of others, and the very notion of death itself, have turned their dream of love into a nightmare of disdain and disgust.

Despite the despair which settles over their once-passionate union, Katrina and Edward continue to live together as husband and wife, and Edward continues to pursue his career as a playwright. The failure of the couple to attain the passion for each other about which they had once dreamed, however, leads to the events surrounding the second key moment in the novel—and the second event which is, after the Delavan fire, significant for the Albany cycle as a whole. This event, known as the Love Nest killings, was alluded to in part in *Billy Phelan's Greatest Game*, and the story of these killings also includes the affair between Edward Daugherty and Melissa Spencer which is so important to that earlier book. *The Flaming Corsage* not only expands on what we know about the affair from *Billy Phelan*, but it also reveals that the scandal was as much an effect of the unhappy marriage of Edward and Katrina as it was a cause of that unhappiness.

The structure of *The Flaming Corsage* makes it difficult to say too closely exactly what happened during the Love Nest scandal itself. The information is not provided in chronological order, and, while some events are dramatized, most are retold (and only in part) through dialogue or narration by individuals whom one cannot trust to be telling the truth. Newspaper clippings and police depositions, themselves not completely trustworthy, are also used, and we also learn some information—or at least get a perception on events—from some of Edward's own dramatic writings. But as these writings are fictionalized dramatizations, it is never clear as we read them how much liberty Edward has taken with the actual facts.

The Love Nest story itself—or what we know of it—is long and complicated, though one could trace its beginnings to a brawl on a barge on June 17, 1906. The brawl involves an inveterate criminal named Cully Watson. Some time after the brawl, Edward and his and Katrina's friend, Dr. Giles Fitzroy, testify against Watson for his participation in the fight. A few weeks later, Giles, Edward, and several other men play a practical joke on Edward's longtime nemesis, Thomas Maginn. While Maginn and Edward started off together as aspiring writers, Maginn's failures, and his jealousy over Edward's success as a writer and over his marriage to Katrina, have fatally soured the relationship. The joke Edward and his friends play involves tricking Maginn into thinking a relative of Giles is attracted to him. When Maginn goes to the house to visit this woman with Giles and another man named Cadden, a "husband" comes out in anger and fires a gun, and Cadden in turn pretends to be shot. Maginn is terrified that the angry husband will recognize him and hunt him down, so Edward and Giles tell him he needs to have an alibi, and they propose that Maginn get into bed and pretend to be sick. The bed, however, is stuffed with ten pounds of gingersnaps crushed in chicken fat, and the naked Maginn climbs in and suffers the humiliation of immersing himself in the mess. The joke falls flat, however, leaving everyone involved bitter and embarrassed. Maginn and Edward continue to be acquaintances, but it is a relationship much like Edward's marriage, one of twins who despise each other.

A little over two years later, in the climax of the Love Nest Scandal, Giles Fitzroy walks into a hotel room in Manhattan and finds his wife Felicity standing in the room with Edward and Melissa. He shoots and kills Felicity, injures Edward, and then fatally shoots himself. This scene is central to the events of *The Flaming Corsage* and, by consequence, to the Albany cycle as a whole, taking its place alongside such events as the Delavan fire and Francis' dropping of Gerald as formative moments in the lives of some of the Albany citizens. The centrality of the moment is emphasized by Kennedy opening the book with the shooting and then going back in time to discover all the events that led up to that fatal moment.

Despite the significance of the scene in the book and in the Albany cycle as a whole, however, it is never quite clear what happened or what led up to the killings. Why, for example, were the three people in the room when Giles entered? The primary source for our information about the shootings is Edward, but as he is an integral party in the events, one wonders all the time whether he can be trusted. During his investigations, Edward does accumulate evidence from several sources, but one is Cully Watson, a known liar, and another is Melissa herself, a woman whom Edward calls a "virtuoso liar" (142). According to Edward—who does not say much of what he knows himself—he entered an apartment he had been using in the city and found Melissa there along with Felicity, the latter of whom was dressed in a cape. Felicity claimed that Cully Watson had raped her, bathed her, made her wear the cape (which she didn't know existed), and then raped her again. According to Edward, Felicity came over to Melissa for help right before Giles walked in and killed Felicity and himself.

Cully Watson, however, tells a slightly different story than the one Felicity told. According to him, he and Felicity had had sex several times prior to the day of the murders, and on the fatal day itself he had forced both her and Melissa to have sex with him and then had placed them both in the tub together where they seemed to be enjoying each other's company. (The reference to "Melissa and her jealous lesbian lover" when the Love Nest Scandal is described in *Billy Phelan's Greatest Game* seems to confirm some of what Cully says [48].) Cully also claimed to have taken some money and then run because the Albany police were looking for him for some other crimes.

Two years after the murder and suicide, Cully is found hanged by vigilantes in New Orleans. Inspired by this news, Edward searches out Melissa, from whom he has become estranged. They get into bed together, but while they are having sex he sees her wearing pearls that he thinks might have been Felicity's. Melissa is furious at the accusation, and furious too that Edward thinks that anything that Cully said might be true. When Edward confronts her with the news that he knows she bought the cape for Felicity that Felicity herself was wearing when she was killed, Melissa claims that she bought it to help the other woman seduce Edward and consummate her long unexpressed desire for him. Melissa also says she took the cape to Felicity's room the day of the murders and there heard the voices of a man and a woman in the bathroom. According to Melissa, Felicity then later came to Melissa's room and claimed she had been raped.

While the details of the murder scene and the events leading up to it are unclear—What was Felicity doing in the room? Why was she in that cape? What role did Cully Watson have in all of this? Had Felicity been raped? Were Melissa and Felicity willing lovers?—Edward does have a theory about who is to blame, and that culprit is Thomas Maginn. After his talk with Melissa, Edward returns to Albany and reads in one of Katrina's diary entries that Giles had received a poem alluding to a ménage à trois between his wife Felicity, Melissa, and Edward. In addition, as we learn later, a bull's head had been anonymously placed on Giles's porch as a symbol of his being cuckolded. With this information, Edward then goes to talk to Clubber Dooley, a man who helped place the bull's head on the porch. A simple man, Clubber did not (and does not) realize the significance of what he did. He says to Edward that yes, he and Cully Watson had put the bull's head on Giles's porch and they had placed a letter in the mailbox, presumably the poem itself. Then Edward asks Clubber if Maginn had put him and Cully up to it (in retaliation for the joke played on him), but Clubber only asks in response, "'Maginn?'" (149). It seems that just as the reader is about to receive some confirmation of what really happened, of Maginn's complicity in the affair, Kennedy pulls back and refuses to clarify the story.

As if these conflicting and incomplete stories did not complicate the affair enough, readers are also offered hallucinations by Katrina—or, perhaps, memories of hers —visions in which she hears Maginn explaining that people saw Edward, Felicity, and Melissa in bed together. In addition, Edward takes the whole series of events and transforms them into a new play of his, this one entitled—of course—*The Flaming Corsage*. The part of the play that we see (and that Katrina sees in rehearsal) includes a conversation between characters named Marina and Clarissa, combinations and exchanges of Katrina and Melissa. According to the dialogue, a man named Miles shot himself and his wife (just as "Giles" did). Clarissa tells Marina that Miles was wrong, that Marina's husband (i.e., Edward) and Miles's wife (i.e., Felicity) had never been lovers. Marina responds in turn by accusing Clarissa of having an affair with her husband. Clarissa neither confirms nor denies the accusation, and then Marina goes on to explain that her husband, a playwright, blamed another character named "Mangan" (i.e., Maginn) for most of the trouble, an explanation which Clarissa says is due to Mangan's humiliation over the "fireman's-wife joke," the very trick played on Maginn. According to Marina, her husband, not Miles, was the target of Mangan's revenge. Eventually Clarissa accuses Marina of sleeping with a seventeen-year-old neighbor, a direct reference to Katrina's affair with Francis Phelan.

So what can one make of this confusion? Not much, except to see that this confusion is at the very heart of the affair and, consequently, at the very heart of *The Flaming Corsage* (Kennedy's, that is). Marina, Clarissa, Miles, and Mangan all seem to represent respectively Katrina, Melissa, Giles, and Maginn. Edward seems to be the husband-playwright referred to in the script. But as in the novel so in the play: information comes through accusation and is characterized by uncertainty; no one knows anything for sure, no one admits to anything. Prior to the production of the play, Edward tells Melissa that the script includes a playwright involved in an affair identical to the Love Nest Scandal and this playwright in turn writes a play which is to "'synthesize events, discover answers,'" just as Edward himself is doing with *The Flaming Corsage* (137). But Edward's fictional playwright, as Edward says himself, "'discovers little,'" and then, just as he is about to frame a "'conclusion on the cause of the killings, he turns up facts that dramatically contradict his conclusion'"(137). An inconclusive play within an inconclusive play within a novel of the same: one distorting mirror within others: the truth constantly receding.

Katrina herself is startled by the play when she sees it in rehearsal, impressed with what Edward seems to know and impressed too by his "giving shape to the chaos that overtook us" (171). She decides that she will answer some questions about what she knows for sure, and she determines that a letter would be the right form in which to do it. But just as she is about to start writing this letter she falls asleep, and when she awakens she realizes that the school next to her house is on fire. Knowing that the flames will soon consume the house, Katrina sits down at Edward's desk and lets the fire overtake her. Just as we are about to have some clarification on the affair (again), Katrina kills herself, a not unexpected end to a woman obsessed with death and with fire. Katrina's death leaves the chaos in the shape Edward gave to it, but it is a shape as chaotic as the chaos it dramatizes.

Edward's play about the Love Nest Scandal, *The Flaming Corsage*—one result of his attempt to "dramatize the mind of Katrina" (67)—was scheduled to debut on May 11, 1912, only four days after Katrina's death. But the day before it is to go on stage, Edward admits to himself that the play is a failure. It "did not end," he thinks, "it aborted. Three years of writing and he had produced a ridiculous lie, an evasion, a travesty of the truth" (178). Inspired by Katrina's death, Edward rewrites the ending of the play, handing the new script to the frustrated director and actors the evening before the opening.

While Edward may be pleased with his revisions, the city of Albany is not. The play, in fact, closes after only one performance because of the scandal it causes. In a fictional

newspaper article describing the cancellation of the production, an unnamed author writes that "seasoned theatre-
goers who saw the play" agreed that it was "little more than
a self-exculpation by the playwright, an apologia for his
involvement in the Love Nest Scandal" (181). The characters,
the article claims, were "changed so slightly from their real-
life counterparts that all are recognizable" (181). If the play
is an exculpation and a redramatization of events, however,
the reader of the novel is, once again, never privy to what was
revealed by way of exculpation. As earlier we received contradictory information about the Love Nest Scandal from
various sources, all of them untrustworthy in some way, here
Kennedy withholds information by not actually showing us
the revised or complete play, much in the same way he has
Katrina sit down to confess her involvement and then commit
suicide before revealing what she knows. While this lack of
information may frustrate readers in their pursuit of learning
what happened, one wonders how valuable the play or the
letter would even have been. After all, how much could we
trust Edward or Katrina in light of the passions that were
driving them and the self-interest that moved them to tell
their stories?

While readers may be uncertain about what happened,
Edward Daugherty himself is not. Several months after the
closing of his play, Edward is working on another one, again
involving the characters of the scandal. In fact, this time, the
main characters assume their real selves: Maginn is strapped
into an electric chair, Giles Fitzroy is supervising the execution, and Edward himself—though dead—stands by watching
(not an unexpected event in a Kennedy novel). In the one
scene we get from this play, Daugherty, though dead,
observes Maginn's nearly senile monologues and Giles attempting to execute him in the electric chair. Maginn,
however, does not die easy, and he is still alive at the end of
the scene despite his having been shocked several times. The

comment is obvious: Giles deserves revenge, Edward has figuratively died from the tragedy, and Maginn deserves to die but Giles (or Edward) cannot kill him, literally or figuratively.

Edward, however, will soon get a chance in real life to get some revenge. After having talked to Clubber and after having seen Katrina's diary, Edward realizes that what probably happened during the scandal was that Maginn had tried to set up Edward and Giles in an act of revenge and jealousy. Edward believes he was "the true target" (195) of Maginn's deadly and tragic joke, a sentiment echoed in Edward's play. Like the fireman's wife joke played on Maginn, this joke too backfired, and the victims were Felicity and Giles.

After the closing of *The Flaming Corsage*, Edward confronts Maginn where he is working as a bartender and pimp. Maginn admits that he was the one who goaded Giles on, but he said he had no intention of the joke turning fatal. Is any of this true? Possibly, but then Maginn claims that he and Melissa slept together the morning of the shooting and that Melissa had put Cully Watson up to raping Felicity so that Melissa could watch and later comfort the victim. Maginn also claims he lied to Cully about the police wanting him so that Cully would flee the area after the shootings and be out of the way, but he says nothing when Edward accuses him of killing Cully himself. Later in the conversation Edward himself claims he has evidence for all of Maginn's doings—a formerly unknown confession from Cully, testimony from Clubber and Melissa, and a man who claims that someone who looked like Maginn payed the thugs who hanged Cully. While Maginn says nothing about all this evidence, his actions make him look guilty: he knocks Edward unconscious and leaves town that evening with the women who work for him. But just when we think that the situation has at last been clarified, Edward admits after regaining consciousness that he had made up the story about Cully's confession.

Edward, in effect, confesses to being a "virtuoso liar" himself, even if it is in the cause of searching out the truth. Once again, we are left wondering exactly what transpired, though Edward himself is satisfied. He was pleased to think of "Maginn, with fewer teeth, and fettered with whores, forced into midnight exile by the power of fiction" (204). Neither Giles nor Edward can kill Maginn in Edward's play, but in real life fiction can at least exile Maginn to a life on the run.

After he goes to the hospital to have his wounds treated, Edward begins to regret that he hadn't done better with *The Flaming Corsage*. He believes it will never be done again,[6] and he regrets that he didn't use real names. He thinks he'd like to redo some scenes, and then imagines one in particular in which he and Katrina discuss honestly what had happened at the Delavan and what had happened with Giles. He imagines too an honest discussion about Katrina's obsession with death and one about Edward's own behavior throughout the scandal. Edward's reflections comprise a brief scene, but is it memory or fantasy or fiction or revision? The text appears as a script of a play, but when the character named "Edward" speaks, is this character Edward Daugherty's or William Kennedy's? And what of the next brief scene, also written in the form of a script of a play, a scene in which the dying Katrina lays in Edward's arm and asks, "I loved you? Quite likely. I forget" (208). The reader is not certain on which aesthetic or psychological level to interpret these moments. Are they real or are they fictionalized? And whose fictions are they, Edward's or Kennedy's?

Edward's last few imagined plays—if that is what they are—as well as *The Flaming Corsage* itself (the play, that is, not the novel), reveal Edward's longstanding attempt to fuse his art with "reality," whether that reality be the public history he used in *The Baron of Ten Broek Street* or his own personal history with Katrina Taylor. In both cases, Edward attempts to understand the history from which he emerges and in which he is now living. It is, of course, a familiar task in Kennedy's fiction. Edward's own son Martin will use his artistic talents in a similar way in *Billy Phelan's Greatest Game*, though without much success, as he pursues answers to his own troubled past. Daniel Quinn, Francis Phelan, Molly Phelan, Orson Purcell, Peter Phelan—these are some of the other Albany cycle heroes who attempt in one way or another to understand or transform the history from which they emerge and which shapes who they are in the present. Orson Purcell and Peter Phelan, like Edward, even use art as a means to achieve those transformations.

But if *The Flaming Corsage* embodies many of the earlier themes and practices of the other Albany novels, it does distinguish itself perhaps by the way in which it ends. While most of the endings of the other Albany novels are ambiguous, in one way or another they do portray a redemption or transcendence of the circumstances of the past which are so much a concern for them: Legs's soul rises, Billy Phelan returns to Broadway, Martin forgives his own father and son, Francis would arrive "home," Quinn consummates his love with Maud, and Orson finds a family. But Edward's endeavor fails miserably. If for several years he does live the life of a famous artist and upperclass Irishman, by the end of the novel, after the Love Nest Scandal and Katrina's death, he is a complete failure. He's come to a "bad end" (190) and, in fact, returns to live in North Albany, the area he was supposed to rise above, because there's "no place else to go" (191). Maginn even teases him when he first sees Edward in the bordello by saying that he "looks well for a man whose life has been destroyed" (196). Our knowledge of Edward's future from *Billy Phelan*, where he lies senile in a nursing home, only confirms our sense of Edward's tragic life.

The last vision we have of Edward is of him sitting by himself on the porch of the old Daugherty family home, early on the morning after he was roughed up at Maginn's. He is thinking about bacon, and wants it so badly that he can almost smell it. He decides he'll have some and goes in to cook it, a decision which signals how far he has come from the young Edward Daugherty who issued his Manifesto on Love and History, the playwright who was going to raise himself up and then his entire race. Instead of changing the world, he cooks himself some bacon.

And yet, as one might expect in Kennedy's work, Edward does not seem to be finished off: life is a cycle of which even death is a part, as Edward's return to the Daugherty home signals. As Francis Phelan found redemption in his embracing his violent, fugitive self, and as Peter Phelan "saved" his family by acknowledging the insanity and violence in the family history, so Edward sees in the bacon and his desire for it a sign of his willingness and power to go on. "A pig is turned into bacon," Edward thinks, and "bacon becomes food that gives unity and purpose to the imagination" (209). How or why this is so is not clear, but Edward concludes that he "would stay up and outlast" his father (now dead) as well as his son (alienated from Edward) (209). Like Francis, Edward seems to show the promise that he will endure, a promise signaled by the significance Kennedy applies to this enigmatic breakfast: after Edward finishes the early-morning whiskey he is having on the porch, he goes into cook the "bacon, which will always be with us" (209). The bacon becomes, in effect, a form of Eucharist or manna, a symbolic or holy meal which provides unlimited sustenance for the endurance Edward seems to be assigning himself as his new mission.

In one way Edward's compromised stand at the end of *The Flaming Corsage* is familiar—Orson Purcell and Francis Phelan both have notable ambiguities or compromises in their final discoveries—but Edward's end is certainly the most tragic of all so far in the Albany cycle. He is left at the conclusion of the book with only himself, but unlike Francis Phelan, who ends with the same possession of self, Edward started off with so much more: Edward fell—from artistic

success, from love, from passion, hope, fame, and wealth
—where Francis spun in place. They might have ended up in
the same place, a resigned acceptance of who they are and
what remains to them, but Francis' journey resulted in his
finding what he hadn't had before whereas Edward's ended
up in his returning to that which he wanted to escape. This
is especially ironic when one considers that Edward, as much
as any other Albany hero, was sensitive to the power of
history and of art, the sources of so much redemption in the
Kennedy cycle. Edward, as one reviewer wrote, "defies fate
with his art,"[7] but it is an act of defiance which destroys him.

What remains for Edward at the end is the small
consolation of the enduring power of little gifts such as bacon
for breakfast. His Manifesto of Love and History is replaced
by his struggle to get through the day. In Kennedy's fiction,
the past has frequently been a source of redemption for those
living in the present: "then" infuses and sanctifies "now." But
that power of redemption resides in the inescapable presence
of the past in Kennedy's Albany, a presence one must respect.
Edward Daugherty recognized this presence and struggled to
understand it, but he also wanted to rise above it, a desire, a
pride, which resulted in the end in his unwillingly returning
to the very history from which he wished to escape, the North
Albany home of his father. This home was the beginning and
is now the end, at least figuratively, for Edward. It is a refuge
and a source of small blessings such as bacon; it is a sign of
all that Edward has lost and how much he has failed; it is a
reminder that, in Kennedy's Albany, "then" merges indis-
tinguishably into "now," as Edward returns to the past he
had so long struggled to understand and dramatize and rise
above, a past where he must confront, as always, the truth of
who he is.

NOTES

1. See Chapter 3 of this study.
2. Edward's complaint that his "history has not yet been written"

of course echoes Stephen Dedalus's desire to "forge in the smithy of my soul the uncreated conscience of my race" (253) in Joyce's *Portrait of the Artist as a Young Man.*

3. The word "race" to describe the Irish is not chosen as a statement on what constitutes a racial or ethnic group. Instead, it is chosen to draw attention to the similarity between what Edward is doing with his art and what Stephen Dedalus dreams of doing in *A Portrait of the Artist as a Young Man.* See endnote 2 above.

4. From R. Z. Sheppard, "Living with the Ashes" (*Time,* 13 May, 1996: 92–93). Kennedy's practice of incorporating (and transforming) real history into his fiction appears in his work in such guises as the opening cataclysm of *Quinn's Book* and in the use of the historical character Legs Diamond in *Legs.*

5. The scar left behind by this stick has been mentioned before in *Billy Phelan's Greatest Game,* most notably when Martin Daugherty engaged in his Oedipal lovemaking with Melissa Spencer and "studied the portion of her neck and breast where his mother had been scarred by the point of a flaming, flying stick" (209).

6. As we know from *Billy Phelan's Greatest Game,* the play will be done again, though by that time Edward is too senile to appreciate its production.

7. Sheppard, R. Z., "Living with the Ashes." *Time* 13 May 1996: 93.

CHAPTER EIGHT

THE ALBANY NOVELS OF THE ALBANY CYCLE

*W*illiam Kennedy is hardly unique among writers in his production in the Albany cycle of an inter-related series of literary works. Examples of such series abound both in literary and popular fiction. At times the novels or stories in these series are explicitly related to each other in the way they all follow one single plot. Many of the so-called fantasy novels, in fact, such as those in J. R. R. Tolkein's *The Lord of the Rings* trilogy, are as much parts of a series with one continuous story line as they are discrete works. When a single plot does not directly connect together the works in a series, one overarching title for the collection may still indicate the intended close relationship among the works. John Dos Passos's *U.S.A.* trilogy or Sherwood Ander-son's *Winesburg, Ohio* are two notable examples.

Not all works in a series, however, are so explicitly connected as to share a plot line or be labeled under a uni-fying title. At times the novels in a series are related more haphazardly, sharing common material and interests but without the overarching formal structure of a titled trilogy or story collection, such as those works of William Faulkner's which deal with his imaginary Yoknapatawpha County. It is to Faulkner's Yoknapatawpha novels, in fact, that Kennedy's Albany cycle is most readily and most frequently compared.

271

Both authors reuse an imaginary landscape—Yoknapatawpha and Albany respectively—in many of their books, but for neither writer is there any formally titled "Yoknapatawpha" or "Albany" series, only a group of novels related by their shared interest in a place and by the reappearance in their narratives of a consistent body of characters and events. There is also no continuous plot line along which the Yoknapatawpha and Albany novels proceed from one to the other; the works are related and dependent upon a common body of information but nonetheless discrete.

It is perhaps wise to acknowledge this particular characteristic of Kennedy's (and Faulkner's) novels at the end of a study which has shown how similar all of Kennedy's novels are, for while Kennedy's works may share characters and place (the Phelans and Daughertys and Quinns of Albany) and even replicate within their narratives a consistent theme (the past penetrating the present), the novels themselves, like Faulkner's, are notably discrete works, so much so that their differences are as noteworthy as their similarities. A reader who approaches Kennedy's work after reading a study such as this one will probably first be struck at how different each of Kennedy's novels actually are one from the other. Not only is there no single plot line or title connecting the novels, but each work presents a unique plot, narrative structure, and theme (other than the theme of the presence of the past that each of the novels share). It is the differences between the various Albany books, in fact, that was one of the few praises reserved for the generally poorly received *Quinn's Book*. While most critics found little to praise in the novel, some of them did honor Kennedy for departing so radically from the formula he successfully used in *Ironweed*, the book published immediately prior to *Quinn's Book*.[1]

The most noticeable difference between the six Albany novels thus far is of course their different plots or, to say it a different way, the various struggles each of the protagonists endure. While the theme of the past penetrating the present may be a consistent one in characterizing each protagonist's struggle, that struggle itself is nonetheless different in each of the works. In *Legs*, Jack Diamond attempts to maintain his criminal empire and Marcus Gorman attempts to explain not only the myth of Legs but also his own gradual immersion into Diamond's world and lifestyle. In *Billy Phelan's Greatest Game*, Billy struggles to maintain both his code of honor and his gambling business and Martin Daugherty attempts to reconcile himself with his father and his son. *Ironweed* is concerned with the struggles of a single individual, Francis Phelan, as he tries to come to terms with his own past and his own current misfortune. *Quinn's Book* differs from each of the prior novels in that the quests of its protagonist, Daniel Quinn, are subsumed into a larger concern with depicting an "age" in America, particularly the age of mid-nineteenth century New York state. *Very Old Bones* returns to a concern with the struggles of individuals to come to terms with their pasts, much like the quests of Francis Phelan and even Martin Daugherty, but the struggles are decidedly different from those found in previous works—Orson Purcell tries to overcome his bastard state; Molly Phelan, the first real female protagonist of the cycle, wishes to redeem the "sin" of her stillborn child; and Peter Phelan attempts to purify the history of the entire Phelan family, including his own shameful history of denying his fatherhood. This familial redemption is replaced in *The Flaming Corsage* with a concern with the power of art, at least as Edward Daugherty practices it, to rectify the past and elevate the individual; the limitations of that power are made evident as the history that the art attempts to overcome eventually overcomes the artist himself.

Differences in plot are, of course, obvious, and they are necessary if one is to distinguish one novel from another. But a more striking difference between the books in the Albany cycle lies in the narrative structure of each of the novels, in their individually unique use and manipulation of point of view and chronology.[2] The differences between the narrative structures of the books are so noticeable, in fact, that it makes the notion of the shared thematic concerns of the novels all the more intriguing: Kennedy maintains his interest with history and the past, with archetype and myth, but he never does so in the same way twice.

The differences in narrative structure among the Albany novels might not be surprising when one considers how the very first of these novels, *Legs*, itself differs from more traditional works that share its first-person mode of narration. *Legs* is the first of three stories in the cycle ostensibly told from the first-person point of view, in this case by the lawyer Marcus Gorman (the other two first-person novels are *Quinn's Book* and *Very Old Bones*); but if it introduces the use of a first-person narrator, *Legs* also introduces Kennedy's willingness to forego one traditional restriction of first-person point of view, namely that the narrating character must have knowledge in some legitimate way of the story he is telling, either by observing what is happening himself or hearing about it in some way. Although Gorman presents himself toward the beginning of the work as the narrator of the novel, he could not be a witness to all the events that he tells about and he does not always offer explanations as to how he might know about those events. Gorman does not explain, for example, how he knows what happened between Jack and the canaries in the hold of the ship in which Diamond is traveling on his return to the United States from Europe. If we as readers felt the need, we could certainly imagine that some witness, perhaps even Jack himself, retold the events to Gorman, but Gorman himself offers no such explanation.

This curious narrative tactic in *Legs* combines the consistency of the point of view of a traditional novel with the experimental approach of a postmodernist work. But in several ways, the question about the legitimacy of what Gorman knows is obviated by the structure and style of the novel itself. The narration originates, after all, with several of Gorman's friends sitting down to talk about Legs Diamond, so the book itself could be perceived in some ways as a narrative told in a collective voice, or at least in one voice (Gorman's) which is relating what several characters know. More importantly, the events of the narrative stretch the limits of the believable to such a degree that they overwhelm any similar questions we might have about the believability of the narrator. Why would we be concerned, for example, with how Gorman could possibly know what happened to Diamond's clothes as Jack undressed himself alone in his room before being killed? The more startling aspect of this scene is that the laws of physics itself are abandoned in the way the clothes fall to the floor, not that Gorman could not be the narrator of such an event. And if we can accept that the dead Diamond can eventually comment on his own death, then what do we care about whether or not Gorman is or could be the narrator during the scene? Our credulousness is more challenged by the mystical events of the narrative than by the likelihood of Gorman's being able to describe those events. As in *Ironweed*, in which the narrative itself asks us to accept that several moments in time are collapsed together, here in *Legs* we are similarly asked by the magical nature of events not to expect a traditional first-person narration. The narrative is not limited to what is realistic, and neither is its point of view.

Legs, like *Very Old Bones* later, begins in a moment in time and then goes backward to relate what happened in the past prior to that moment. The difference between this first Albany novel and *Very Old Bones*, however, is that once the narrative in *Legs* does return to the past, it proceeds through a generally straightforward chronology from the time Gorman meets Jack up until the point of Diamond's death. The narrative of *Very Old Bones*, on the other hand, moves in and out of the past and the present, constantly spiraling backward and forward. Of all the Albany novels, *Legs* is the only one both to use this notion of a reminiscent narrator and then to proceed in a generally chronological way within that reminiscence.

Billy Phelan's Greatest Game, unlike *Legs*, contains both a traditional third-person point of view and a straightforward chronological progression through a brief period in time (less than a week). Of all the novels, this one is the most traditional in terms of its narrative structure. The point of view (or points of view) is generally limited to two characters, Billy Phelan and Martin Daugherty, each of whom serves as a filtering consciousness observing the action, and the characters themselves do not go back in time (as happens in a way with Francis Phelan in *Ironweed*) except in such figurative moments as Martin's observing himself as a child on stage during Melissa's performance or his reenacting his earlier "debauch" with her. The events of the narrative generally move forward, not backward as happens at the beginning of *Legs* or cyclically as happens in *Very Old Bones*. Like a traditional story, *Billy Phelan's Greatest Game* has a beginning, a middle, and an end—a crisis, resolution, and dénouement.

Being aware of this traditional narrative point of view in *Billy Phelan*[3] makes the structure of the next novel, *Ironweed*, all the more startling. It follows, for the most part, the highly traditional use of a single third-person point of view—in this case, that of the character Francis Phelan—and yet within that traditional concept it abandons most radically the limitations of realistic narrative. As we have seen, *Ironweed* does not take place in any readily identifiable moment in space or time: we do not move forward or backward so much as we exist in numerous places and moments simultaneously. Traditional linear time is collapsed, and in that collapsing the traditional third-person point of view is itself emphatically altered. We are for much of the book limited to the consciousness of Francis Phelan, but that consciousness itself is not limited to perceiving what is happening in the Albany of 1938. Instead, Francis' mind opens up a whole history of itself, even history it could not observe but from which it emerges, such as Francis' own conception. This point of view makes that history part of the present moment, not merely as memory, as in the case of Martin Daugherty, and not merely as stories retold, as happens in *Legs*, but rather as a living moment in the present time frame in which the narrative takes place. The plot of the novel concerns only three days in the life of Francis Phelan, but those three days are part of a highly complex chronological structure in which linear notions of time moving forward are replaced with a three-dimensional conception in which all time exists now.

After this imaginative manipulation of third-person point of view in *Ironweed*, Kennedy switches back in *Quinn's Book*, his next novel, to the first-person point of view he used in *Legs*. And as in *Legs*, Kennedy again violates the traditional expectations of this point of view, though the violation this time derives more from a focus on the historical than on the mystical. This focus in *Quinn's Book* on the historical—on America rather than on Daniel Quinn—produces a novel in which the narrator, the "I" speaking about events, often cannot be the actual Daniel Quinn himself, at least not one understood to be a realistic character in a realistic novel. Sometimes it seems that the novel simply switches from first- to third-person point of view—from Quinn to a narrative voice independent of any character—and sometimes it seems that Quinn himself is narrating about events that occur outside of what he could possibly know.

Although similar violations of traditional points of view occur in *Legs* and *Ironweed*, *Quinn's Book* is unique in the way it repeatedly and inconsistently violates its announced narrative stance. While *Ironweed* may violate traditional conceptions of third-person point of view, for example, it does so with consistency (in fact, it is this consistency which allows us to realize that the events are more than hallucination). And while *Legs* does stretch our credulity in its use of Gorman as narrator, it at least does so in a way that is both unobtrusive and consistent with the mystical nature of the plot itself. *Quinn's Book,* on the other hand, switches points of view abruptly and in no identifiable pattern, does not concern itself with coordinating the events being narrated with the most likely point of view which could legitimately observe those events, and covers material well beyond that which is directly within the scope of Daniel Quinn's life. One gets the sense that the collision of myth and history which describes Kennedy's treatment of the opening flood carries over into his treatment of point of view: the accuracy of historical detail combines in this point of view with the universally available knowledge of myth. Or perhaps the point of view in the novel embodies the attitude of Daniel Quinn at the end of the book as he embraces the power and freedom of the imagination over the limitations of journalistic reporting.

Quinn's Book, as we noted in an earlier chapter, is also different from all the other Albany novels thus far in its exclusive concern with nineteenth century America. The time covered in *Quinn's Book* is also the longest for those works which consistently move forward chronologically in their narrative. *Billy Phelan's Greatest Game* and *Ironweed,* the other two novels which can be said to follow a straightforward movement in terms of the events of the plot, each take place within a week's time. The events in *Quinn's Book* take fifteen years and cover what happens not only to the primary protagonist, Daniel Quinn, but also to other characters such as Maud Fallon, Magdalena Colón, and John the Brawn as well as to historical phenomena such as horse racing, slavery, and journalism.

For its part *Very Old Bones* employs a highly imaginative first-person point of view, and it also extensively manipulates its chronology, as we said above, by frequently switching between various moments of time. Orson Purcell, the narrator of the novel, "witnesses" and describes events he could not possibly see. But unlike Marcus Gorman in *Legs,* who also violates this limitation of the first-person point of view, Orson acknowledges what he is doing as narrator, justifying his narrative tricks by claiming to have the powers of a Keatsian "negative capability" as it applies to a narrator of fiction; specifically, Orson argues that he has the capability to know what is happening in places he is not through the force of his imagination.[4] Kennedy, in other words, uses Orson's explicitly stated argument rather than mere narrative (as he does in *Ironweed*) to try to get the reader to believe in a narrative point of view which is not credible in simply realistic terms. Again Kennedy seems to be combining his penchant for historical realism with his post-modern and magical sensibilities, a combination akin perhaps to the simultaneous historical and archetypal contexts in which he views Albany itself.[5] Orson does not apologize for speaking of events he has not seen or describing the emotions of others that he could not know, but rather he simply asks us to believe that he can legitimately speak of such things. In none of the other Albany novels is there such a self-conscious narrator, in part because *Very Old Bones* announces itself as Orson's own memoir, so that Orson actually is, in a figurative sense, the author of the book we are reading.

In addition to this self-conscious and unusual first-person narration, *Very Old Bones* also stands apart from the other novels for its unusually complex time scheme. As we saw earlier, after the beginning of the story in July of 1958, the novel then proceeds in fits and starts through numerous different periods, jumping backward and then forward again, from one date to another, sometimes through Orson's remembering or telling, sometimes through a story or memory retold by a character other than Orson, and sometimes through no identifiable consciousness at all. In no other novel is linear time both respected and yet so radically manipulated.

Readers unfamiliar with Kennedy's generous manip-ulation with point of view might scratch their heads at the difficulties engendered by Kennedy's narrative approach in the final book of this study, *The Flaming Corsage*. Although Edward Daugherty's point of view is the most significant in the book, it is countered at times by a more omniscient narrator and by Katrina's point of view as well as by a succession of independently presented works such as police reports or scripts of plays. The ontological status of these works within the story—whether they are memory or fiction or dream—is sometimes uncertain, as is the credibility of their authors: the self-interest of each of the characters, the questionable reputations of a Melissa Spencer or Cully Watson or Thomas Maginn, the uncertainty of how much truth Edward translates into his plays, Katrina's mental state—these uncertainties combine throughout the story to render the truth an impossible goal to achieve. As so often happens in Kennedy's work, the form of the novel here embodies one of its themes: as *Legs* carries on the very mythicization it dramatizes, *The Flaming Corsage* embodies the uncertainty which haunts Edward Daugherty as he tries to unravel the mystery of the Love Nest Scandal and to understand the mysteries of his enigmatic wife. In this case the uncertainty is embodied in Kennedy's manipulation of the point of view itself.

What this brief survey of the various narrative structures of the Albany novels reveals is how Kennedy continually alters the structure of those narratives while nonetheless maintaining his concern in his stories with the presence of the past. While these different narrative structures are perhaps the most radical differences between each of the novels, one should note too how the six Albany novels also differ in terms of those thematic concerns of theirs that lie beyond their shared notion of the past as being always present. *Legs*, for example, is unique among the Albany novels for its concern with the process of "mythicization," of how an individual is transformed into a myth. Mythology also plays a key role in *Ironweed*, and transformed or altered history is part of the story in *Quinn's Book*, but only in *Legs* is the process of history-turning-into-myth both explored and dramatized in such depth.

For its part, *Billy Phelan* offers two themes wholly different from those presented in *Legs* or any other of the works in the Albany cycle. Billy's primary concern is with his keeping his code of honor when he is asked to spy on a suspected kidnapper, and Kennedy not only attempts to dramatize the difficulty of maintaining such a code—as Hemingway might do—but he also questions the validity of doing so: What kind of a code is it, after all, if it means jeopardizing the life of an innocent man? This adherence to a code is what attracts Martin Daugherty to Billy, but through Daugherty, Kennedy explores not so much the nature of radical individualism as it is inherent in a personal code but rather the difficulty of maintaining "generational communion," the ability of fathers and sons to understand each other.

The third novel, *Ironweed*, pursues the theme of an individual's existential struggle with himself rather than his struggle against the expectations of and duties in society. There are no McCalls or alienated fathers for Francis to fight, merely his own obsessive concern with his irresponsibility and guilt and with the past in which his sins are forever preserved. Unlike *Billy Phelan's Greatest Game*, *Ironweed* does not offer a dramatic cleansing of the sins of the past—there is no reversal such as Martin's eventual understanding of his son and father or the McCalls' reopening of Albany nightlife to Billy. Instead, *Ironweed* presents a character who survives by deciding to embrace his past and his faults rather than trying to escape them. The past is not overcome and purified as much as it is accepted in all its ugliness. The (compromised) Christian vision of forgiveness evident in the actions of the McCalls and Martin Daugherty, for both Billy Phelan and Martin's father and son respectively, is replaced in *Ironweed* by an existential though nonetheless heroic resignation toward one's inescapably flawed condition.

Although *Quinn's Book* is the least interested in its characters of all the Albany novels—a characteristic many would identify as an artistic flaw—this fourth Albany novel nonetheless pursues more emphatically than any of the other books questions about the art of writing itself. In its attempt to dramatize and understand a historical age, the novel has its protagonist ask himself questions about the meaning of such attempts, and his answer to these questions is finally found in the realm of aesthetics—namely, that the repetition of fact, specifically of historical fact, offers no answers to understanding the world; instead, one must concede to the essentially mysterious nature of the world, a mystery that can only be contemplated, and then only through acts of the imagination, specifically for Quinn in writing. This power of the imagination to approach the truth that fact cannot is a mystery as profound as the mystery of love, a realization emphasized by Daniel Quinn's discovering the wisdom of the imagination at the same time that he consummates his desire for Maud Fallon.

Very Old Bones, much like *Quinn's Book*, also pursues questions about art and comes to similar conclusions—that art is able to grasp and reveal an essential truth about the world, in this case the truth about the Phelan family and its history. But in *Very Old Bones* this power of art can also work as a restorative, curing the ills that one's history might have caused. For *Very Old Bones* this restoration is emphatically aimed at the "family" in particular, for this novel, more so than any of its predecessors, pursues the question of the nature of family, especially as it serves to define one's identity in the world. The novel seems to say in its conclusion, in the reuniting and celebrating of the hobbled remnant of the Phelan family at the reading of Peter

Phelan's will, that a crippled family is better than no family at all. The events point out that an awareness of one's own history, no matter how scandalous that history, is better than floating in an ahistorical world—Orson the Phelan is better than Orson the bastard.

Like the other novels, *The Flaming Corsage* also concerns itself with history. But unlike them, history becomes a source of failure or warning rather than redemption, and this despite the fact that the protagonist of the novel, Edward Daugherty, is explicitly concerned with the nature of history in his art. At first his concern is for public history, for the story of members of his Irish race in Albany, but then he confronts his own life, specifically in the form of his wife, Katrina. But in both cases Edward's art or his mind is not up to the task. His social plays create only animosity, and when he tires of this struggle and turns to Katrina, his imaginative talents fail to conquer the power that Katrina's own personal history and her own obsession with death have over her. Edward's sin is not ignorance but pride: a Francis Phelan or Orson Purcell understands the power of history and accepts it; Edward thinks he can overcome and manipulate history for his own self-centered ends. The result of such pride is apt, for Edward returns to the home from which he wanted to escape, to the history which he wanted to overcome and rise above. The theme of this last of the Albany novels to date is a mirror image of many of the other works: history can redeem us, but that is because it has power over us, a power we must respect.

Each of these Albany novels, of course, offers other minor themes and issues and questions, even as each of them also addresses the concern with the presence of the past that has been the focus of this study. Yet what these various themes reveal, as do also the unique struggles of each of the protagonists and the highly different narrative structures of these works, is how variously Kennedy maintains his consistent emphasis on the conflation of the historical, and the archetypal, on the interpenetration of past, present and future. Whether it be in terms of plot, point of view, chronological structure, or theme, no two novels in the Albany cycle duplicate each other, and yet all of these novels not only rely on a common imaginary history and set of characters but they also invariably revolve around a similar conception of the power of the past always and emphatically to be present.

Kennedy has written that it is his "task" while writing his books "to peer into the heart of [the] always-shifting past," an endeavor which we have seen he has done with consistency in the six novels discussed here (OA, 7). This task has led to a group of stories in which history, as the introduction to this book put it, is resurrected, overcome, purified, forgiven, or endured, and this always occurs through a process in which this history, what happened back "then," is transformed into what is always happening "now." Such consistency does not mean, however, that the modes of these fictional transformations are all identical. In Kennedy's fiction, the past is always present, but it always comes forward in a different way. The Albany cycle spins forward from one book to the next; it does not simply spin in place.

NOTES

1. Paul Gray writes that "*Quinn's Book* may at first prompt some head scratching, since it looks like a startling departure from the fiction that established Kennedy's reputation" (*Time*, May 16, 1988: 92). *Publishers Weekly*, in an anonymous review, says, "All praise to Kennedy for a bold departure from the books that (finally) made his great reputation—the Albany cycle culminating in *Ironweed*. His new novel [*Quinn's Book*] is, as they say, something completely different" (March 18, 1988: 71). In a review that is somewhat critical, Loxley F. Nichols nonetheless adds that "*Quinn's Book* marks a departure in style more than a diminution of talent" (47). Peter A. Quinn notes that *Quinn's Book* "carries the Cycle back in time to its mid-nineteenth century origins but is neither mere genealogy nor a clone of stories already told" (*Commonweal*, May 20, 1988: 308).

2. By narrative structure is meant here both the point of view of the story (a specific character, say, or an omniscient or limited third-person

narrator) and also the time frame in the novel (the moment from which the story is told, the amount of time that transpires within that novel, and the ways in which time is manipulated in the narrative).

3. This traditional and realistic point of view, along with the traditional and realistic chronology, is different, of course, from the possibly unrealistic events of parts of the plot. That Martin Daugherty practices an odd and imperfect mysticism and that Billy Phelan hears the voices of ghosts does not mean that the point of view or the chronology itself in the novel is in some way unrealistic.

4. As Orson explains, in evoking Keats's notion of negative capability, he is able to "drain myself of myself, and to project myself into realms of the family where I have no credentials for being, but am there even so" (21). Thus Orson is, in a sense—an artistic, theoretical, Keatsian, and Kennedyesque sense—actually a witness to that which he could never have seen. As we are asked often in the Albany cycle to accept the possibility of the magical, so in *Very Old Bones* Kennedy asks us to accept it in terms of the narrative point of view of the novel itself.

5. See *O Albany!*, p. 7, or the introduction of this study, p. 3.

APPENDIX

Daniel Quinn's Celtic disk. This depiction of the disk appears on the title page of William Kennedy's *Quinn's Book* (Viking, 1988).

From *Quinn's Book* by William Kennedy. Copyright © 1988 by WJK, Inc. Used by permission of Viking Penguin, a division of Penguin Books USA Inc.

WORKS CITED

PRIMARY SOURCES

The following are the major primary sources of William Kennedy's work, although not all of these works are directly cited in this study.

Novels

Billy Phelan's Greatest Game. New York: Viking, 1978 (Penguin, 1983); London: Penguin, 1984.

Ironweed. New York: Viking, 1983; Harmondsworth: Penguin, 1984.

Legs. New York: Coward, McCann, 1975 (Penguin, 1983); London: Cape, 1977.

The Flaming Corsage. New York: Penguin, 1996.

The Ink Truck. New York: Dial, 1969 (Viking, 1984); London: Macdonald, 1970.

Quinn's Book. New York: Viking, 1988. London: Cape, 1988.

Very Old Bones. New York: Penguin, 1992.

Nonfiction

O Albany! Improbable City of Political Wizards, Fearless Ethnics, Spectacular Aristocrats, Splendid Nobodies, and Underrated Scoundrels. New York: Viking; Albany, NY: Washington Park Press, 1983.

"Why It Took So Long." *New York Times Book Review* 20 May 1990: 1, 32–34.

Riding the Yellow Trolley Car. New York: Viking, 1993.

Short Fiction

"The Concept of Being Twenty-Two." *The San Juan Review* 1 June 1964: 18–20, 27–29.

"Figgy Blue." *The San Juan Review* 3 February 1966: 36–38.

"The Secrets of Creative Love." *Harper's* July 1983: 54–58.

"An Exchange of Gifts." *Glen Falls Review* 3 1985/86: 7–9.

"A Cataclysm of Love." *Esquire* November 1986: 241–53. [The opening section of *Quinn's Book*.]

"Jack's Alive." *The Big Book of American Irish Culture.* Ed. Bob Callahan. New York: Viking Penguin, 1987. 218–22. [The opening section of *Legs*.]

"The Hills and the Creeks (Albany 1850)." *Harper's* March 1988: 55–62. [Adaptation of part of *Quinn's Book*.]

Screenplays

The Cotton Club (with Francis Ford Coppola). Orion, 1984. New York: St. Martin's Press, 1986.

Ironweed. Tri-Star, 1987.

SECONDARY SOURCES

Articles and Reviews

Agrest, Susan. "Tough Guy with a Golden Touch." *Hudson Valley Magazine* July 1987: 42–49, 72.

Birkerts, Sven. "O Albany." *The New Republic* 27 June 1988: 41–42.

Black, David. "The Fusion of Past and Present in William Kennedy's *Ironweed*." *Critique* 27 1986: 177–84.

Campbell, Joseph. *The Hero with a Thousand Faces.* Princeton: Princeton University Press, 1968.

Chamberlain, Lori. "Magicking the Real: Paradoxes of Postmodern Writing." *Postmodern Fiction: a Bio-Bibliographical Guide.* Ed. Larry McCaffery. Westport, Conn.: Greenwood Press, Inc., 1986. 5–22.

Clarke, Peter P. "Classical Myth in William Kennedy's Ironweed." *Critique* 27 1986: 167–76.

Clute, John. "The Rituals of Redemption." *TLS* 27 May–2 June 1988: 584.

Cobb, Gerald T. Rev. of "Very Old Bones." *America* 21 Nov. 1992: 410–12.

De Hora, Sean. "Triumph of the Dimestore Novel." *Commonweal* 9 Sept. 1983: 472–73.

Edwards, Thomas R. "Family Values." *The New York Review of Books*, 13 Aug. 1992: 54–55.

Fitzgerald, F. Scott. *The Great Gatsby*. New York: Charles Scribner's Sons, 1925.

Gibb, Robert. *The Life of the Soul: William Kennedy, Magical Realist*. Dissertation. Lehigh University, 1986.

Gilbert, Stuart. *James Joyce's* Ulysses: *A Study*. New York: Viking, 1958.

Gray, Paul. "An Eyewitness to Paradox." *Time* 16 May 1988: 92, 95.

Griffin, Paul F. "The Moral Implications of Annie Phelan's Jell-O." *San Jose Studies* 14.3 1988: 85–95.

— "Susan Sontag, Franny Phelan, and the Moral Implications of Photographs." *Midwest Quarterly: A Journal of Contemporary Thought* 29.2 1988: 194–203.

Hamilton, Edith. *Mythology*. Boston: Little, Brown and Co., 1942.

Hunt, George W. "William Kennedy's Albany Triology." *America* 19 May 1984: 373–75.

Rev. of "Ironweed." *The New Yorker*, 7 February 1983: 121.

Joyce, James. *A Portrait of the Artist as a Young Man*. The Viking Critical Library. Ed. Chester G. Anderson. New York: Viking Press, 1968.

Murtaugh, Daniel M. "Fathers and Their Sons: William Kennedy's Hero-Transgressors." *Commonweal* 19 May 1989: 298–302.

Nichols, Loxley F. "William Kennedy Comes of Age." *National Review*, 9 August 1985: 46–48.

Ott, Bill. Rev. of "Very Old Bones." *Booklist*, 15 February 1992: 1066.

Quinn, Peter A. "Incandescent Albany." *Commonweal* 20 May 1988: 308–09.

Rev. of "Quinn's Book." *Publishers Weekly* 18 March 1988: 71.

Reilly, Edward C. "Dante's *Purgatorio* and Kennedy's *Ironweed*: Journeys to Redemption." *Notes on Contemporary Literature* 17.3 1987: 5–8.

— "The Pigeons and Circular Flight in Kennedy's *Ironweed*." *Notes on Contemporary Literature* 16.2 1986: 8.

— *William Kennedy*. Twayne's United States Authors Series, 570. Ed. Frank Day. Boston: G. K. Hall & Co. 1991.

Sheppard, R. Z. "Living with the Ashes." *Time* 13 May 1996: 122-23.

Taylor, Anya. "*Ironweed*, Alcohol, and Celtic Heroism." *Critique: Studies in Contemporary Fiction* 33.2 1992: 107-20.

Tierce, Michael. "William Kennedy's Odyssey: The Travels of Francis Phelan." *Classical and Modern Literature: A Quarterly* 8.4 1988: 247-263.

Van Dover, J. K. *Understanding William Kennedy*. Columbia: University of South Carolina Press, 1991.

Rev. of "Very Old Bones." *The Antioch Review* 51 (1992): 313-14.

Rev. of "Very Old Bones." *Bookman's Weekly* 10 August 1992: 444-45.

Rev. of "Very Old Bones." *The New Yorker* 27 April 1992: 106.

Whittaker, Stephen. "The Lawyer as Narrator in William Kennedy's *Legs*." *Legal Studies Forum* 9.2 1985: 157-164.

Yetman, Michael G. "*Ironweed*: The Perils and Purgatories of Male Romanticism." *PLL: Papers on Language and Literature* 27.1 1991: 84-104.

Interviews

Allen, Douglas R. and Mona Simpson. *The Paris Review* 31 1989: 34-59.

Bonetti, Kay. "An Interview with William Kennedy." *The Missouri Review* 8.2 1985: 69-86.

McCaffery, Larry, and Sinda Gregory. "An Interview with William Kennedy." *Fiction International* 15 1984: 157-79. Rpt. in *Alive and Writing: Interviews with American Writers of the 1980's*. Ed. Larry McCaffery and Sinda Gregory. Urbana: University of Illinois Press, 1987. 151-74.

Quinn, Peter. "William Kennedy: An Interview." *The Recorder: A Journal of the American Irish Historical Society* 1 1985: 65-81.

Reilly, Edward C. "On an Averill Park Afternoon with William Kennedy." *South Carolina Review* 21.2 1989: 11-24.

Thomson, David. "The Man Has Legs." *Film Comment* 21 1985: 54-59.

INDEX